More Praise for *Prisoners of Geography*

"In an ever more complex, chaotic, and interlinked world, *Prisoners of Geography* is a concise and useful primer on geopolitics."

—*Newsweek*

"A convincing analysis of Russian geopolitical thinking . . . Also makes clear the terrible price the world has had to pay because European officials decided to create nation states with borders that completely ignored cultural geography."

—*The Washington Post*

"Marshall is excellent on some of the highways and byways of geopolitics."

—*Financial Times*

"Fans of geography, history, and politics (and maps) will be enthralled."

—*Fort Worth Star-Telegram*

"This is not a book about environmental determinism—the geography of a region is never presented as fatalistic; but it does send a timely reminder that despite technological advances, geography is always there, often forcing the hand of world leaders."

—*Geographical* magazine

"Lively and perceptive political and historical analyses are frequent. The chapter on China is excellent; the chapter on Africa combines geography and history in a convincing way; the chapter on Western Europe . . . is a brilliant narrative of European relations, particularly between France and Germany. The superb chapter on the Middle East makes for a clear indictment of the Sykes-Picot agreements and of their tracing of artificial borders. The chapter on the Arctic is precise and informative . . . A very lively, sensible, and informative series of country reports in which geography occupies its rightful place along with shrewd historical reminders and political judgments."

—*Survival: Global Politics and Strategy*

"Sharp insights into the way geography shapes the choices of world leaders."

—*The World*, the *Financial Times* news blog

ALSO BY TIM MARSHALL

"Dirty Northern B*st*rds!" and Other Tales from the Terraces:
The Story of Britain's Football Chants

Shadowplay: The Inside Story of
the Overthrow of Slobodan Milosevic

PRISONERS

of

GEOGRAPHY

Ten Maps That Explain
Everything About the World

Tim Marshall

SCRIBNER
New York   London   Toronto   Sydney   New Delhi

To Joanna Simone: *"L'histoire de ma vie—c'est toi."*

_____

Scribner
An Imprint of Simon & Schuster, Inc.
1230 Avenue of the Americas
New York, NY 10020

First Scribner paperback edition October 2016

SCRIBNER and design are registered trademarks of The Gale Group, Inc., used under license by Simon & Schuster, Inc., the publisher of this work.

For information about special discounts for bulk purchases, please contact Simon & Schuster Special Sales at 1-866-506-1949 or business@simonandschuster.com.

The Simon & Schuster Speakers Bureau can bring authors to your live event. For more information or to book an event, contact the Simon & Schuster Speakers Bureau at 1-866-248-3049 or visit our website at www.simonspeakers.com.

Interior design by Jill Putorti

Manufactured in the United States of America

10 9 8

Library of Congress Cataloging-in-Publication Data is available.

ISBN 978-1-5011-2146-3
ISBN 978-1-5011-2147-0 (pbk)
ISBN 978-1-5011-2148-7 (ebook)

CONTENTS

Introduction   1

1 Russia   11

2 China   40

3 United States   68

4 Western Europe   92

5 Africa   116

6 The Middle East   142

7 India and Pakistan   182

8 Korea and Japan   208

9 Latin America   230

10 The Arctic   256

Conclusion   273

Acknowledgments   279

Bibliography   281

Index   287

INTRODUCTION

Vladimir Putin says he is a religious man, a great supporter of the Russian Orthodox Church. If so, he may well go to bed each night, say his prayers, and ask God: "Why didn't you put some mountains in Ukraine?"

If God had built mountains in Ukraine, then the great expanse of flatland that is the North European Plain would not be such encouraging territory from which to attack Russia repeatedly. As it is, Putin has no choice: he must at least attempt to control the flatlands to the west. So it is with all nations, big or small. The landscape imprisons their leaders, giving them fewer choices and less room to maneuver than you might think. This was true of the Athenian Empire, the Persians, the Babylonians, and before; it was true of every leader seeking high ground from which to protect their tribe.

The land on which we live has always shaped us. It has shaped the wars, the power, politics, and social development of the peoples that now inhabit nearly every part of the earth. Technology may seem to overcome the distances between us in both mental and physical space, but it is easy to forget that the land where we live, work, and raise our children is hugely important and that the choices of those who lead the seven billion inhabitants of this planet will to some degree always be shaped by the rivers, mountains, deserts, lakes, and seas that constrain us all—as they always have.

Overall there is no one geographical factor that is more important than any other. Mountains are no more important than deserts, nor rivers than jungles. In different parts of the planet different geographical features are among the dominant factors in determining what people can and cannot do.

Broadly speaking, geopolitics looks at the ways in which international affairs can be understood through geographical factors: not just the physical landscape—the natural barriers of mountains or connections of river networks, for example—but also climate, demographics, cultural regions, and access to natural resources. Factors such as these can have an important impact on many different aspects of our civilization, from political and military strategy to human social development, including language, trade, and religion.

The physical realities that underpin national and international politics are too often disregarded in both writing about history and in contemporary reporting of world affairs. Geography is clearly a fundamental part of the "why" as well as the "what." Take, for example, China and India: two massive countries with huge populations that share a very long border but are not politically or culturally aligned. It wouldn't be surprising if these two giants had fought each other in several wars, but in fact, apart from one monthlong battle in 1962, they never have. Why? Because between them is the highest mountain range in the world, and it is practically impossible to advance large military columns through or over the Himalayas. As technology becomes more sophisticated, of course, ways are emerging of overcoming this obstacle, but the physical barrier remains a deterrent, and so both countries focus their foreign policy on other regions, while keeping a wary eye on each other.

Individual leaders, ideas, technology, and other factors all play a role in shaping events, but they are temporary. Each new generation will still face the physical obstructions created by the Hindu Kush and the Himalayas, the challenges created by the rainy season, and the disadvantages of limited access to natural minerals or food sources.

I first became interested in this subject when covering the wars in the Balkans in the 1990s. I watched close at hand as the leaders of various peoples, be they Serbian, Croat, or Bosniak, deliberately reminded their "tribes" of the ancient divisions and, yes, ancient suspicions in a region crowded with diversity. Once they had pulled the peoples apart, it didn't take much to then push them against each other.

The River Ibar in Kosovo is a prime example. Ottoman rule over Serbia was cemented by the Battle of Kosovo Polje in 1389, fought near where the Ibar flows through the city of Mitrovica. Over the following centuries the Serb population began to withdraw behind the Ibar as Muslim Albanians gradually descended from the mountainous Malesija region into Kosovo, where they became a majority by the mideighteenth century. Fast-forward to the twentieth century and there was still a clear ethnic-religious division roughly marked by the river. Then in 1999, battered by NATO from the air and the Kosovo Liberation Army on the ground, the Yugoslav (Serbian) military retreated across the Ibar, quickly followed by most of the remaining Serb population. The river became the de facto border of what some countries now recognize as the independent state of Kosovo.

Mitrovica was also where the advancing NATO ground forces came to a halt. During the three-month war, there had been veiled threats that NATO intended to invade all of Serbia. In truth, the restraints of both geography and politics meant the NATO leaders never really had that option. Hungary had made it clear that it would not allow an invasion from its territory, as it feared reprisals against the 350,000 ethnic Hungarians in northern Serbia. The alternative was an invasion from the south, which would have gotten them to the Ibar in double-quick time; but NATO would then have faced the mountains above them.

I was working with a team of Serbs in Belgrade at the time and asked what would happen if NATO came: "We will put our cameras down, Tim, and pick up guns" was the response. They were liberal Serbs, good friends of mine and opposed to their government, but they still pulled out the maps and showed me where the Serbs would defend their territory in the mountains, and where NATO would grind to a halt. It was some relief to be given a geography lesson in why NATO's choices were more limited than the Brussels PR machine made public.

An understanding of how crucial the physical landscape was in reporting news in the Balkans stood me in good stead in the years that followed. For example, in 2001, a few weeks after 9/11, I saw a demonstration of how, even with today's modern technology, climate still dictates the military possibilities of even the world's most powerful armies. I was in northern Afghanistan, having crossed the border river from Tajikistan on a raft, in order to link up with the Northern Alliance (NA) troops who were fighting the Taliban.

The American fighter jets and bombers were already overhead, pounding Taliban and al-Qaeda positions on the cold, dusty plains and hills east of Mazar-e-Sharif in order to pave the way for the advance on Kabul. After a few weeks it was obvious that the NA were gearing up to move south. And then the world changed color.

The most intense sandstorm I have ever experienced blew in, turning everything a mustard-yellow color. At the height of the storm you couldn't see more than a few yards ahead of you, and the only thing clear was that the Americans' satellite technology, at the cutting edge of science, was helpless, blind in the face of the climate of this wild land. Everyone, from President Bush and the Joint Chiefs of Staff to the NA troops on the ground, just had to wait. Then it rained and the sand that had settled on everything turned into mud. The rain came down so hard that the baked-mud huts we were living in looked as if they were melting. Again it was clear that the move south was on hold until geography finished having its say. The rules of geography, which Hannibal, Sun Tzu, and Alexander the Great all knew, still apply to today's leaders.

More recently, in 2012, I was given another lesson in geostrategy: As Syria descended into full-blown civil war, I was standing on a Syrian hilltop overlooking a valley south of the city of Hama and saw a hamlet burning in the distance. Syrian friends pointed out a much larger village about a mile away, from where they said the attack had come. They then explained that if one side could push enough people from the other faction out of the valley, then the valley could be joined onto other land that led to the country's only motorway, and as such would be useful in carving out a piece of contiguous, viable territory that one day could be used to create a mini-statelet if Syria could not be put back together again. Where before I saw only a burning hamlet, I could now see its strategic importance and understand how political realities are shaped by the most basic physical realities.

Geopolitics affects every country, whether at war, as in the examples above, or at peace. There will be instances in every region you can name. In these pages I cannot explore each one: Canada, Australia, and Indonesia, among others, get no more than a brief mention, although a whole book could be devoted to Australia alone and the ways in which its geography has shaped its connections with other parts of the world, both physically and culturally. Instead I have focused on the powers and regions that best illustrate the key points of the book, covering the legacy of geopolitics from the past (nation-forming); the most pressing situations we face today (the troubles in Ukraine, the expanding influence of China); and looking to the future (growing competition in the Arctic).

In Russia we see the influence of the Arctic, and how it limits Russia's ability to be a truly global power. In China we see the limitations of power without a global navy and how in 2016 it became obvious the speed at which China is seeking to change this. The chapter on the United States illustrates how shrewd decisions to expand its territory in key regions allowed it to achieve its modern destiny as a two-ocean superpower. Europe shows us the value of flatland and navigable rivers in connecting regions and producing a culture able to kick-start the modern world, while Africa is a prime example of the effects of isolation.

The chapter on the Middle East demonstrates why drawing lines on maps while disregarding the topography and, equally important, the geographical cultures in a given area is a recipe for trouble. We will continue to witness that trouble this century. The same theme surfaces in the chapters on Africa and India/Pakistan. The colonial powers used ink to draw lines that bore no relation to the physical realities of the region, and created some of the most artificial borders the world has seen. In the Middle East, an attempt is now being made to redraw them in blood.

Very different from the examples of Kosovo or Syria are Japan and Korea, in that they are mostly ethnically homogenous. But they have other problems: Japan is an island nation devoid of natural resources, while the division of the Koreas is a problem still waiting to be solved. Meanwhile, Latin America is an anomaly. In its far south it is so cut off from the outside world that global trading is difficult, and its internal geography is a barrier to creating a trading bloc as successful as the EU.

Finally, we come to one of the most uninhabitable places on

earth—the Arctic. For most of history, humans have ignored it, but in the twentieth century we found energy there, and twenty-first-century diplomacy will determine who owns—and sells—that resource.

Seeing geography as a decisive factor in the course of human history can be construed as a bleak view of the world, which is why it is disliked in some intellectual circles. It suggests that nature is more powerful than man and that we can go only so far in determining our own fate. However, other factors clearly have an influence on events, too. Any sensible person can see that technology is now bending the iron rules of geography. It has found ways over, under, or through some of the barriers. The Americans can now fly a plane all the way from Missouri to Mosul on a bombing mission without needing to land to refuel. That, along with their great aircraft carrier battle groups, means they no longer absolutely have to have an ally or a colony in order to extend their global reach around the world. Of course, if they *do* have an air base on the island of Diego Garcia, or permanent access to the port in Bahrain, then they have more options; but it is less essential.

So airpower has changed the rules, as, in a different way, has the Internet. But geography, and the history of how nations have established themselves within that geography, remains crucial to our understanding of the world today and to our future.

The conflict in Iraq and Syria is rooted in colonial powers ignoring the rules of geography, whereas the Chinese occupation of Tibet is rooted in obeying them. America's global foreign policy is dictated by them, and even the power projection of the last superpower standing can only mitigate the rules that nature, or God, handed down.

What are those rules? The place to begin is in the land where power is hard to defend, and so for centuries its leaders have compensated by pushing outward. It is the land without mountains to its west: Russia.

OCEAN

UNITED STATES
Alaska

••••••••••• Europe–Asia divide
———————— State border
------------- Disputed border

Bering Strait

Severnaya
Zemlya

Novosibirsk
Islands

Bering Sea

Arctic Circle

b   e   r   i

a

S   I   A

Kamchatka
Peninsula

Sea of
Okhotsk

PACIFIC OCEAN

Sakhalin

Lake
Baikal

MONGOLIA

Vladivostok

Sea of
Japan

NORTH
KOREA

JAPAN

H   I   N   A

SOUTH
KOREA

Yellow
Sea

1000 miles   1000 km

RUSSIA

Vast, vaster, vastest (adj):
of very great area or extent; immense

Russia is vast. It is the vastest. Immense. It is six-million-square-miles vast, eleven time zones vast; it is the largest country in the world.

Its forests, lakes, rivers, frozen tundra, steppe, taiga, and mountains are all vast. This size has long seeped into our collective conscious. Wherever we are, there is Russia, perhaps to our east, or west, to our north or south—but there is the Russian Bear.

It is no coincidence that the bear is the symbol of this immense size. There it sits, sometimes hibernating, sometimes growling, majestic, but ferocious. *Bear* is a Russian word, but the Russians are also wary of calling this animal by its name, fearful of conjuring up its darker side. They call it *medved*, "the one who likes honey."

At least 120,000 of these *medveds* live in a country that bestrides Europe and Asia. To the west of the Ural Mountains is European Russia. To their east is Siberia, stretching all the way to the Bering Sea and the Pacific Ocean. Even in the twenty-first century, to cross it by train takes six days. Russia's leaders must look across these distances, and differences, and formulate policy accordingly; for several centuries now they have looked in all directions, but concentrated mostly westward.

When writers seek to get to the heart of the bear they often use Winston Churchill's famous observation of Russia, made in 1939: "It is a riddle wrapped in a mystery inside an enigma," but few go on to complete the sentence, which ends "but perhaps there is a key. That key is Russian national interest." Seven years later he used that key to unlock his version of the answer to the riddle, asserting, "I am convinced that there is nothing they admire so much as strength, and there is nothing for which they have less respect than for weakness, especially military weakness."

He could have been talking about the current Russian leadership, which despite being now wrapped in the cloak of democracy, remains authoritarian in its nature with national interest still at its core.

When Vladimir Putin isn't thinking about God, and mountains, he's thinking about pizza. In particular, the shape of a slice of pizza—a wedge.

The thin end of this wedge is Poland. Here, the vast North European Plain stretching from France to the Urals (which extend a thousand miles south to north, forming a natural boundary between Europe and Asia) is only three hundred miles wide. It runs from the Baltic Sea in the north to the Carpathian Mountains in the south. The North European Plain encompasses all of western and northern France, Belgium, the Netherlands, northern Germany, and nearly all of Poland.

From a Russian perspective this is a double-edged sword. Poland represents a relatively narrow corridor into which Russia could drive its armed forces if necessary and thus prevent an enemy from advancing toward Moscow. But from this point the wedge begins to broaden; by the time you get to Russia's borders it is more than two thousand miles wide, and is flat all the way to Moscow and beyond. Even with a large army you would be hard-pressed to defend in strength along this line. However, Russia has never been conquered from this direction partially due to its strategic depth. By the time an army approaches Moscow it already has unsustainably long supply lines, a mistake that Napoleon made in 1812, and that Hitler repeated in 1941.

Likewise, in the Russian Far East it is geography that protects Russia. It is difficult to move an army from Asia up into Asian Russia; there's not much to attack except for snow and you could get only as far as the Urals. You would then end up holding a massive piece of territory, in difficult conditions, with long supply lines and the ever-present risk of a counterattack.

You might think that no one is intent on invading Russia, but that is not how the Russians see it, and with good reason. In the past five hundred years they have been invaded several times from the west. The Poles came across the North European Plain in 1605, followed by the Swedes under Charles XII in 1708, the French under Napoleon in 1812, and the Germans—twice, in both world wars, in 1914 and 1941. Looking at it another way, if you count from Napoleon's invasion of 1812, but this time include the Crimean War of 1853–56 and the two world wars up to 1945, then the Russians were fighting on average in or around the North European Plain once every thirty-three years.

At the end of the Second World War in 1945, the Russians occupied the territory conquered from Germany in Central and Eastern Europe, some of which then became part of the USSR, as it increasingly began to resemble the old Russian empire. In 1949, the North Atlantic Treaty Organization (NATO) was formed by an association of European and North American states, for the defense of Europe and the North Atlantic against the danger of Soviet aggression. In response, most of the Communist states of Europe—under Russian leadership—formed the Warsaw Pact in 1955, a treaty for military defense and mutual aid. The pact was supposed to be made of iron, but with hindsight, by the early 1980s it was rusting, and after the fall of the Berlin Wall in 1989 it crumbled to dust.

President Putin is no fan of the last Soviet president, Mikhail Gorbachev. He blames him for undermining Russian security and has referred to the breakup of the former Soviet Union during the 1990s as a "major geopolitical disaster of the century."

Since then the Russians have watched anxiously as NATO has crept steadily closer, incorporating countries that Russia claims it was promised would not be joining: the Czech Republic, Hungary, and Poland in 1999; Bulgaria, Estonia, Latvia, Lithuania, Romania, and Slovakia in 2004; and Albania in 2009. NATO says no such assurances were given.

Russia, like all great powers, is thinking in terms of the next one hundred years and understands that in that time anything could happen. A century ago, who could have guessed that American armed forces would be stationed a few hundred miles from Moscow in Poland and the Baltic States? By 2004, just fifteen years after 1989, every single former Warsaw Pact state bar Russia was in NATO or the European Union.

The Moscow administration's mind has been concentrated by that, and by Russia's history.

Russia as a concept dates back to the ninth century and a loose federation of East Slavic tribes known as Kievan Rus, which was based in Kiev and other towns along the Dnieper River, in what is now Ukraine. The Mongols, expanding their empire, continually attacked the region from the south and east, eventually overrunning it in the thirteenth century. The fledgling Russia then relocated northeast in and around the city of Moscow. This early Russia, known as the Grand Principality of Muscovy, was indefensible. There were no mountains, no deserts, and few rivers.

In all directions lay flatland, and across the steppe to the south and east were the Mongols. The invader could advance at a place of his choosing, and there were few natural defensive positions to occupy.

Enter Ivan the Terrible, the first tsar. He put into practice the concept of attack as defense—i.e., beginning your expansion by consolidating at home and then moving outward. This led to greatness. Here was a man to give support to the theory that individuals can change history. Without his character, of both utter ruthlessness and vision, Russian history would be different.

The fledgling Russia had begun a moderate expansion under Ivan's grandfather, Ivan the Great, but that expansion accelerated after he came to power in 1533. It encroached east on the Urals, south to the Caspian Sea, and north toward the Arctic Circle. It gained access to the Caspian, and later the Black Sea, thus taking advantage of the Caucasus Mountains as a partial barrier between it and the Mongols. A military base was built in Chechnya to deter any would-be attacker, be they the Mongol Golden Horde, the Ottoman Empire, or the Persians.

There were setbacks, but over the next century Russia would push past the Urals and edge into Siberia, eventually incorporating all the land to the Pacific coast far to the east.

Now the Russians had a partial buffer zone and a hinterland—strategic depth—somewhere to fall back to in the case of invasion. No one was going to attack them in force from the Arctic Sea, nor fight their way over the Urals to get to them. Their land was becoming what we now know as Russia, and to get to it from the south or southeast you had to have a huge army and a very long supply line and you had to fight your way past defensive positions.

In the eighteenth century, Russia, under Peter the Great—who founded the Russian Empire in 1721—and then Empress Catherine the Great, looked westward, expanding the empire to become one of the great powers of Europe, driven chiefly by trade and nationalism. A more secure and powerful Russia was now able to occupy Ukraine and reach the Carpathian Mountains. It took over most of what we now know as the Baltic States—Lithuania, Latvia, and Estonia. Thus it was protected from any incursion via land that way, or from the Baltic Sea.

Now there was a huge ring around Moscow that was the heart of the country. Starting at the Arctic, it came down through the Baltic region, across Ukraine, then the Carpathians, the Black Sea, the Caucasus, and the Caspian, swinging back around to the Urals, which stretched up to the Arctic Circle.

In the twentieth century, Communist Russia created the Soviet Union. Behind the rhetoric of "Workers of the World Unite" the USSR was simply the Russian Empire writ large. After the Second World War it stretched from the Pacific to Berlin, from the Arctic to the borders of Afghanistan—a superpower economically, politically, and militarily, rivaled only by the United States.

How big is the biggest country in the world? Russia is twice the size of the United States or China, five times the size of India, seventy times the size of the UK. However, it has a relatively small population (144 million), fewer people than Nigeria or Pakistan. Its agricultural growing season is short and it struggles to adequately distribute what is grown around the eleven time zones that Moscow governs.

Russia, up to the Urals, is a European power insofar as it borders the European landmass, but it is not an Asian power despite bordering Kazakhstan, Mongolia, China, and North Korea, and having maritime borders with several countries, including Japan and the United States.

Former US vice presidential candidate Sarah Palin was mocked when she was reported as saying "You can actually see Russia from land here in Alaska," a line which morphed in media coverage to "You can see Russia from my house." What she really said was "You can see Russia from land here in Alaska, from an island in Alaska." She was right. A Russian island in the Bering Strait is two and a half miles from an American island in the Strait, Little Diomede Island, and can be seen with the naked eye. You can indeed see Russia from America.

High up in the Urals there is a cross marking the place where Europe stops and Asia starts. When the skies are clear, it is a beautiful spot and you can see through the fir trees for miles toward the east. In winter it is snow-covered, as is the Siberian Plain you see below you stretching toward the city of Yekaterinburg. Tourists like to visit to put one foot in Europe and one in Asia. It is a reminder of just how big Russia is when you realize that the cross is placed merely a quarter of the way into the country. You may have traveled 1,500 miles from Saint Petersburg, through western Russia, to get to the Urals, but you still have another 4,500 miles to go before reaching the Bering Strait, and a possible sighting of Mrs. Palin, across from Alaska in the United States.

Shortly after the fall of the Soviet Union, I was in the Urals, at the point where Europe becomes Asia, accompanied by a Russian camera crew. The cameraman was a taciturn, stoic, grizzled veteran of filming, and was the son of the Red Army's cameraman who had filmed a great deal of footage during the German siege of Stalingrad. I asked him, "So, are you European or are you Asian?" He reflected on this for a few seconds then replied, "Neither—I am Russian."

Whatever its European credentials, Russia is not an Asian power for many reasons. Although 75 percent of its territory is in Asia, only 22 percent of its population lives there. Siberia may be Russia's "treasure chest," containing the majority of the mineral wealth, oil, and gas, but it is a harsh land, freezing for months on end, with vast forests (taiga), poor soil for farming, and large stretches of swampland. Only two railway networks run west to east—the Trans-Siberian and the Baikal-Amur Mainline. There are few transport routes leading north to south and so no easy way for Russia to project power southward into modern Mongolia or China: it lacks the manpower and supply lines to do so.

China may well eventually control parts of Siberia in the long run, but this would be through Russia's declining birthrate and Chinese immigration moving north. Already as far west as the swampy West Siberian Plain, between the Urals in the west and the Yenisei River one thousand miles to the east, you can see Chinese restaurants in most of the towns and cities. Many different businesses are coming. The empty depopulating spaces of Russia's Far East are even more likely to come under Chinese cultural, and eventually political, control.

When you move outside of the Russian heartland, much of the population in the Russian Federation is not ethnically Russian and pays little allegiance to Moscow, which results in an aggressive security system similar to the one in Soviet days. During that era, Russia was effectively a colonial power ruling over nations and people who felt they had nothing in common with their masters; parts of the Russian Federation—for example, Chechnya and Dagestan in the Caucasus—still feel this way.

Late in the last century overstretch, spending more money than was available, the economics of the madhouse in a land not designed for people, and defeat in the mountains of Afghanistan led to the fall of the USSR and saw the Russian Empire shrink back to the shape of more or less the pre–Communist era with its European borders ending at Estonia, Latvia, Belarus, Ukraine, Georgia, and Azerbaijan. The Soviet invasion of Afghanistan in 1979, in support of the Communist Afghan government against anti-Communist Muslim guerrillas, had never been about bringing the joys of Marxist-Leninism to the

Afghan people. It was always about ensuring that Moscow controlled that space in order to prevent anyone else from doing so.

Crucially, the invasion of Afghanistan also gave hope to the great Russian dream of its army being able to "wash their boots in the warm waters of the Indian Ocean," in the words of the ultra-nationalistic Russian politician Vladimir Zhirinovsky, and thus achieve what it never had: a warm-water port where the water does not freeze in winter, with free access to the world's major trading routes. The ports on the Arctic, such as Murmansk, freeze for several months each year: Vladivostok, the largest Russian port on the Pacific Ocean, is ice-locked for about four months and is enclosed by the Sea of Japan, which is dominated by the Japanese. This does not just halt the flow of trade; it prevents the Russian fleet from operating as a global power. In addition, waterborne transport is much cheaper than land or airborne routes.

However, the "warm-water open sea-lanes" dream has seeped away from Moscow, further now perhaps than for two hundred years. The Afghan experience is sometimes called "Russia's Vietnam," but it was more than that; the plains of Kandahar and the mountains of the Hindu Kush proved the rule that Afghanistan is the "Graveyard of Empires."

This lack of a warm-water port with direct access to the oceans has always been Russia's Achilles' heel, as strategically important to it as the North European Plain. Russia is at a geographical disadvantage, saved from being a much weaker power only because of its oil and gas. No wonder, in his will of 1725, that Peter the Great advised his descendants to "approach as near as possible to Constantinople and India. Whoever governs there will be the true sovereign of the world. Consequently, excite continual wars, not only in Turkey, but in Persia. . . . Penetrate as far as the Persian Gulf, advance as far as India."

When the Soviet Union broke apart, it split into fifteen countries. Geography had its revenge on the ideology of the Soviets, and a more logical picture reappeared on the map, one where mountains, rivers, lakes, and seas delineate where people live, how they are separated from each other and, thus, how they developed different languages and customs. The exception to this rule are the "stans," such as Tajikistan, whose borders were deliberately drawn by Stalin so as to weaken each state by ensuring it had large minorities of people from other states.

If you take the long view of history—and most diplomats and military planners do—then there is still everything to play for in each of the states that formerly made up the USSR, plus some of those previously in the Warsaw Pact military alliance. They can be divided three ways: those that are neutral, the pro-Western group, and the pro-Russian camp.

The neutral countries—Uzbekistan, Azerbaijan, and Turkmenistan—are those with fewer reasons to ally themselves with Russia or the West. This is because all three produce their own energy and are not beholden to either side for their security or trade.

In the pro-Russian camp are Kazakhstan, Kyrgyzstan, Tajikistan, Belarus, and Armenia. Their economies are tied to Russia in the way that much of eastern Ukraine's economy is (another reason for the rebellion there). The largest of these, Kazakhstan, leans toward Russia diplomatically and its large Russian-minority population is well integrated. Of the five, Kazakhstan, Belarus, Armenia, and Kyrgyzstan have joined the Russian-led Eurasian Economic Union (a sort of poor man's EU), which celebrated its first anniversary in January 2016. All, including Tajikistan, are in a military alliance with Russia called the Collective Security Treaty Organization. The CSTO suffers from not having a name you can boil down to one word, and from being a watered-down Warsaw Bloc. Russia maintains a military presence in Kyrgyzstan, Tajikistan, and Armenia.

Then there are the pro-Western countries formerly in the Warsaw Pact but now all in NATO and/or the EU: Poland, Latvia, Lithuania, Estonia, the Czech Republic, Bulgaria, Hungary, Slovakia, Albania, and Romania. By no coincidence, many are among the states that suffered most under Soviet tyranny. Add to these Georgia, Ukraine, and Moldova, who would all like to join both organizations but are being held at arm's length because of their geographic proximity to Russia and because all three have Russian troops or pro-Russian militia on their soil. NATO membership of any of these three could spark a war.

All of the above explains why, in 2013, as the political battle for the direction of Ukraine heated up, Moscow concentrated hard.

As long as a pro-Russian government held sway in Kiev, the Russians could be confident that its buffer zone would remain intact and guard the North European Plain. Even a studiedly neutral Ukraine, which would promise not to join the EU or NATO and to uphold the lease Russia had on the warm-water port at Sevastopol in Crimea, would be acceptable. That Ukraine was reliant on Russia for energy also made its increasingly neutral stance acceptable, albeit irritating. But a pro-Western Ukraine with ambitions to join the two great Western alliances and that threw into doubt Russia's access to its Black Sea port? A Ukraine that one day might even host a NATO naval base? That could not stand.

President Viktor Yanukovych of Ukraine tried to play both sides. He flirted with the West, but paid homage to Moscow—thus Putin tolerated him. When he came close to signing a massive trade agreement with the EU, one which could lead to membership, Putin began turning the screw.

For the Russian foreign policy elite, membership in the EU is simply a stalking horse for membership in NATO, and for Russia, Ukrainian membership in NATO is a red line. Putin piled the pressure on Yanukovych, made him an offer he chose not to refuse, and the Ukrainian president scrambled out of the EU deal and made a pact with Moscow, thus sparking the protests that were eventually to overthrow him.

The Germans and Americans had backed the opposition parties, with Berlin in particular seeing former world boxing champion turned politician Vitali Klitschko as their man. The West was pulling Ukraine intellectually and economically toward it while helping pro-Western Ukrainians push it westward by training and funding some of the democratic opposition groups.

Street fighting erupted in Kiev and demonstrations across the country grew. In the east, crowds came out in support of the president. In the west of the country, in cities such as L'viv, which used to be in Poland, they were busy trying to rid themselves of any pro-Russian influence.

By mid-February 2014, L'viv, and other urban areas, were no longer controlled by the government. Then on February 22, after dozens of deaths in Kiev, the president, fearing for his life, fled. Anti-Russian factions, some of which were pro-Western and some pro-fascist, took over the government. From that moment the die was cast. President Putin did not have much of a choice—he had to annex Crimea, which contained not only many Russian-speaking Ukrainians but most important the port of Sevastopol. This geographic imperative and the whole eastward movement of NATO is exactly what Putin had in mind when, in a speech about the annexation, he said "Russia found itself in a position it could not retreat from. If you compress the spring all the way to its limit, it will snap back hard. You must always remember this."

Sevastopol is Russia's only true major warm-water port. However, access out of the Black Sea into the Mediterranean is restricted by the Montreux Convention of 1936, which gave Turkey—now a NATO member—control of the Bosporus. Russian naval ships do transit the strait, but in limited numbers, and this would not be permitted in the event of conflict. Even after crossing the Bosporus the Russians need to navigate the Aegean Sea before accessing the Mediterranean, and would still have either to cross the Strait of Gibraltar to gain access to the Atlantic Ocean, or be allowed down the Suez Canal to reach the Indian Ocean.

The Russians do have a small naval presence in Tartus on Syria's Mediterranean coast (this partially explains their support for the Syrian government when fighting broke out in 2011), but it is a limited-supply and replenishment base, not a major force.

Another strategic problem is that in the event of war the Russian navy cannot get out of the Baltic Sea, either, due to the Skagerrak Strait, which connects to the North Sea. The narrow strait is controlled by NATO members Denmark and Norway; and even if the ships made it, the route to the Atlantic goes through what is known as the GIUK (Greenland/Iceland/UK) gap in the North Sea—which we will see more of when we look at Western Europe.

Having annexed Crimea, the Russians are wasting no time. They are building up the Black Sea fleet at Sevastopol and constructing a new naval port in the Russian city of Novorossiysk, which, although it does not have a natural deep harbor, will give the Russians extra capacity. Eighty new ships are being commissioned as well as several submarines. The fleet will still not be strong enough to break out of the Black Sea during wartime, but its capacity is increasing. In July 2015, Russia published its new naval doctrine and, there, right at the top of the list of threats to Russian interests, was NATO. It called NATO's positioning of troops and hardware closer to its borders "inadmissible," which was just short of fighting talk.

To counter this, in the next decade we can expect to see the United States encouraging its NATO partner Romania to boost its fleet in the Black Sea while relying on Turkey to hold the line across the Bosporus.

Crimea was part of Russia for two centuries before being granted to the Soviet Republic of Ukraine in 1954 by President Khrushchev at a time when it was envisaged that Soviet man would live forever and so be controlled by Moscow forever. Now that Ukraine was no longer Soviet, nor even pro-Russian—Putin knew the situation had to change. Did the Western diplomats know? If they didn't, then they were unaware of rule A, lesson one, in "Diplomacy for Beginners": When faced with what is considered an existential threat, a great power will use force. If they were aware, then they must have considered Putin's annexation of Crimea a price worth paying for pulling Ukraine into modern Europe and the Western sphere of influence.

A generous view is that the United States and the Europeans were looking forward to welcoming Ukraine into the democratic world as a full member of its liberal institutions and the rule of law and that there wasn't much Moscow could do about it. That is a view that does not take into account the fact that geopolitics still exists in the twenty-first century and that Russia does not play by the rule of law.

Flushed with victory, the new interim Ukrainian government had immediately made some foolish statements, not least of which was the intention to abolish Russian as the official second language in various regions. Given that these regions were those with the most

Russian speakers and pro-Russian sentiment, and indeed included Crimea, this was bound to spark a backlash. It also gave President Putin the propaganda he needed to make the case that ethnic Russians inside Ukraine needed to be protected.

The Kremlin has a law that compels the government to protect "ethnic Russians." A definition of that term is, by design, hard to come by because it will be defined as Russia chooses in each of the potential crises that may erupt in the former Soviet Union. When it suits the Kremlin they will be defined simply as people who speak Russian as their first language. At other times the new citizenship law will be used, which states that if your grandparents lived in Russia, and Russian is your native language, you can take Russian citizenship. Given that, as the crises arise, people will be inclined to accept Russian passports to hedge their bets, this will be a lever for Russian entry into a conflict.

Approximately 60 percent of Crimea's population is "ethnically Russian," so the Kremlin was pushing against an open door. Putin helped the anti-Kiev demonstrations and stirred up so much trouble that eventually he "had" to send his troops out of the confines of the naval base and onto the streets to protect people. The Ukrainian military in the area was in no shape to take on both the people and the Russian army and swiftly withdrew. Crimea was once again de facto a part of Russia.

You could make the argument that President Putin did have a choice: he could have respected the territorial integrity of Ukraine. But, given that he was dealing with the geographic hand God has dealt Russia, this was never really an option. He would not be the man who "lost Crimea" and with it the only proper warm-water port his country had access to.

No one rode to the rescue of Ukraine as it lost territory equivalent to the size of Belgium, or the state of Maryland. Ukraine and its neighbors knew a geographic truth: that unless you are in NATO, Moscow is near, and Washington, DC, is far away. For Russia this was an existential matter: they could not cope with losing Crimea, but the West could.

The EU imposed limited sanctions—limited because several European countries, Germany among them, are reliant on Russian energy to heat their homes in winter. The pipelines run east to west and the Kremlin can turn the taps on and off.

Energy as political power will be deployed time and again in the coming years, and the concept of "ethnic Russians" will be used to justify whatever moves Russia makes.

In a speech in 2014, President Putin briefly referred to "Novorossiya" or "New Russia." The Kremlin watchers took a deep breath. He had revived the geographic title given to what is now southern and eastern Ukraine, which Russia had won from the Ottoman Empire during the reign of Catherine the Great in the late eighteenth century. Catherine went on to settle Russians in these regions and demanded that Russian be the first language. Novorossiya was ceded to the newly formed Ukrainian Soviet Socialist Republic only in 1922. "Why?" asked Putin rhetorically. "Let God judge them." In his speech he listed the Ukrainian regions of Kharkiv, Luhansk, Donetsk, Kherson, Mykolaiv, and Odessa before saying, "Russia lost these territories for various reasons, but the people remained."

Several million ethnic Russians still remain inside what was the USSR but outside Russia.

It is no surprise that, after seizing Crimea, Russia went on to encourage the uprisings by pro-Russians in the Ukrainian eastern industrial heartlands in Luhansk and Donetsk. Russia could easily drive militarily all the way to the eastern bank of the Dnieper River in Kiev. But it does not need the headache that would bring. It is far less painful, and cheaper, to encourage unrest in the eastern borders of Ukraine and remind Kiev who controls energy supplies, to ensure that Kiev's infatuation with the flirtatious West does not turn into a marriage consummated in the chambers of the EU or NATO.

Covert support for the uprisings in eastern Ukraine was also logistically simple and had the added benefit of deniability on the international stage. Barefaced lying in the great chamber of the UN Security Council is simple if your opponent does not have concrete proof of your actions and, more important, doesn't want concrete proof in case he or she has to do something about it. Many politicians in the West breathed a sigh of relief and muttered quietly, "Thank goodness Ukraine isn't in NATO or we would have had to act."

The annexation of Crimea showed how Russia is prepared for military action to defend what it sees as its interests in what it calls its "near abroad." It took a rational gamble that outside powers would not intervene and Crimea was "doable." It is close to Russia, could be supplied across the Black Sea and the Sea of Azov, and could rely on internal support from large sections of the population of the peninsula.

Russia has not finished with Ukraine yet, nor elsewhere. Unless it feels threatened, Russia will probably not send its troops all the way into the Baltic States, or any farther forward than it already is in Georgia; but it will push its power in Georgia, and in this volatile period further military action cannot be ruled out.

However, just as Russia's actions in its war with Georgia in 2008 were a warning to NATO to come no closer, so NATO's message to

Russia in the summer of 2014 was "This far west and no farther." A handful of NATO warplanes were flown to the Baltic States, military exercises were announced in Poland, and the Americans began planning to "pre-position" extra hardware as close to Russia as possible. At the same time there was a flurry of diplomatic visits by defense and foreign ministers to the Baltic States, Georgia, and Moldova to reassure them of support.

Some commentators poured scorn on the reaction, arguing that six RAF Eurofighter Typhoon jets flying over Baltic airspace were hardly going to deter the Russian hordes. But the reaction was about diplomatic signaling, and the signal was clear—NATO is prepared to fight. Indeed it would have to, because if it failed to react to an attack on a member state, it would instantly be obsolete. The Americans—who are already edging toward a new foreign policy in which they feel less constrained by existing structures and are prepared to forge new ones as they perceive the need arises—are deeply unimpressed with the European countries' commitment to defense spending.

In the case of the three Baltic States, NATO's position is clear. As they are all members of the alliance, armed aggression against any of them by Russia would trigger Article 5 of NATO's founding charter, which states: "An armed attack against one or more [NATO member states] in Europe or North America shall be considered an attack against them all," and goes on to say NATO will come to the rescue if necessary. Article 5 was invoked after the terrorist attacks in the United States on September 11, 2001, paving the way for NATO involvement in Afghanistan.

President Putin is a student of history. He appears to have learned the lessons of the Soviet years, in which Russia overstretched itself and was forced to contract. An overt assault on the Baltic States would likewise be overstretching and is unlikely, especially if NATO and its political masters ensure that Putin understands their signals. At the beginning of 2016, the Russian president sent his own signal. He changed the wording of Russia's overall military strategy document and went further than the naval strategy paper of 2015. For the first time the US was named as an "external threat" to Russia.

Russia does not have to send an armored division into Latvia, Lithuania, or Estonia to influence events there, but if it ever does, it would justify the action by claiming that the large Russian communities there are being discriminated against. In both Estonia and Latvia, approximately one in four people are ethnically Russian and in Lithuania it is 5.8 percent. In Estonia, the Russian speakers say they are underrepresented in government and thousands do not have any form of citizenship. This does not mean they want to be part of Russia, but they are one of the levers Russia can pull to influence events.

The Russian-speaking populations in the Baltics can be stirred up to making life difficult. There are existing, fully formed political parties already representing many of them. Russia also controls the central heating in the homes of the Baltic people. It can set the price people pay for their heating bills each month, and, if it chooses, simply turn the heating off.

Russia will continue to push its interests in the Baltic States. They are one of the weak links in its defense since the collapse of the USSR, another breach in the wall they would prefer to see forming an arc from the Baltic Sea, south, then southeast, connecting to the Urals.

This brings us to another gap in the wall and another region Moscow views as a potential buffer state. Firmly in the Kremlin's sights is Moldova.

A number of countries that were once members of the Soviet Union aspire to closer ties with Europe, but with certain regions, such as Transnistria in Moldova, remaining heavily pro-Russian, there is potential for future conflict.

Moldova presents a different problem for all sides. An attack on the country by Russia would necessitate crossing through Ukraine, over the Dnieper River, and then over another sovereign border into Moldova. It could be done—at the cost of significant loss of life and by using Odessa as a staging post—but there would no deniability. Although it might not trigger war with NATO (Moldova is not a member), it would provoke sanctions against Moscow at a level hitherto unseen, and confirm what this writer believes to already be the case; that the cooling relationship between Russia and the West is already the New Cold War.

Why would the Russians want Moldova? Because as the Carpathian Mountains curve around southwest to become the Transylvanian

Alps, to the southeast is a plain leading down to the Black Sea. That plain can also be thought of as a flat corridor into Russia, and just as the Russians would prefer to control the North European Plain at its narrow point in Poland, so they would like to control the plain by the Black Sea—also known as Moldova—in the region formerly known as Bessarabia.

After the Crimean War (fought between Russia and Western European allies to protect Ottoman Turkey from Russia), the 1856 Treaty of Paris returned parts of Bessarabia to Moldova, thus cutting Russia off from the Danube River. It took Russia almost a century to regain access to it, but with the collapse of the USSR, once more Russia had to retreat eastward.

However, in effect, the Russians do already control part of Moldova—a region called Transnistria, part of Moldova east of the Dniester River that borders Ukraine. Stalin, in his wisdom, settled large numbers of Russians there, just as he had in Crimea after deporting much of the Tatar population.

Modern Transnistria is now at least 50 percent Russian- or Ukrainian-speaking, and that part of the population is pro-Russian. When Moldova became independent in 1991 the Russian-speaking population rebelled and, after a brief period of fighting, declared a breakaway Republic of Transnistria. It helped that Russia had soldiers stationed there, and it retains a force of two thousand troops to this day.

A Russian military advance in Moldova is unlikely, but the Kremlin can and does use its economic muscle and the volatile situation in Transnistria to try to influence the Moldovan government not to join the EU or NATO.

Moldova is reliant on Russia for its energy needs, its crops go eastward, and Russian imports of the excellent Moldovan wine tend to rise or fall according to the state of the relationship between the two countries.

Across the Black Sea from Moldova lies another wine-producing nation: Georgia. It is not high on Russia's list of places to control for two reasons. First, the Georgia–Russian war of 2008 left large parts of the country occupied by Russian troops, who now fully control the regions of Abkhazia and South Ossetia. Second, it lies south of the Caucasus Mountains and Russia also has troops stationed in neighboring Armenia. Moscow would prefer an extra layer to their buffer zone, but can live without taking the rest of Georgia. That situation could potentially change if Georgia looked close to becoming a NATO member. This is precisely why it has so far been rebuffed by the NATO governments, which are keen to avoid the inevitable conflict with Russia.

A majority of the population in Georgia would like closer ties with the EU countries, but the shock of the 2008 war, when then president Mikheil Saakashvili naively thought the Americans might ride to his rescue after he provoked the Russians, has caused many to consider that hedging their bets may be safer. In 2013 they elected a government and president, Giorgi Margvelashvili, far more conciliatory to Moscow. As in Ukraine, people instinctively know the truism everyone in the neighborhood recognizes: that Washington is far away, and Moscow is near.

Russia's most powerful weapons now, leaving to one side nuclear missiles, are not the Russian army and air force, but gas and oil. Russia is second only to the United States as the world's biggest supplier of natural gas, and of course it uses this power to its advantage. The better your relations with Russia, the less you pay for energy; for example, Finland gets a better deal than the Baltic States. This policy has been used so aggressively, and Russia has such a hold over Europe's energy needs that moves are afoot to blunt its impact. Many countries in Europe are attempting to wean themselves off their dependency on Russian energy, not via alternative pipelines from less aggressive countries but by building ports.

On average, 25 percent of Europe's gas and oil comes from Russia; but often the closer a country is to Moscow, the greater its dependency. This in turn reduces that country's foreign policy options. Latvia, Slovakia, Finland, and Estonia are 100 percent reliant on Russian gas; the Czech Republic, Bulgaria, and Lithuania are 80 percent dependent; and Greece, Austria, and Hungary 60 percent. About half of Germany's gas supply comes from Russia, which, along with extensive trade deals, is partly why German politicians tend to be slower to criticize the Kremlin for aggressive behavior than a country such as Britain, which not only has 13 percent dependency, but also has its own gas-producing industry, including reserves of up to nine months' supply.

There are several major pipeline routes running east to west out of Russia, some for oil and some for gas. It is the gas lines that are the most important.

In the north, via the Baltic Sea, is the Nord Stream route, which connects directly to Germany. Below that, cutting through Belarus, is the Yamal pipeline, which feeds Poland and Germany. In the south is the Blue Stream, taking gas to Turkey via the Black Sea. Until early 2015 there was a planned project called South Stream, which was due to use the same route but branch off to Hungary, Austria, Serbia, Bulgaria, and Italy. South Stream was Russia's attempt to ensure that even during disputes with Ukraine it would still have a major route to large markets in Western Europe and the Balkans. Several

EU countries put pressure on their neighbors to reject the plan, and Bulgaria effectively pulled the plug on the project by saying the pipelines would not come across its territory. President Putin reacted by reaching out to Turkey with a new proposal, sometimes known as Turk Stream.

Russia's South Stream and Turk Stream projects to circumvent Ukraine followed the price disputes between the two states of 2005–10, which at various times cut the gas supply to eighteen countries. European nations that stood to benefit from South Stream were markedly more restrained in their criticism of Russia during the Crimea crisis of 2014.

Enter the Americans, with a win-win strategy for the United States and Europe. Noting that Europe wants gas, and not wanting to be seen to be weak in the face of Russian foreign policy, the Americans believe they have the answer. The massive boom in shale gas production in the United States is not only enabling it to be self-sufficient in energy, but also to sell its surplus to one of the great energy consumers—Europe.

To do this, the gas needs to be liquefied and shipped across the Atlantic. This in turn requires liquefied natural gas (LNG) terminals and ports to be built along the European coastlines to receive the cargo and turn it back into gas. Washington is already approving licenses for export facilities, and Europe is beginning a long-term project to build more LNG terminals. Poland and Lithuania are constructing LNG terminals; other countries such as the Czech Republic want to build pipelines connecting to those terminals, knowing they could then benefit not just from American liquefied gas, but also supplies from North Africa and the Middle East. The Kremlin would no longer be able to turn the taps off.

The Russians, seeing the long-term danger, point out that piped gas is cheaper than LNG, and President Putin, with a *What did I ever do wrong?* expression on his face, says that Europe already has a reliable and cheaper source of gas coming from his country. LNG is unlikely to completely replace Russian gas, but it will strengthen what is a weak European hand in both price negotiation and foreign policy. To prepare for a potential reduction in revenue, Russia is planning pipelines heading southeast and hopes to increase sales to China.

This is an economic battle based on geography and one of the modern examples where technology is being utilized in an attempt to beat the geographic restraints of earlier eras.

A lot was made of the economic pain Russia suffered in 2014 when the price of oil fell below $50 a barrel, and lower still in 2015. Moscow's 2016 budget—and predicted spending for 2017—was based on prices of $50, and even though Russia began pumping record levels of oil, it knows it cannot balance the books. Russia loses about $2 billion in revenue for each dollar drop in the oil price and the Russian economy duly took the hit, bringing great hardship to many ordinary people, but predictions of the collapse of the state were wide of the mark. Russia will struggle to fund its huge increase in military spending, but despite the difficulties the World Bank predicts that in the second half of this decade the economy will grow slightly. If the new discoveries of vast amounts of oil in the Arctic's Kara Sea can be brought to shore, that growth will be healthier.

Away from the heartland Russia does have a global political reach and uses its influence, notably in Latin America, where it buddies up to whichever South American country has the least friendly relationship with the United States, for example, Venezuela. It tries to check American moves in the Middle East, or at least ensure it has a say in matters, it is spending massively on its Arctic military forces, and it consistently takes an interest in Greenland to maintain its territorial claims. Since the fall of Communism it has focused less on Africa, but maintains what influence it can there, albeit in a losing battle with China.

Competitors they may be, but the two giants also cooperate on various levels. Moscow, knowing that the Europeans have a long-term ambition to wean themselves off dependency on Russian energy, is looking to China as an alternative customer. China has the upper hand in what is a buyers' market, but the lines of communication are cordial and well used. From 2018 Russia will supply China with 38 billion cubic meters of gas a year in a $400 billion thirty-year deal.

The days when Russia was considered a military threat to China have passed and the idea of Russian troops occupying Manchuria, as they did in 1945, is inconceivable, although they do keep a wary eye on each other in places in which each would like to be the dominant power, such as Kazakhstan. However, they are not in competition for the ideological leadership of global Communism and this has freed each side to cooperate at a military level where their interests coincide. What seems like an odd example came in May 2015 when they conducted joint military live fire exercises in the Mediterranean. Beijing's push into a sea 9,000 miles from home was part of its attempt to extend its naval reach around the globe. Moscow has designs on the gas fields found in the Mediterranean, is courting Greece, and wants to protect its small naval port on the Syrian coast. In addition, both sides are quite happy to annoy the NATO powers in the region, including the American 6th Fleet based in Naples.

At home it is facing many challenges, not least of which is demographic. The sharp decline in population growth may have been arrested, but it remains a problem. The average life span for a Russian man is below sixty-five, ranking Russia in the bottom half of the world's 193 UN member states, and there are now only 144 million Russians (excluding Crimea).

From the Grand Principality of Muscovy, through Peter the Great, Stalin, and now Putin, each Russian leader has been confronted by the same problems. It doesn't matter if the ideology of those in control is czarist, Communist, or crony capitalist—the ports still freeze, and the North European Plain is still flat.

Strip out the lines of nation states, and the map Ivan the Terrible confronted is the same one Vladimir Putin is faced with to this day.

2

CHINA

China is a civilization pretending to be a nation.
—Lucian Pye, political scientist

In October 2006, a US Naval Super Carrier Group led by the thousand-foot USS *Kitty Hawk* was confidently sailing through the East China Sea between southern Japan and Taiwan, minding everyone's business, when, without warning, a Chinese navy submarine surfaced in the middle of the group.

An American aircraft carrier of that size is surrounded by about twelve other warships, with air cover above and submarine cover below. The Chinese vessel, a Song-class attack submarine, may well be very quiet when running on electric power, but, still, this was the equivalent to Pepsi-Cola's management popping up in a Coca-Cola board meeting after listening under the table for half an hour.

The Americans were amazed and angry in equal measure. Amazed because they had no idea a Chinese sub could do that without being noticed, angry because they hadn't noticed and because they regarded the move as provocative, especially as the sub was within torpedo range of the *Kitty Hawk* itself. They protested, perhaps too much, and the Chinese said: "Oh! What a coincidence, us surfacing in the middle of your battle group that is off our coast, we had no idea."

This was twenty-first-century reverse gunboat diplomacy; whereas the British used to heave a man-of-war off the coast of some minor power to signal intent, the Chinese heaved into view off their own coast with a clear message: "We are now a maritime power, this is our time, and this is our sea." It has taken four thousand years, but the Chinese are coming to a port—and a shipping lane—near you.

Until now China has never been a naval power—with its large landmass, multiple borders, and short sea routes to trading partners, it had no need to be, and it was rarely ideologically expansive. Its merchants have long sailed the oceans to trade goods, but its navy did not seek territory beyond its region, and the difficulty of patrolling the great sea-lanes of the Pacific, Atlantic, and Indian Oceans was not worth the effort. It was always a land power, with a lot of land and a lot of people—now nearly 1.4 billion.

The concept of China as an inhabited entity began almost four thousand years ago. The birthplace of Chinese civilization is the region known as the North China Plain, which the Chinese refer to as the Central Plain. A large, low-lying tract of nearly 160,000 square miles, it is situated below Inner Mongolia, south of Manchuria, in and around the Yellow River and down past the Yangtze River, which both run west to east. It is now one of the most densely populated areas in the world.

The Yellow River basin is subject to frequent and devastating floods, earning the river the unenviable sobriquet "scourge of the Sons of Han." The industrialization of the region began in earnest in the 1950s and has been rapidly accelerating in the last three decades.

The terribly polluted river is now so clogged with toxic waste that it sometimes struggles even to reach the sea. Nevertheless, the Yellow River is to China what the Nile is to Egypt—the cradle of its civilization, where its people learned to farm, and to make paper and gunpowder.

To the north of this proto-China were the harsh lands of the Gobi Desert in what is now Mongolia. To the west the land gradually rises until it becomes the Tibetan Plateau, reaching to the Himalayas. To the southeast and the south lies the sea.

The heartland, as the North China Plain is known, was and is a large, fertile plain with two main rivers and a climate that allows rice and soybeans to be harvested twice a season (double-cropping), which encouraged rapid population growth. By 1500 BCE in this heartland, out of hundreds of mini city-states, many warring with each other, emerged the earliest version of a Chinese state—the Shang dynasty. This is where what became known as the Han people emerged, protecting the heartland and creating a buffer zone around them.

The Han now make up more than 90 percent of China's population and they dominate Chinese politics and business. They are differentiated by Mandarin, Cantonese, and many other regional languages, but united by ethnicity and at a political level by the geopolitical impulsion to protect the heartland. Mandarin, which originated in the northern part of the region, is by far the dominant language and is the medium of government, national state television, and education. Mandarin is similar to Cantonese and many other languages when written, but very different when spoken.

The heartland is the political, cultural, demographic, and—crucially—the agricultural center of gravity. About a billion people live in this part of China, despite its being just half the size of the

United States, which has a population of 322 million. Because the terrain of the heartland lent itself to settlement and an agrarian lifestyle, the early dynasties felt threatened by the non-Han regions that surrounded them, especially Mongolia, with its nomadic bands of violent warriors.

China chose the same strategy as Russia: attack as defense, leading to power. As we shall see, there were natural barriers that—if the Han could reach them and establish control—would protect them. It was a struggle over millennia, fully realized only with the annexation of Tibet six decades ago.

By the time of the famous Chinese philosopher Confucius (551–479 BCE) there was a strong feeling of Chinese identity and of a divide between civilized China and the "barbarous" regions that surrounded it. This was a sense of identity shared by 60 million or so people.

By 200 BCE, China had expanded toward, but not reached, Tibet in the southwest, north to the grasslands of central Asia, and south all the way down to the South China Sea. The Great Wall (known as the Long Wall in China) had been first built by the Qin dynasty (221–207 BCE), and on the map China was beginning to take on what we now recognize as its modern form. It would be more than two thousand years before today's borders were fixed, however.

Between 605 and 609 CE, the Grand Canal, centuries in the making and today the world's longest man-made waterway, was extended and finally linked the Yellow River to the Yangtze. The Sui dynasty (581–618 CE) had harnessed the vast numbers of workers under its control and used them to connect existing natural tributaries into a navigable waterway between the two great rivers. This tied the northern and southern Han to each other more closely than ever before. It took several million slaves five years to do the work, but the ancient problem of how to move supplies south to north had been solved—but not the problem that exists to this day, that of flooding.

The Han still warred with each other, but increasingly less so, and by the early eleventh century CE they were forced to concentrate their attention on the waves of Mongols pouring down from the north. The Mongols defeated whichever dynasty, north or south, they came up against, and by 1279 their leader, Kublai Khan, became the first foreigner to rule all of the country as emperor of the Mongol dynasty. It was almost ninety years before the Han would take charge of their own affairs with the establishment of the Ming dynasty.

By now there was increasing contact with traders and emissaries from the emerging nation states of Europe, such as Spain and Portugal. The Chinese leaders were against any sort of permanent European presence, but increasingly opened up the coastal regions to trade. It remains a feature of China to this day that when China opens up, the coastland regions prosper but the inland areas are neglected. The prosperity engendered by trade has made coastal cities such as Shanghai wealthy, but that wealth has not been reaching the countryside. This has added to the massive influx of people into urban areas and accentuated regional differences.

In the eighteenth century, China reached into parts of Burma and Indochina to the south, and Xinjiang in the northwest was conquered, becoming the country's biggest province. An area of rugged mountains and vast desert basins, Xinjiang is 642,820 square miles, twice the size of Texas—or, to put it another way, you could fit the UK, France, Germany, Austria, Switzerland, the Netherlands, and Belgium into it and still have room for Luxembourg. And Lichtenstein.

But, in adding to its size, China also added to its problems. Xinjiang, a region populated by Muslims, was a perennial source of instability, indeed insurrection, as were other regions; but for the Han, the buffer was worth the trouble, even more so after the fate that befell the country in the nineteenth and twentieth centuries with the coming of the Europeans.

The imperial powers arrived, the British among them, and carved the country up into spheres of influence. It was, and is, the greatest humiliation the Chinese suffered since the Mongol invasions. This is a narrative the Communist Party uses frequently; it is in part true, but it is also useful in covering up the party's own failures and repressive policies.

Later, the Japanese—expanding their territory as an emerging world power –invaded, attacking first in 1932 and then again in 1937, after which they occupied most of the heartland as well as Manchuria and Inner Mongolia. Japan's unconditional surrender to the Americans at the end of the Second World War in 1945 led to the withdrawal of Japanese troops, although in Manchuria they were replaced by the advancing Soviet army, which then withdrew in 1946.

A few outside observers thought the postwar years might bring liberal democracy to China. It was wishful thinking akin to the naive nonsense Westerners wrote during the early days of the recent Arab Spring, which, as with China, was based on a lack of understanding of the internal dynamics of the people, politics, and geography of the region.

Instead, nationalist forces under Chiang Kai-shek and Communist armies under Chairman Mao battled for supremacy until 1949, when the Communists emerged victorious and the nationalists withdrew to Taiwan. That same year, Radio Beijing announced: "The People's

Liberation Army must liberate all Chinese territories, including Tibet, Xinjiang, Hainan, and Taiwan."

Mao centralized power to an extent never seen in previous dynasties. He blocked Russian influence in Inner Mongolia and extended Beijing's influence into Mongolia. In 1951, China annexed Tibet (another vast non-Han territory) and by then Chinese school textbook maps began to depict China as stretching even into the central Asian republics. The country had been put back together; Mao would spend the rest of his life ensuring it stayed that way and consolidating Communist Party control in every facet of life but turning away from much of the outside world. The country remained desperately poor, especially away from the coastal areas, but unified.

Mao's successors tried to turn his Long March to victory into an economic march toward prosperity. In the early 1980s, the Chinese leader Deng Xiaoping coined the term "socialism with Chinese Characteristics," which appears to translate as "total control for the Communist Party in a capitalist economy." China was becoming a major trading power and a rising military giant. By the end of the 1990s it had recovered from the shock of the Tiananmen Square massacre of 1989, regained Hong Kong and Macau from the British and Portuguese, respectively, and could look around its borders, assess its security, and plan for its great move out into the world.

If we look at China's modern borders we see a great power now confident that it is secured by its geographical features, which lend themselves to effective defense and trade. In China, the points of the compass are always listed in the order east-south-west-north, but let's start in the north and move clockwise.

In the north we see the 2,906-mile-long border with Mongolia. Straddling this border is the Gobi Desert. Nomadic warriors from ancient times might have been able to attack south across it, but a modern army would be spotted amassing there weeks before it was ready to advance, and it would have incredibly long supply lines running across inhospitable terrain before it got into Inner Mongolia (part of China) and toward the heartland. There are few roads fit to move heavy armor, and few habitable areas. The Gobi Desert is a massive early warning system–cum–defensive line. Any Chinese expansion northward will come not via the military but from trade deals as China attempts to sweep up Mongolia's natural resources, primarily minerals. This will bring with it increased migration of the Han into Mongolia.

Next door, to the east, is China's border with Russia, which runs all the way to the Pacific Ocean—or at least the Sea of Japan subdivision of it. Above this is the mountainous Russian Far East, a huge, inhospitable territory with a tiny population. Below it is Manchuria, which the Russians would have to push through if they wanted to reach the Chinese heartland. The population of Manchuria is 100 million and growing; in contrast, the Russian Far East has only seven million people and no indications of population growth. Large-scale migration south to north can be expected, which will in turn give China more leverage in its relations with Russia. From a military perspective the best place to cross would be near the Russian Pacific port of Vladivostok, but there are few reasons, and no current intentions, to do so. Indeed, the recent Western sanctions against Russia due to the crisis in Ukraine have driven Russia into massive economic deals with China on terms that help keep Russia afloat, but are favorable to the Chinese. Russia is the junior partner in this relationship.

Below the Russian Far East, along the coast, are China's Yellow, East China, and South China Seas, which lead to the Pacific and

Indian Oceans, have many good harbors, and have always been used for trade. But across the waves lie several island-size problems—one shaped like Japan, which we shall come to shortly. Continuing clockwise, we come to the next land borders: Vietnam, Laos, and Burma. Vietnam is an irritation for China. For centuries the two have squabbled over territory and, unfortunately for both, this is the one area to the south that has a border an army can get across without too much trouble—which partially explains the thousand-year domination and occupation of Vietnam by China from 111 BCE to 938 CE and their brief cross-border war of 1979. However, as China's military prowess grows, Vietnam will be less inclined to get drawn into a shooting match and will either cozy up even closer to the Americans for protection or quietly begin shifting diplomatically to become friends with Beijing. That both countries are nominally ideologically Communist has little to do with the state of their relationship: it is their shared geography that has defined relations. Viewed from Beijing, Vietnam is only a minor threat and a problem that can be managed.

The border with Laos is hilly jungle terrain, difficult for traders to cross—and even more complicated for the military. As they move clockwise to Burma, the jungle hills become mountains until at the western extreme they are approaching twenty thousand feet and begin to merge into the Himalayas.

This brings us to Tibet and its importance to China. The Himalayas run the length of the Chinese-Indian border before descending to become the Karakoram Range bordering Pakistan, Afghanistan, and Tajikistan. This is nature's version of a Great Wall of China, or—looking at it from New Delhi's side—the Great Wall of India. It cuts the two most populous countries on the planet off from each other both militarily and economically.

They have their disputes: China claims the Indian province of Arunachal Pradesh, India says China is occupying Aksai Chin; but despite pointing their artillery at each other high up on this natural wall, both sides have better things to do than reignite the shooting match that broke out in 1962, when a series of violent border disputes culminated in vicious large-scale mountain fighting. Nevertheless, the tension is ever present and each side needs to handle the situation with care.

Very little trade has moved between China and India over the centuries, and that is unlikely to change soon. Of course, the border is really the Tibetan-Indian border—and that is precisely why China has always wanted to control it.

This is the geopolitics of fear. If China did not control Tibet, it would always be possible that India might attempt to do so. This would give India the commanding heights of the Tibetan Plateau and a base from which to push into the Chinese heartland, as well as control of the Tibetan sources of three of China's great rivers, the Yellow, Yangtze, and Mekong, which is why Tibet is known as "China's Water Tower." China, a country with approximately the same volume of water usage as the United States, but with a population five times as large, will clearly not allow that.

It matters not whether India wants to cut off China's river supply, only that it would have the power to do so. For centuries China has tried to ensure that it could never happen. The actor Richard Gere and the Free Tibet movement will continue to speak out against the injustices of the occupation, and now settlement, of Tibet by Han Chinese; but in a battle between the Dalai Lama, the Tibetan independence movement, Hollywood stars, and the Chinese Communist Party—which rules the world's second-largest economy—there is going to be only one winner.

When Westerners, be they Mr. Gere or President Obama, talk about Tibet, the Chinese find it deeply irritating. Not dangerous, not subversive—just irritating. They see it not through the prism of human rights, but that of geopolitical security, and can only believe that the Westerners are trying to undermine their security. However, Chinese security has not been undermined and it will not be, even if there are further uprisings against the Han. Demographics and geopolitics oppose Tibetan independence.

The Chinese are building "facts on the ground" on the "roof of the world." In the 1950s, the Chinese Communist People's Liberation Army began building roads into Tibet, and since then they have helped to bring the modern world to the ancient kingdom; but the roads, and now railways, also bring the Han.

It was long said to be impossible to build a railway through the permafrost, the mountains, and the valleys of Tibet. Europe's best engineers, who had cut through the Alps, said it could not be done. As late as 1988 the travel writer Paul Theroux wrote in his book *Riding the Iron Rooster*: "The Kunlun Range is a guarantee that the railway will never get to Lhasa." The Kunlun separated Xinjiang province from Tibet, for which Theroux gave thanks: "That is probably a good thing. I thought I liked railways until I saw Tibet, and then I realized that I liked wilderness much more." But the Chinese built it. Which, perhaps, only they could have done. The line into the Tibetan capital, Lhasa, was opened in 2006 by the then Chinese president Hu Jintao. Now passenger and goods trains arrive from as far away as Shanghai and Beijing, four times a day, every day.

They bring with them many things, such as consumer goods from across China, computers, color televisions, and cell phones. They bring tourists who support the local economy, they bring modernity to an ancient and impoverished land, a huge improvement in living standards and health care, and they bring the potential to carry Tibetan goods out to the wider world. But they have also brought several million Han Chinese settlers.

The true figures are hard to come by: the Free Tibet movement claims that in the wider cultural Tibetan region Tibetans are now a minority, but the Chinese government says that in the official Tibet Autonomous Region more than 90 percent of people are Tibetan. Both sides are exaggerating, but the evidence suggests the government is the one with the greater degree of exaggeration. Its figures do not include Han migrants, who are not registered as residents, but the casual observer can see that Han neighborhoods now dominate the Tibetan urban areas.

Once, the majority of the population of Manchuria, Inner Mongolia, and Xinjiang were ethnically Manchurian, Mongolian, and Uighur; now all three are majority Han Chinese, or approaching the majority. So it will be with Tibet.

This means that resentment of the Han will continue to manifest itself in rioting such as that of 2008, when anti-Chinese Tibetan protesters in Lhasa burned and looted Han properties, twenty-one people died, and hundreds were injured. The authorities' crackdown will continue, the Free Tibet movement will continue, monks will continue to set themselves on fire to bring the plight of the Tibetans to the world's attention—and the Han will keep coming.

China's massive population, mostly crammed into the heartland, is looking for ways to expand. Just as the Americans looked west, so do the Chinese, and just as the iron horse brought the European settlers to the lands of the Comanche and the Navajo, so the modern iron roosters are bringing the Han to the Tibetans.

Finally, the clock hand moves around past the borders with Pakistan, Tajikistan, and Kyrgyzstan (all mountainous) before reaching the border with Kazakhstan, which leads back around north to Mongolia. This is the ancient Silk Route, the land trade bridge from the middle kingdom to the world. Theoretically it's a weak spot in China's defense, a gap between the mountains and desert, but it is far from the heartland, the Kazakhs are in no position to threaten China, and Russia is several hundred miles distant.

Southeast of this Kazakh border is the restive "semiautonomous" Chinese province of Xinjiang and its native Muslim population of the Uighur people, who speak a language related to Turkish. Xinjiang borders eight countries: Russia, Mongolia, Kazakhstan, Kyrgyzstan, Tajikistan, Afghanistan, Pakistan, and India.

There was, is, and always will be trouble in Xinjiang. The Uighurs have twice declared an independent state of "East Turkestan," in the 1930s and 1940s. They watched the collapse of the Russian Empire result in their former Soviet neighbors in the stans becoming sovereign states, were inspired by the Tibetan independence movement, and many are now again calling to break away from China.

Interethnic rioting erupted in 2009, leading to more than two hundred deaths. Beijing responded in three ways: it ruthlessly suppressed dissent, it poured money into the region, and it continued to pour in Han Chinese workers. For China, Xinjiang is too strategically important to allow an independence movement to get off the ground: it not only borders eight countries, thus buffering the heartland, but it also has oil, and is home to China's nuclear weapons testing sites. The territory is also key to the Chinese economic strategy of "One Belt, One Road." The road is, oddly enough, the sea route: the creation of an oceangoing highway for goods, the belt is the "Silk Road

Economic Belt," a land-based route based on the old Silk Route that goes straight through Xinjiang and will in turn connect down southward to the massive deep-water port China is building in Gwadar in Pakistan. In late 2015, China signed a forty-year lease on the port. This is part of the way in which "the belt and the road" will be connected.

Most of the new towns and cities springing up across Xinjiang are overwhelmingly populated by Han Chinese attracted by work in the new factories in which the central government invests. A classic example is the city of Shihezi, eighty-five miles northwest of the capital, Ürümqi. Of its population of 650,000, it is thought that at least 620,000 are Han. Overall, Xinjiang is reckoned to be 40 percent Han, at a conservative estimate—and even Ürümqi itself may now be majority Han, although official figures are difficult to obtain and not always reliable due to their political sensitivity.

There is a World Uighur Congress based in Germany, and the East Turkestan Liberation Organization set up in Turkey; but Uighur separatists lack a Dalai Lama–type figure upon whom foreign media can fix, and their cause is almost unknown around the world. China tries to keep it that way, ensuring it stays on good terms with as many border countries as possible in order to prevent any organized independence movement from having supply lines or somewhere to which it could fall back. Beijing also paints separatists as Islamist terrorists. Al-Qaeda and other groups, which have a foothold in places like Tajikistan, are indeed attempting to forge links with the Uighur separatists, but the movement is nationalist first, Islamic second. However, gun, bomb, and knife attacks in the region against state and/or Han targets over the past few years do look as if they will continue and could escalate into a full-blown uprising. In early 2016, local government officials said that deradicalization efforts had "markedly weakened" the nascent Islamist movement. However, given that the Turkish army said it had arrested 324 suspected jihadists from Xinjiang en route to Syria in 2015, that seems unlikely.

China will not cede this territory and, as in Tibet, the window for independence is closing. Both are buffer zones, one is a major land trade route, and—crucially—both offer markets (albeit with a limited income) for an economy that must keep producing and selling goods if China is to continue to grow and to prevent mass unemployment. Failure to do so would likely lead to widespread civil disorder, threatening the control of the Communist Party and the unity of China.

There are similar reasons for the party's resistance to democracy and individual rights. If the population were to be given a free vote, the unity of the Han might begin to crack or, more likely, the countryside and urban areas would come into conflict. That in turn would embolden the people of the buffer zones, further weakening China. It is only a century since the most recent humiliation of the rape of China by foreign powers; for Beijing, unity and economic progress are priorities well ahead of democratic principles.

The Chinese look at society very differently from the West. Western thought is infused with the rights of the individual; Chinese thought prizes the collective above the individual. What the West thinks of as the rights of man, the Chinese leadership thinks of as dangerous theories endangering the majority, and much of the population accepts, at the least, that the extended family comes before the individual.

I once took a Chinese ambassador in London to a high-end French restaurant in the hope he would repeat Prime Minister Chou En-lai's much quoted answer to President Richard Nixon's question "What is the impact of the French Revolution?" to which the prime minister replied, "It's too soon to tell." Sadly, this was not forthcoming, but I was treated to a stern lecture about how the full imposition of "what you call human rights" in China would lead to widespread violence and death and was then asked, "Why do you think your values would work in a culture you don't understand?"

The deal between the party leaders and the people has been, for a generation now, "We'll make you better off—you will follow our orders." So long as the economy keeps growing, that grand bargain may last. If it stops, or goes into reverse, the deal is off. The current level of demonstrations and anger against corruption and inefficiency are testament to what would happen if the deal breaks.

Another growing problem for the party is its ability to feed the population. More than 40 percent of arable land is now either polluted or has thinning topsoil, according to their Ministry of Agriculture.

China is caught in a catch-22. It needs to keep industrializing as it modernizes and raises standards of living, but that very process threatens food production. If it cannot solve this problem there will be unrest.

There are now around five hundred mostly peaceful protests a day across China over a variety of issues. If you introduce mass unemployment, or mass hunger, that tally will explode in both number and the degree of force used by both sides.

So, on the economic side, China now also has a grand bargain with the world—"We'll make the stuff for cheap—you buy it for cheap."

Leave to one side the fact that already labor costs are rising in China and it is being rivaled by Thailand and Indonesia, for price if not volume. What would happen if the resources required to make the stuff dried up, if someone else got them first, or if there was a naval blockade of your goods—in and out? Well, for that, you'd need a navy.

The Chinese were great sea voyagers, especially in the fifteenth century, when they roamed the Indian Ocean; Admiral Zheng He's expedition ventured as far as Kenya. But these were moneymaking exercises, not power projections, and they were not designed to create forward bases that could be used to support military operations.

Having spent four thousand turbulent years consolidating its landmass, China is now building a blue-water navy. A green-water navy patrols its maritime borders, a blue-water navy patrols the oceans. It will take another thirty years (assuming economic progression) for China to build naval capacity to seriously challenge the most powerful seaborne force the world has ever seen—the US Navy. But in the medium to short term, as it builds, and trains, and learns, the Chinese navy will bump up against its rivals in the seas; and how those bumps are managed—especially the Sino-American ones—will define great power politics in this century.

The young seamen now training on the secondhand aircraft carrier that China salvaged from a Ukrainian junkyard will be the ones who, if they make it to the rank of admiral, may have learned enough to know how to take a twelve-ship carrier group across the world and back—and if necessary fight a war along the way. As some of the richer Arab nations came to realize, you cannot buy an efficient military off the shelf. A Chinese-built aircraft carrier is nearing completion, and in early 2016 China announced plans for a third to be ready by late 2021. It is doubtful it will be nuclear-powered, and it will lack the capabilities of US carriers; nevertheless, it will give China more reach, and more options.

Gradually the Chinese will put more and more vessels into the seas off their coast and into the Pacific. Each time one is launched there will be less space for the Americans in the China seas. The Americans know this, and know the Chinese are working toward a land-based antiship missile system to double the reasons why the US Navy, or any of its allies, might one day want to think hard about sailing through the South China Sea. Or indeed, any other "China sea." China's increasing long distance-shore-to ship artillery firepower will free up its growing navy to venture farther from its coastline because the navy will be become less vital for defense. There was hint of this in September 2015 when the Chinese (lawfully) sailed five vessels through American territorial waters off the coast of Alaska. That this took place just before President Xi's visit to the United States was not a coincidence. The Bering Strait is the quickest way for Chinese vessels to reach the Arctic Ocean. We will see more of them off the Alaskan coast in the coming years. And all the while, the developing Chinese space project will be watching every move the Americans make, and those of its allies.

So, having gone clockwise around the land borders, we now look east, south, and southwest toward the sea.

Under the water China is playing catch-up in submarine warfare. It may be able to surface a sub next to a US carrier group, but its underwater fleet is too noisy to hunt enemy submarines. While it works on this problem it is deploying anti-submarine ships and is busy installing a network of underwater sensors in the East and South China Seas.

Between China and the Pacific is the archipelago that Beijing calls the "first island chain." There is also the "nine-dash line," more recently turned into ten dashes in 2013 to include Taiwan, which

China says marks its territory. This dispute over ownership of more than two hundred tiny islands and reefs is poisoning China's relations with its neighbors. National pride means China wants to control the passageways through the chain; geopolitics dictates it has to. It provides access to the world's most important shipping lanes in the South China Sea. In peacetime the route is open in various places, but in wartime it could very easily be blocked, thus blockading China. All great nations spend peacetime preparing for the day war breaks out.

The South China Sea is a hotly contested area between China and its neighbors that leads to disputes over ownership of islands, natural resources, and control of the seas and shipping lanes.

Free access to the Pacific is first hindered by Japan. Chinese vessels emerging from the Yellow Sea and rounding the Korean Peninsula would have to go through the Sea of Japan and up through La Perouse Strait above Hokkaido and into the Pacific. Much of this is Japanese or Russian territorial waters, and at a time of great tension, or even hostilities, would be inaccessible to China. Even if they made it they would still have to navigate through the Kuril Islands northeast of Hokkaido, which are controlled by Russia but claimed by Japan.

Japan is also in dispute with China over the uninhabited island chain it calls Senkaku and the Chinese know as Diaoyu, northeast of Taiwan. This is the most contentious of all territorial claims between the two countries. If instead Chinese ships pass through, or indeed set off from, the East China Sea off Shanghai and go in a straight line toward the Pacific, they must pass the Ryukyu Islands, which include Okinawa—upon which there is not only a huge American military base, but also as many shore-to-ship missiles as the Japanese can pile at the tip of the island. The message from Tokyo is: "We know you're going out there, but don't mess with us on the way out."

Another potential flare-up with Japan centers on the East China Sea's gas deposits. Beijing has declared an "Air Defense Identification Zone" over most of the sea, requiring prior notice before anyone else flies through it. The Americans and Japanese are trying to ignore it, but it will become a hot issue at a time of their choosing or due to an accident that is mismanaged.

Below Okinawa is Taiwan, which sits off the Chinese coast and separates the East China Sea from the South China Sea. China claims Taiwan as its twenty-third province, but it is currently an American ally with a navy and air force armed to the teeth by Washington. It came under Chinese control in the seventeenth century but has only been ruled by China for five years in the last century (from 1945 to 1949).

Taiwan's official name is the Republic of China (ROC) to differentiate it from the People's Republic of China, although the ROC claims it should govern both territories. This is a name Beijing can live with, as it does not state that Taiwan is a separate state. America is committed to defending Taiwan in the event of a Chinese invasion under the Taiwan Relations Act of 1979. However, if Taiwan declares full independence from China, which China would consider an act of war, the United States is not to come to its rescue, as the declaration would be considered provocative.

The two governments vie for recognition for themselves and non-recognition of the other in every single country in the world, and in most cases Beijing wins. When you can offer a potential market of 1.4 billion people as opposed to 23 million, most countries don't need long to consider. However, there are twenty-two countries (mostly developing states; for example, Swaziland, Burkina Faso, and the island nation of São Tomé and Principe) that do opt for Taiwan and that are usually handsomely rewarded.

The Chinese are determined to have Taiwan but are nowhere near being able to challenge for it militarily. Instead they are using soft power by increasing trade and tourism between the two states. China wants to woo Taiwan back into its arms. During the 2014 student protests in Hong Kong, one of the reasons the authorities did not quickly batter them off the streets—as they would have done in, for example, Ürümqi—was that the world's cameras were there and would have captured the violence. In China much of this footage would be blocked, but in Taiwan people would see what the rest of the world saw and ask themselves how close a relationship they wanted with such a power. Beijing hesitated; it is playing the long game.

The soft-power approach is to persuade the people of Taiwan they have nothing to fear in rejoining the "motherland." The Air Defense Identification Zone, the surfacing near US ships, and the buildup of a navy are part of a long-term plan to weaken American resolve to defend an island 140 miles off the coast of mainland China, but 6,400 miles from the West Coast of the United States.

From the South China Sea, Chinese ships would still have problems, whether they headed toward the Pacific or the Indian Ocean—which is the world's waterway for the gas and oil without which China would collapse.

To go westward toward the energy-producing states of the Gulf they must pass Vietnam, which as we have noted has recently been making overtures to the Americans. They must go near the Philippines, a US ally, before trying to get through the Strait of Malacca between Malaysia, Singapore, and Indonesia, all of which are diplomatically and militarily linked to the United States. The strait is approximately five hundred miles long and at its narrowest point is less than two miles wide. It has always been a choke point—and the Chinese remain vulnerable to being choked, which is why by the fall of 2016 the Chinese were nearing the completion of extending the capacity of the port in Gwadar, Pakistan, and linking it by highway to China. All of the states along the strait, and near its approaches, are anxious about Chinese dominance and most have territorial disputes with Beijing.

China claims almost the entire South China Sea, and the energy supplies believed to be beneath it, as its own. However, Malaysia, Taiwan, Vietnam, the Philippines, and Brunei also have territorial claims against China and one another. For example, the Philippines and China argue bitterly over the Mischief Islands, a large reef in the Spratly Islands in the South China Sea, which one day could live up to their name. Every one of the hundreds of disputed atolls, and sometimes just rocks poking out of the water, could be turned into a diplomatic crisis, as surrounding each rock is a potential dispute about fishing zones, exploration rights, and sovereignty.

To further these aims, China, using dredging and land reclamations methods, has embarked on turning a series of reefs and atolls in disputed territory into islands. For example, one, whose name, Fiery Cross Reef, described what it was, has been turned into an island complete with port and runway in the Spratly Islands. Another has had artillery units stationed on it. The runway could host fighter jets giving China far more control of the skies over the region than it currently has.

Speaking in the summer of 2015, US Defense Secretary Ash Carter said, "Turning an underwater rock into an airfield simply does not afford the rights of sovereignty or permit restrictions on international air or maritime transit." This was shortly after China announced it was switching its military posture in the region from defense to both offense and defense. The move underlines China's intention to be the rule maker in the region and for that it will both court and threaten its neighbors.

China must secure these routes, both for its goods to get to market and for the items required to make those goods—oil, gas, and precious metals among them—to get into China. It cannot afford to be blockaded. Diplomacy is one solution; the ever-growing navy is another; but the best guarantees are pipelines, roads, and ports.

Diplomatically they will attempt to pull the Southeast Asian nations away from the United States using both carrot and stick. Too much stick and the countries will tie themselves ever closer into defense treaties with Washington; too much carrot and they may not bend to Beijing's will. At the moment they still look across the Pacific for protection.

The maps of the region that the Chinese now print show almost the whole of the South China Sea as theirs. This is a statement of intent, backed by aggressive naval patrols and official statements. Beijing intends to change its neighbors' ways of thinking and to change America's way of thinking and behaving—pushing and pushing an agenda until its competitors back off. At stake here is the concept of international waters and free passage in peacetime; it is not something that will easily be given up by the other powers.

The geopolitical writer Robert D. Kaplan expounds the theory that the South China Sea is to the Chinese in the twenty-first century what the Caribbean was to the United States at the beginning of the twentieth century. The Americans, having consolidated their landmass, had become a two-ocean power (Atlantic and Pacific), and then moved to control the seas around them, pushing the Spanish out of Cuba.

China also intends to become a two-ocean power (Pacific and Indian). To achieve this, China is investing in deep-water ports in Burma, Bangladesh, Pakistan, and Sri Lanka—an investment that buys it good relations, the potential for its future navy to have friendly bases to visit or reside in, and trade links back home.

The Indian Ocean and Bay of Bengal ports are part of an even bigger plan to secure China's future. Its lease on the new deep-water port at Gwadar in Pakistan will (if the Pakistan region of Baluchistan is stable enough) be key to creating an alternative land route up to China. From Burma's west coastline, China has built natural gas and oil pipelines linking the Bay of Bengal up into southwest China—China's way of reducing its nervous reliance on the Strait of Malacca, through which almost 80 percent of its energy supplies pass. This partially explains why, when the Burmese junta began to slowly open up to the outside world in 2010, it wasn't just the Chinese who beat a path to their door. The Americans and Japanese were quick to establish better relations, with both President Obama and Prime Minister Shinzo Abe of Japan going to pay their respects in person. If they can influence Burma, they can help keep China in check. So far, the Chinese are winning this particular game on the global chessboard, but the Americans may be able to outmuscle them as long as the Burmese government is confident Washington will stand by it.

The Chinese are also building ports in Kenya, railroad lines in Angola, and a hydroelectric dam in Ethiopia. They are scouring the length and breadth of the whole of Africa for minerals and precious metals.

Chinese companies and workers are spread out across the world; slowly, China's military will follow. With great power comes great responsibility. China will not leave the sea-lanes in its neighborhood to be policed by the Americans. There will be events that require the Chinese to act out of region. A natural disaster or a terrorist/hostage incident involving large numbers of Chinese workers would require China to take action, and that entails forward bases, or at least agreements from states that China could pass through their territory. There are now tens of millions of Chinese around the world, in some cases housed in huge complexes for workers in parts of Africa.

China will struggle to become agile over the next decade. It could barely maneuver the People's Army's equipment to help in the aftermath of the devastating 2008 earthquake in Sichuan. It mobilized the army, but not their matériel; moving abroad at speed would be an even greater challenge.

This will change. China is not weighed down or motivated diplomatically or economically by human rights in its dealings with the world. It is secure in its borders, straining against the bonds of the first island chain, and now moving around the globe with confidence. If it can avoid a serious conflict with Japan or the United States, then the only real danger to China is itself.

There are 1.4 billion reasons why China may succeed, and 1.4 billion reasons why it may not surpass America as the greatest power in the world. A great depression such as in the 1930s could set it back decades. China has locked itself into the global economy. If we don't buy, they don't make. And if they don't make, there will be mass unemployment. If there is mass and long-term unemployment, in an age when the Chinese are a people packed into urban areas, the inevitable social unrest could be—like everything else in modern China—on a scale hitherto unseen.

CAN

Washington

Oregon

Montana

Idaho

Wyoming

Nevada

Sierra Nevada

California

Utah

Colorado

Arizona

New Mexico

North Dakot

South Dako

Nebrask

Kans

Okla

Texas

R o c k y   M o u n t a i n s

G r e a t   P l a i n s

PACIFIC

OCEAN

Rio Grande

MEXICO

500 miles   500 km

State border
Administrative border
Mississippi basin

3

UNITED STATES

Reports of my death have been greatly exaggerated.
—Mark Twain, 1897

Location, location, location. If you won the lottery, and were look-ing to buy a country to live in, the first one the real estate agent would show you would be the United States of America.

Twain was referring to the erroneous reporting of his death, but he could have been talking about the overreporting of the demise of the United States.

It's in a wonderful neighborhood, the views are marvelous, and there are some terrific water features, the transport links are excel-lent, and the neighbors? The neighbors are great, no trouble at all.

If you broke this living space up into numerous sections it would considerably lower its value, especially if the tenants did not all speak the same language and paid the rent in different currencies, but as one home, for one family—it can't be bettered.

There are fifty American states, but they add up to one nation in a way the twenty-eight sovereign states of the European Union never can. Most of the EU states have a national identity far stronger, more defined, than any American state. It is easy to find a French person who is French first, European second, or one who pays little allegiance to the idea of Europe, but an American identifies with their Union in a way few Europeans do theirs. This is explained by the geography, and the history of the unification of the United States.

Painting this vast country in bold, broad brushstrokes from east to west, you can divide it into three.

First, there is the East Coast Plain leading to the Appalachian Mountains, an area well watered by short but navigable rivers and with fertile soil. Then, heading farther west, you have the Great Plains stretching all the way to the Rocky Mountains, and within this section lies the Mississippi basin with its network of huge, navigable rivers flowing into the Mississippi River all the way down to the Gulf of Mexico, which is sheltered by the peninsula of Florida and several islands. Once over the massive mountain range that is the Rockies you get to the desert, the Sierra Nevada Mountains, a narrow coastal plain, and finally to the shores of the Pacific Ocean.

To the north, above the Great Lakes, lies the Canadian Shield, the world's largest area of Precambrian rock, much of which forms a barrier to human settlement. To the southwest—desert. Geography had determined that if a political entity could get to and then control the land "from sea to shining sea," it would be a great power, the greatest history has known. Once that power was achieved, the Union would become militarily impossible to invade. As we say with Russia, there is "strategic depth" for a defending force to fall back into. Equally important, anyone stupid enough to contemplate invading America would soon reflect on the fact that it contains hundreds of millions of guns, which are available to a population that takes its life, liberty, and pursuit of happiness very seriously. In addition to the formidable US Armed Forces, there is the National Guard, state police, and as we've seen recently, an urban police force that can quickly resemble a military unit. In the event of an invasion every US Folsom, Fairfax, and Farmerville would quickly resemble an Iraqi Fallujah.

The size of Canada (and to a lesser extent Mexico) is also an asset. Any hostile power approaching in strength from the sea would have incredibly long supply lines, a truism for any similar land force as well. But, to achieve this rare geographical position of near invulnerability from conventional attack, first the space had to be acquired and unified. Considering the continent is three thousand miles from coast to coast, this was achieved in an astonishingly quick time.

When the Europeans first began to land and stay in the early seventeenth century, they quickly realized that the east coast of this "virgin" territory was packed with natural harbors and fertile soil. Here was a place where they could live and, unlike their home countries, a place where they hoped they could live freely. Their descendants would go on to deny the native inhabitants their freedom, but that was not the intention of the first settlers. Geography pulled them across the Atlantic in ever greater numbers.

The last of the original thirteen colonies to be established was Georgia in 1732. The thirteen became increasingly independent minded all the way up to the American Revolutionary War (1775–83). At the beginning of this period, the colonies, which gradually began to connect to one another, stretched one thousand miles from Massachusetts in the north, down to Georgia, and had an estimated combined population of approximately 2.5 million people. They were bounded by the Atlantic to their east and the Appalachian Mountains to their west. The Appalachians, 1,500 miles long, are impressive, but compared to the Rockies not particularly high. Nevertheless, they still formed a formidable barrier to westward movement for the early settlers, who were busy consolidating what territory they had subdued and preparing to govern it themselves. The colonists had another barrier, this one political. The British government forbade settlement west of the Appalachians, as it wanted to ensure that trade, and taxes, remained on the Eastern Seaboard.

The Declaration of Independence (1776) states: "When in the course of human events, it becomes necessary for one people to dissolve the political bands which have connected them with another, and to assume among the Powers of the earth, the separate and equal station to which the Laws of Nature and of Nature's God entitle them, a decent respect to the opinions of mankind requires that they should declare the causes which impel them to the separation." It goes on to outline at some length those causes, and to state (with no hint of slave-owning irony) that it was self-evident that all men were created equal. These noble sentiments helped to fuel the victory in the War of Independence, which in turn gave birth to a new nation state.

In the early 1800s this new country's leadership still had little idea that it was thousands of miles from the "south sea," or Pacific. Using Native American trails, a few explorers, for whom the word *intrepid* could have been coined, had pushed through the Appalachians and reached the Mississippi. There they thought they might find a waterway leading to the ocean and thus joining up with the vast tracts of lands the Spanish had explored across the southwestern and Pacific coastal regions, including what are now Texas and California.

At this point the fledgling United States was far from secure, and if it had been restricted to its then boundaries it would have struggled to become a great power. Its citizens already had access to the Ohio

River, just west of the Appalachians, but that led to the Mississippi, whose western bank was controlled by the French all the way down to the city of New Orleans. This gave the French command of American trade heading out to the Old World from the Gulf of Mexico, as well as the vast territory to the west in what is now the American heartland. In 1802, a year after Thomas Jefferson assumed the presidency, he wrote: "There is on the globe one single spot, the possessor of which is our natural and habitual enemy. It is New Orleans."

So France was the possessor and the problem; but the solution, unusually, was not warfare.

In 1803, the United States simply bought control of the entire Louisiana Territory from France. The land stretched from the Gulf of Mexico northwest up to the headwaters of the tributaries of the Mississippi River in the Rocky Mountains. It was an area equivalent in size to modern-day Spain, Italy, France, the UK, and Germany combined. With it came the Mississippi basin, from which flowed America's route to greatness.

At the stroke of a pen, and the handing over of $15 million, the Louisiana Purchase of 1803 doubled the size of the United States and gave it mastery over the greatest inland water transport route in the world. As the American historian Henry Adams wrote, "Never did the United States get so much for so little."

The greater Mississippi basin has more miles of navigable river than the rest of the world put together. Nowhere else are there so many rivers whose source is not in highland and whose waters run smoothly all the way to the ocean across vast distances. The Mississippi, fed by much of the basin river system, begins near Minneapolis and ends 1,800 miles south in the Gulf of Mexico. So the rivers were the natural conduit for ever-increasing trade, leading to a great port and all using waterborne craft that was, and is, many times cheaper than road travel.

The Americans now had strategic geographical depth, a massive fertile land, and an alternative to the Atlantic ports with which to conduct business. They also had ever-expanding routes east to west linking the East Coast to the new territory, and then the river systems flowing north to south to connect the then sparsely populated lands with one another, thus encouraging America to form as a single entity.

There was now a sense that the nation would become a colossus, a continental power. They pushed onward, ever westward, but with an eye on the south and the security of the jewel in the crown—the Mississippi.

By 1814 the British had gone, and the French had given up on Louisiana. The trick now was to get the Spanish to go. It wasn't too difficult. The Spanish were exhausted by the war in Europe against Napoleon; the Americans were pushing the Seminole nation into Spanish Florida, and Madrid knew that waves of settlers would be following. In 1819 the Spanish ceded Florida to the United States and with it a massive amount of territory.

The Louisiana Purchase had given the United States the heartland, but the Transcontinental Treaty of 1819 gave them something almost as valuable. The Spanish accepted that the US would have jurisdiction in the far west above the 42nd parallel on what is now the border of California and Oregon while Spain would control what lay below, west of the American territories. The United States had reached the Pacific.

At the time, most Americans thought the great victory of 1819 was getting Florida, but Secretary of State John Quincy Adams wrote in his diary: "The acquisition of a definite line of boundary to the [Pacific] forms a great epoch in our history."

But there was another Spanish-speaking problem—Mexico.

Because the Louisiana Purchase doubled the size of the United States, when Mexico became independent of Spain in 1821 its border was just two hundred miles from the port of New Orleans. In the twenty-first century, Mexico poses no territorial threat to the United States, although its proximity causes America problems, as it feeds its northern neighbor's appetite for illegal labor and drugs.

In 1821 that was different. Mexico controlled land all the way up to Northern California, which the United States could live with, but it also stretched out east, including what is now Texas, which, then as now, borders Louisiana. Mexico's population at the time was 6.2 million, the United States's 9.6 million. The US army may have been able to see off the mighty British, but they had been fighting three thousand miles from home with supply lines across an ocean. The Mexicans were next door.

Quietly, Washington, DC, encouraged Americans, and new arrivals, to begin to settle on both sides of the US–Mexican border. Waves of immigrants came and spread west and southwest. There was little chance of them putting down roots in the region we now know as modern Mexico, thus assimilating, and boosting, the population numbers there. Mexico is not blessed in the American way. It has poor-quality agricultural land, no river system to use for transport, and was wholly undemocratic, with new arrivals having little chance of ever being granted land.

While the infiltration of Texas was going on, Washington, DC, issued the Monroe Doctrine (named after President James Monroe) in 1823, which boiled down to warning the European powers that they could no longer seek land in the Western Hemisphere, and that if they lost any parts of their existing territory they could not reclaim them. Or else.

By the mid-1830s there were enough white settlers in Texas to force the Mexican issue. The Mexican, Catholic, Spanish-speaking population numbered in the low thousands, but there were approximately twenty thousand white Protestant settlers. The Texas Revolution of 1835–36 drove the Mexicans out, but it was a close-run thing, and had the settlers lost then, the Mexican army would have been in a position to march on New Orleans and control the southern end of the Mississippi. It is one of the great what-ifs of modern history.

However, history turned the other way and Texas became independent, via American money, arms, and ideas. The territory went on to join the Union in 1845 and together they fought the 1846–48 Mexican War, in which they crushed their southern neighbor, which was required to accept that Mexico ended in the sands of the southern bank of the Rio Grande.

With California, New Mexico, and land that is now Arizona, Nevada, Utah, and part of Colorado included, the borders of the continental United States then looked similar to those of today, and they are in many ways natural borders. In the south, the Rio Grande runs through desert; to the north are the Great Lakes and rocky land with few people close to the border, especially in the eastern half of the continent; and to the east and west are the great oceans. However, in the twenty-first century, in the southwest the cultural historical memory of the region as Hispanic land is likely to resurface, as the demographics are changing rapidly and Hispanics will be the majority population within a few decades.

But back to 1848. The Europeans had gone, the Mississippi basin was secure from land attack, the Pacific was reached, and it was obvious that the remaining Native American nations would be subdued: there was no threat to the United States. It was time to make some money, and then venture out across the seas to secure the approaches to the three coastlines of the superpower-to-be.

The California gold rush of 1848–49 helped, but the immigrants were heading west anyway; after all, there was a continental empire to build, and as it developed, more immigrants followed. The Homestead Act of 1862 awarded 160 acres of federally owned land to anyone who farmed it for five years and paid a small fee. If you were a poor man from Germany, Scandinavia, or Italy, why go to Latin America and be a serf, when you could go to the United States and be a free land-owning man?

In 1867, Alaska was bought from Russia. At the time it was known as "Seward's Folly," named for the secretary of state, William Seward, who agreed to the deal. He paid $7.2 million, or two cents, an acre. The press accused him of purchasing snow, but minds were changed with the discovery of gold in 1896. Decades later, huge reserves of oil were also found.

Two years on, in 1869, came the opening of the transcontinental railroad. Now you could cross the country in a week, whereas it had previously taken several hazardous months.

As the country grew, and grew wealthy, it began to develop a blue-water navy. For most of the nineteenth century, foreign policy was dominated by expanding trade and avoiding entanglements outside the neighborhood, but it was time to push out and protect the approaches to the coastlines. The only real threat was from Spain—it may have been persuaded to leave the mainland, but it still controlled the islands of Cuba, Puerto Rico, and part of what is now the Dominican Republic.

Cuba in particular kept American presidents awake at night, as it would again in 1962 during the Cuban Missile Crisis. The island sits just off Florida, giving it access to and potential control of the Straits of Florida and the Yucatán Channel in the Gulf of Mexico. This is the exit and entry route for the port of New Orleans.

Spain's power may have been diminishing toward the end of the nineteenth century, but it was still a formidable military force. In 1898, the US declared war on Spain, routed its military, and gained control of Cuba, with Puerto Rico, Guam, and the Philippines thrown in for good measure. They would all come in useful, but Guam in particular is a vital strategic asset and Cuba a strategic threat if controlled by a major power.

In 1898 that threat was removed by war with Spain. In 1962 it was removed by the threat of war with the Soviet Union after they blinked first. Today no great power sponsors Cuba and it appears destined to come under the cultural, and probably political, influence of the United States again.

America was moving quickly. In the same year it secured Cuba, the Straits of Florida, and to a great extent the Caribbean. It also annexed the Pacific island of Hawaii, thus protecting the approaches to its own West Coast. In 1903, America signed a treaty leasing it exclusive rights to the Panama Canal. Trade was booming.

The time was right for the United States to show it had more than arrived on the world stage, and what better way to demonstrate that than a show of force circumnavigating the globe.

President Theodore Roosevelt was speaking relatively softly—but in essence he "sailed" a large stick around the world. Sixteen navy battleships from the Atlantic force set out from the United States in December 1907. Their hulls were painted white, the navy's peacetime color, and this impressive example of diplomatic signaling became known as "the Great White Fleet." Over the following fourteen months the fleet called on twenty ports, including ones in Brazil, Chile, Mexico, New Zealand, Australia, the Philippines, Japan, China, Italy, and Egypt. Of these the most important was Japan, who was put on notice that in extremis America's Atlantic fleet could be deployed to the Pacific. The voyage, a mixture of hard and soft power, preceded the military term *force projection*, but that is what it was, and it was duly noted by every major power in the world.

Most subsequent presidents bore in mind George Washington's advice in his farewell address in 1796 not to get involved in "inveterate antipathies against particular nations, and passionate attachments for others," and to "steer clear of permanent alliances with any portion of the foreign world."

Apart from a late—albeit crucial—entry into the First World War, twentieth-century America did manage, mostly, to avoid entanglements and alliances until 1941.

The Second World War changed everything. The United States was attacked by an increasingly militaristic Japan after Washington imposed economic sanctions on Tokyo that would have brought the country to its knees. The Americans came out swinging. They projected their now vast power around the world, and in order to keep things that way, this time they didn't go home.

As the world's greatest economic and military postwar power, America now needed to control the world's sea-lanes, to keep the peace, and get the goods to market.

They were "the last man standing." The Europeans had exhausted themselves; their economies, like their towns and cities, were in ruins. Meanwhile, the Japanese were crushed; the Chinese were both devastated and at war with each other; and the Russians weren't even in the capitalist game.

A century earlier, the British had learned they needed forward bases and coaling stations from which to project and protect their naval power. Now, with Britain in decline, the Americans looked lasciviously at the British assets and said, "Nice bases—we'll have them."

The price was right. In the autumn of 1940, the British desperately needed more warships. The Americans had fifty to spare and so, with what was called the Destroyers for Bases Agreement, the British swapped their ability to be a global power for help in remaining in the war. Almost every British naval base in the Western Hemisphere was handed over.

This was, and is still, for all countries, about concrete. Concrete for the building of ports, runways, hardened aircraft hangars, fuel depots, dry docks, and Special Forces training areas. In the East, after the defeat of Japan, America seized the opportunity to build these all over the Pacific. Guam, halfway across, they already had; now they had bases right up to the Japanese island of Okinawa in the East China Sea.

The Americans also looked to the land. If they were going to pay to reconstruct Europe through the Marshall Plan of 1948–51, they had to ensure that the Soviet Union wouldn't wreck the place and reach the Atlantic coast. The doughboys didn't go home. Instead they set up shop in Germany and faced down the Red Army across the North European Plain.

In 1949, Washington led the formation of NATO and with it effectively assumed command of the Western world's surviving military might. The civilian head of NATO may well be a Belgian one year, a Brit the next, but the military commander is always an American, and by far the greatest firepower within NATO is American.

No matter what the treaty says, NATO's Supreme Commander

ultimately answers to Washington. The UK and France would learn at their expense during the Suez Crisis of 1956—when they were compelled by American pressure to cease their occupation of the canal zone, losing most of their influence in the Middle East as a result—that a NATO country does not hold a strategic naval policy without first asking Washington.

With Iceland, Norway, Britain, and Italy (all founding members of NATO) having granted the United States access and rights to their bases, it now dominated the North Atlantic and the Mediterranean as well as the Pacific. In 1951, it extended its domination there down to the south by forming an alliance with Australia and New Zealand, and also to the north following the Korean War of 1950–53.

There were now two maps of the United States. The familiar one stretching diagonally down from Seattle on the Pacific coast to the panhandle in the Sargasso Sea, and the part real/part conceptual one of America's geopolitical-power footprint.

This map consisted of the bases, ports, and runways you could mark on the page, but also the conceptual map, the one that told you that in the event of situation A happening in region B, country C could be relied upon to side with the United States and vice versa. If a major power wanted to play anywhere, it knew that if it chose to, the United States could have a dog in the fight. A superpower had arrived.

In the 1960s, the United States's failure in Vietnam damaged its confidence and made it more cautious about foreign entanglements. However, what was effectively a defeat did not substantially alter America's global strategy.

There were now only three places from which a challenge to American hegemony could come: a united Europe, Russia, and China. All would grow stronger, but two would reach their limits.

The dream of some Europeans of an EU with "ever closer union" and a common foreign and defense policy is dying slowly before our eyes, and even if it were not, the EU countries spend so little on defense that ultimately they remain reliant on the United States. The economic crash of 2008 has left the European powers reduced in capacity and with little appetite for foreign adventures. The gradual splintering of the idea of unity was magnified by the UK's decision to hold a referendum on its membership in the EU in the summer of 2016. The complicated aftermath of the Brexit vote has brought confusion to the continent. It also disappointed Washington, DC, which always favored having the UK inside the EU as its eyes and ears

In 1991, the Russian threat had been seen off due to their own staggering economic incompetence, military overstretch, and failure to persuade the subjected masses in their empire that gulags and the overproduction of state-funded tractors was the way ahead. The recent pushback by Putin's Russia is a thorn in America's side, but not a serious threat to America's dominance. When President Obama described Russia as "no more than a regional power" in 2014, he may have been needlessly provocative, but he wasn't wrong. The bars of Russia's geographical prison, as seen in chapter one, are still in place: they still lack a warm-water port with access to the global sea-lanes and still lack the military capacity in wartime to reach the Atlantic via the Baltic and North Seas, or the Black Sea and the Mediterranean.

The United States was partially behind the change of government in Ukraine in 2014. It wanted to extend democracy in the world, and it wanted to pull Ukraine away from Russian influence and thus weaken President Putin. Washington knows that during the last decade, as America was distracted in Iraq and Afghanistan, the Russians took advantage in what they call their "near abroad," regaining a solid footing in places such as Kazakhstan and seizing territory in Georgia. Belatedly, and somewhat half-heartedly, the Americans have been trying to roll back Russian gains.

Americans care about Europe, they care about NATO, and they will sometimes act (if it is in the American interest), but Russia is now, for the Americans, mostly a European problem, albeit one they keep an eye on.

That leaves China, and China rising.

Most analysis written over the past decade assumes that by the middle of the twenty-first century China will overtake the United States and become the leading superpower. For reasons partially discussed in chapter two, I am not convinced. It may take a century.

Economically the Chinese are on their way to matching the Americans, and that buys them a lot of influence and a place at the top table, but militarily and strategically they are decades behind. The United States will spend those decades attempting to ensure it stays that way, but it feels inevitable that the gap will close.

The concrete costs a lot. Not just to mix and pour, but to be allowed to mix and pour it where you want to. As we saw with the Destroyers for Bases Agreement, American assistance to other governments is not always entirely altruistic. Economic and, equally important, military assistance buys permission to pour the concrete, but much more as well, even if there is also an added cost.

For example, Washington might be outraged at human rights abuses in Syria (a hostile state) and express its opinions loudly, but its outrage at abuses in Bahrain might be somewhat more difficult to hear, muffled as it has been by the engines of the US 5th Fleet, which is based in Bahrain as the guest of the Bahraini government. On the other hand, assistance does buy the ability to suggest to government B (say Burma) that it might want to resist the overtures of government

C (say China). In that particular example, the United States is behind the curve because the Burmese government only recently began to open up to most of the outside world and Beijing has a head start.

However, when it comes to Japan, Thailand, Vietnam, South Korea, Singapore, Malaysia, Indonesia, and others, the Americans are pushing at a door already open due to those countries' anxiety about their giant neighbor and keenness to engage with Washington. They may all have issues with one another, but those issues are dwarfed by the knowledge that if they do not stand together they will be picked off one by one and eventually fall under Chinese hegemony.

The United States is still in the opening phase of what in 2011 then secretary of state Hillary Clinton called "the pivot to China." It was an interesting phrase, taken by some to mean the abandonment of Europe; but a pivot toward one place does not mean the abandonment of another. It is more a case of how much weight you put on which foot. Extra weight for the pivot was shown in the summer of 2016 when the U.S. 3rd Fleet, operating out of San Diego, "forward deployed" more ships than ever into the Western Pacific (alongside the 7th Fleet) whereas traditionally it operated only in the Eastern Pacific.

Many US government foreign policy strategists are persuaded that the history of the twenty-first century will be written in Asia and the Pacific. Half of the world's population lives there, and if India is included it is expected to account for half of the global economic output by 2050.

Hence, we will see the United States increasingly investing time and money in East Asia to establish its presence and intentions in the region. For example, in Northern Australia the Americans have set up a base for the US Marine Corps. But in order to exert real influence they may also have to invest in limited military action to reassure their allies that they will come to their rescue in the event of hostilities. For example, if

China begins shelling a Japanese destroyer and it looks as if they might take further military action, the US Navy may have to fire warning shots toward the Chinese navy, or even fire directly, to signal that it is willing to go to war over the incident. Equally, when North Korea fires at South Korea, the South fires back, but currently the United States does not. Instead, it puts forces on alert in a public manner to send a signal. If the situation escalated it would then fire warning shots at a North Korean target, and finally, direct shots. It's a way of escalating without declaring war—and this is when things get dangerous.

The United States is seeking to demonstrate to the whole region that it is in their best interests to side with Washington—China is doing the opposite. So, when challenged, each side must react, because for each challenge it ducks, its allies' confidence, and competitors' fear, slowly drains away until eventually there is an event that persuades a state to switch sides.

Analysts often write about the need for certain cultures not to lose face, or ever be seen to back down, but this is not just a problem in the Arab or East Asian cultures—it is a human problem expressed in different ways. It may well be more defined and openly articulated in those two cultures, but American foreign policy strategists are as aware of the issue as any other power. The English language even has two sayings that demonstrate how deeply ingrained the idea is: "Give them an inch and they'll take a mile," and President Theodore Roosevelt's maxim of 1900, which has now entered the political lexicon: "Speak softly and carry a big stick."

The deadly game in this century will be how the Chinese, Americans, and others in the region manage each crisis that arises without losing face and without building up a deep well of resentment and anger on both sides.

The Cuban Missile Crisis is generally considered an American victory; what is less publicized is that several months after Russia removed its missiles from Cuba, the United States removed its Jupiter missiles (which could reach Moscow) from Turkey. It was actually a compromise, with both sides, eventually, able to tell their respective publics that they had not capitulated.

In the twenty-first-century Pacific there are more great-power compromises to be made. In the short term, most, but not all, are likely to be made by the Chinese—an early example is Beijing's declaration of an Air Defense Identification Zone requiring foreign nations to inform them before entering what is disputed territory, and the Americans deliberately flying through it without telling them. The Chinese gained something by declaring the zone and making it an issue; the United States gained something by being seen not to comply. It is a long game. It is also a game of cat and mouse. In early 2016, for the first time, China landed a plane on one of the runways it has constructed on the artificial islands it is building in the Spratly Islands area of the South China Sea. Vietnam and the Philippines made formal protests as they both have claims on the area and the US described the move as threatening "regional stability." Washington, DC, now watches each construction project, and flight, and has to pick and choose when and where it makes more vigorous protests or sends naval and air force patrols near the disputed territory. Somehow it must reassure its allies it will stand by them and guarantee freedom of navigation in international areas, while simultaneously not going so far as to draw China into a military confrontation.

The US policy regarding the Japanese is to reassure them that they share strategic interests vis-à-vis China and ensure that the US base in Okinawa remains open. The Americans will assist the Japanese Self-Defense Force to be a robust body, but simultaneously restrict

Japan's military ability to challenge the United States in the Pacific.

While all the other countries in the region matter, in what is a complicated diplomatic jigsaw puzzle, the key states look to be Indonesia, Malaysia, and Singapore. These three sit astride the narrow Strait of Malacca. Every day through that strait come 12 million barrels of oil heading for an increasingly thirsty China and elsewhere in the region. As long as these three countries are pro-American, the Americans have a key advantage.

On the plus side, the Chinese are not politically ideological, they do not seek to spread Communism, nor do they covet (much) more territory in the way the Russians did during the Cold War, and neither side is looking for conflict. The Chinese can accept America guarding most of the sea-lanes that deliver Chinese goods to the world, so long as the Americans accept that there will be limits to just how close to China that control extends.

There will be arguments, and nationalism will be used to ensure the unity of the Chinese people from time to time, but each side will be seeking compromise. The danger comes if they misread each other and/or gamble too much.

There are flash points. America's treaty with Taiwan states if the Chinese invade what they regard as their 23rd province, the United States will go to war. A red line for China, which could spark an invasion, is formal recognition of Taiwan by the United States, or a declaration of independence by Taiwan. However, there is no sign of that, and a Chinese invasion cannot be seen on this side of the horizon.

As China's thirst for foreign oil and gas grows, that of the United States declines. This will have a huge impact on its foreign relations, especially in the Middle East, with ramifications for other countries.

Due to offshore drilling in US coastal waters, and underground fracking across huge regions of the country, America looks destined to become not just self-sufficient in energy, but a net exporter of energy by 2020. This will mean that its focus on ensuring a flow of oil and gas from the Gulf region will diminish. It will still have strategic interests there, but the focus will no longer be so intense. If the American attention wanes, the Gulf nations will seek new alliances. One candidate will be Iran, another China, but that will only happen when the Chinese have built their blue-water navy and, equally important, are prepared to deploy it.

The US 5th Fleet is not about to sail away from its port in Bahrain—that is a piece of concrete it would give up reluctantly. However, if the energy supplies of Saudi Arabia, Kuwait, the UAE, and Qatar are no longer required to keep American lights on and cars on the road, the American public and Congress will ask "What is it there for?" If the response is "To check Iran," it may not be enough to quash the debate, especially in light of President Obama's deal with Tehran on its nuclear capabilities.

Elsewhere in the Middle East, US policy in the short term is to attempt to ensure Iran does not become too strong, but at the same time build on that nuclear deal to try and reach what is known as the "grand bargain"—an agreement settling the many issues that divide the two countries, and ending three and a half decades of enmity. With the Arab nations embarking on what may be a decades-long struggle with armed Islamists, Washington looks as if it has given up on the optimistic idea of encouraging Jeffersonian democracies to emerge and will concentrate on attempting to manage the situation, while at the same time desperately trying not to get sand on the boots of US soldiers.

The close relationship with Israel may cool, albeit slowly, as the demographics of the United States change. The children of the Hispanic and Asian immigrants now arriving in the United States will be more interested in Latin America and the Far East than in a tiny country on the edge of a region no longer vital to American interests.

The policy in Latin America will be to ensure that the Panama Canal remains open, to inquire about the rates to pass through the proposed Nicaraguan canal to the Pacific, and to keep an eye on the rise of Brazil in case it gets any ideas about its influence in the Caribbean Sea. Economically the United States will also compete with China throughout Latin America for influence, but only in Cuba would Washington pull out all the stops to ensure it dominates the post-Castro/Communist era. The proximity of Cuba to Florida, the historic relationship (albeit mixed), and Chinese pragmatism should be enough to ensure that the United States will be the dominant power in the new Cuba.

In Africa, the Americans are but one nation seeking the continent's natural wealth, but the nation finding most of it is China. As in the Middle East, the United States will watch the Islamist struggle in North Africa with interest but try not to get involved much closer than thirty thousand feet above the ground.

America's experiment with nation building overseas appears to be over.

In Iraq, Afghanistan, and elsewhere, the United States underestimated the mentality and strength of small powers and of tribes. The Americans' own history of physical security and unity may have led them to overestimate the power of their democratic rationalist argument, which believes that compromise, hard work, and even voting would triumph over atavistic, deep-seated historical fears of "the other," be they Sunni, Shia, Kurd, Arab, Muslim, or Christian. They assumed people would want to come together, whereas in fact many dare not try and would prefer to live apart because of their experiences. It is a sad reflection upon humanity, but it appears throughout many periods of history, and in many places, to be an unfortunate truth. The American actions took the lid off a simmering pot that had temporarily hidden that truth.

This does not make American policy makers "naive," as some of the snootier European diplomats like to believe; but they do have a "can do" and a "can fix" attitude, which inevitably will not always work.

For thirty years it has been fashionable to predict the imminent or ongoing decline of the United States. This is as wrong now as it was in the past. The planet's most successful country is about to become self-sufficient in energy, it remains the preeminent economic power, and it spends more on research and development for its military than the overall military budget of all the other NATO countries combined. Its population is not aging as in Europe and Japan, and a 2013 Gallup Poll showed that 25 percent of all people hoping to emigrate put the United States as their first choice of destination. In the same year, Shanghai University listed what its experts judged the top-twenty universities of the world: seventeen were in the United States.

The Prussian statesman Otto von Bismarck, in a double-edged remark, said more than a century ago that "God has a special providence for fools, drunks, and the United States of America." It appears still to be true.

4

WESTERN EUROPE

Here the past was everywhere, an entire continent sown with memories.
—Miranda Richmond Mouillot,
A Fifty-Year Silence: Love, War, and a Ruined House in France

The modern world, for better or worse, springs from Europe. This western outpost of the great Eurasian landmass gave birth to the Enlightenment, which led to the Industrial Revolution, which has resulted in what we now see around us every day. For that, we can give thanks to, or blame, Europe's location.

The climate, fed by the Gulf Stream, blessed the region with the right amount of rainfall to cultivate crops on a large scale, and the right type of soil for them to flourish in. This allowed for population growth in an area in which, for most, work was possible year-round, even in the height of summer. Winter actually adds a bonus, with temperatures warm enough to work in but cold enough to kill off many of the germs, which to this day plague huge parts of the rest of the world.

Good harvests mean surplus food that can be traded; this in turn builds up trading centers that become towns. It also allows people to think of more than just growing food and to turn their attention to ideas and technology.

Western Europe has no real deserts, the frozen wastes are confined to a few areas in the far north, and earthquakes, volcanoes, and massive flooding are rare. The rivers are long, flat, navigable, and made for trade. As they empty into a variety of seas and oceans, they flow into coastlines that are—west, north, and south—abundant in natural harbors.

If you are reading this trapped in a snowstorm in the Alps, or waiting for floodwaters to subside back into the Danube, then Europe's geographical blessings may not seem too apparent; but, relative to many places, a blessing they are. These are the factors that led to the Europeans creating the first industrialized nation states, which in turn led them to be the first to conduct industrial-scale war.

If we take Europe as a whole, we see the mountains, rivers, and valleys that explain why there are so many nation states. Unlike the United States, in which one dominant language and culture pressed rapidly and violently ever westward, creating a giant country, Europe grew organically over millennia and remains divided between its geographical and linguistic regions.

The various tribes of the Iberian Peninsula, for example, prevented from expanding north into France by the presence of the Pyrenees, gradually came together, over thousands of years, to form Spain and Portugal—and even Spain is not an entirely united country, with Catalonia increasingly vocal about wanting its independence. France has also been formed by natural barriers, framed as it is by the Pyrenees, the Alps, the Rhine, and the Atlantic Ocean.

Europe's major rivers do not meet (unless you count the Sava, which drains into the Danube in Belgrade). This partly explains why there are so many countries in what is a relatively small space. Because they do not connect, most of the rivers act, at some point, as boundaries, and each is a sphere of economic influence in its own right; this gave rise to at least one major urban development on the banks of each river, some of which in turn became capital cities.

Europe's second longest river, the Danube (1,771 miles), is a case in point. It rises in Germany's Black Forest and flows south on its way to the Black Sea. In all, the Danube basin affects eighteen countries and forms natural borders along the way, including those of Slovakia and Hungary, Croatia and Serbia, Serbia and Romania, and Romania and Bulgaria. More than two thousand years ago it was one of the borders of the Roman Empire, which in turn helped it to become one of the great trading routes of medieval times and gave rise to the present capital cities of Vienna, Bratislava, Budapest, and Belgrade. It also formed the natural border of two subsequent empires, the Austro-Hungarian and the Ottoman. As each shrank, the nations emerged again, eventually becoming nation states. However, the geography of the Danube region, especially at its southern end, helps explain why there are so many small nations there in comparison to the bigger countries in and around the North European Plain.

The countries of northern Europe have been richer than those of the south for several centuries. The north industrialized earlier than the south and so has been more economically successful. As many of the northern countries comprise the heartland of Western Europe, their trade links were easier to maintain, and one wealthy neighbor could trade with another—whereas the Spanish, for example, either had to cross the Pyrenees to trade, or look to the limited markets of Portugal and North Africa.

The Danube Basin illustrates the geographical advantages of the terrain in Europe; interconnected rivers on a flat plain provided natural borders and an easily navigable transport network that encouraged a booming trade system.

There are also unprovable theories that the domination of Catholicism in the south has held it back, whereas the Protestant work ethic propelled the northern countries to greater heights. Each time I visit the Bavarian city of Munich, I reflect on this theory, and while driving past the gleaming temples of the headquarters of BMW, Allianz, and Siemens I have cause to doubt it. In Germany, 34 percent of the population is Catholic, and Bavaria itself is predominantly Catholic, yet their religious predilections do not appear to have influenced either their progress or their insistence that Greeks work harder and pay more taxes.

The contrast between northern and southern Europe is also at least partly attributable to the fact that the south has fewer coastal plains suitable for agriculture, and has suffered more from drought and natural disasters than the north, albeit on a lesser scale than in other parts of the world. As we saw in chapter one, the North European Plain is a corridor that stretches from France to the Ural Mountains in Russia, bordered to the north by the North and Baltic Seas. The land allows for successful farming on a massive scale, and the waterways enable the crops and other goods to be moved easily.

Of all the countries in the plain, France was best situated to take advantage of it. France is the only European country to be both a northern and southern power. It contains the largest expanse of fertile land in Western Europe, and many of its rivers connect with one another; one flows west all the way to the Atlantic (the Seine), another south to the Mediterranean (the Rhône). These factors, together with France's relative flatness, were suitable for the unification of regions, and—especially from the time of Napoleon—centralization of power.

But to the south and west many countries remain in the second tier of European power, partially because of their location. The south of Italy, for example, is still well behind the north in terms of development, and although it has been a unified state (including Venice and Rome) since 1871, the strains of the rift between north and south are greater now than they have been since before the Second World War. The heavy industry, tourism, and financial centers of the north have long meant a higher standard of living there, leading to the formation of political parties agitating for cutting state subsidies to the south, or even breaking away from it.

Spain is also struggling, and has always struggled because of its geography. Its narrow coastal plains have poor soil, and access to markets is hindered internally by its short rivers and the Meseta Central, a highland plateau surrounded by mountain ranges, some of which cut through it. Trade with Western Europe is further hampered by the Pyrenees, and any markets to its south on the other side of the Mediterranean are in developing countries with limited income. It was left behind after the Second World War, as under the Franco dictatorship it was politically frozen out of much of modern Europe. Franco died in 1975 and the newly democratic Spain joined the EU in 1986. By the 1990s, it had begun to catch up with the rest of Western Europe, but its inherent geographical and financial weaknesses continue to hold it back and have intensified the problems of overspending and loose central fiscal control. It has been among the countries hit worst by the 2008 economic crisis.

Greece suffers similarly. Much of the Greek coastline comprises steep cliffs and there are few coastal plains for agriculture. Inland are more steep cliffs, rivers that will not allow transportation, and few wide, fertile valleys. What agricultural land there is is of high quality; the problem is that there is too little of it to allow Greece to become a major agricultural exporter, or to develop more than a handful of major urban areas containing highly educated, highly skilled, and technologically advanced populations. Its situation is further exacerbated by its location, with Athens positioned at the tip of a peninsula, almost cut off from land trade with Europe. It is reliant on the Aegean Sea for access to maritime trade in the region—but across that sea lies Turkey, a large potential enemy. Greece fought several wars against Turkey in the late nineteenth and early twentieth centuries, and in modern times it still spends a vast amount of euros, which it doesn't have, on defense.

The mainland is protected by mountains, but there are about 1,400 Greek islands (six thousand if you include various rocks sticking out of the Aegean) of which approximately two hundred are inhabited. It takes a decent navy just to patrol this territory, never mind one strong enough to deter any attempt to take the islands over. The result is a huge cost in military spending that Greece cannot afford. During the Cold War, the Americans, and to a lesser extent the British, were content to underwrite some of the military requirements in order to keep the Soviet Union out of the Aegean and the Mediterranean. When the Cold War ended, so did the checks. But Greece kept spending.

This historical split continues to have an impact to this day in the wake of the financial crash that hit Europe in 2008 and the ideological rift in the eurozone. In 2012, when the European financial bailouts, to keep Greece afloat and in the euro currency zone, began and demands for Greek austerity measures were made, the geographical divide soon became obvious. The donors and demanders were the northern countries, the recipients and supplicants mostly southern. It didn't take long for people in Germany to point out that they were working until sixty-five but paying taxes that were going to Greece so that people could retire at fifty-five. They then asked "Why?" And the answer, "In sickness and in health," was unsatisfactory.

The Germans led the bailout-imposed austerity measures, the Greeks led the backlash. For example, the German finance minister, Wolfgang Schäuble, commented that he was "not yet sure that all political parties in Greece are aware of their responsibility for the difficult situation their country is in." To which the Greek president, Karolos Papoulias, who had fought the Nazis, replied, "I cannot accept Mr. Schäuble insulting my country. . . . Who is Mr. Schäuble to insult Greece? Who are the Dutch? Who are the Finnish?" He also made a pointed reference to the Second World War: "We were always proud to defend not only our freedom, our country, but Europe's freedom, too." The stereotypes of profligate, slack southerners and careful, industrious northerners soon resurfaced with the Greek media responding with constant and crude reminders of Germany's past, including superimposing a Hitler mustache on a front-page photograph of Chancellor Merkel.

The Greek taxpayer—of whom there are not enough to sustain the country's economy—has a very different view, asking: "Why should the Germans dictate to us, when the euro benefits them more than anyone else?" In Greece and elsewhere, austerity measures imposed from the north are seen as an assault on sovereignty.

Cracks are appearing in the edifice of the "family of Europe." On the periphery of Western Europe the financial crisis has left Greece looking like a semidetached member; to the east it has again seen conflict. If the aberration of the past seventy years of peace is to continue through this century, that peace will need love, care, and attention.

The post–Second World War generations have grown up with peace as the norm, but what is different about the current generation is that Europeans find it difficult to imagine the opposite. Wars now seem to be what happens elsewhere or in the past—at worst, they happen on the "periphery" of Europe. The trauma of two world wars, followed by seven decades of peace and then the collapse of the Soviet Union persuaded many people that Western Europe was a "post-conflict" region.

There are reasons to believe that this may still hold true in the future, but potential sources of conflict bubble under the surface, and the tension between the Europeans and the Russians may result in a confrontation. For example, history and geographical shape-shifting haunts Polish foreign policy even if the country is currently at peace, successful, and one of the bigger EU states, with a population of 38 million. It is also physically one of the larger members and its economy has doubled since it emerged from behind the Iron Curtain, but still it looks to the past as it tries to secure its future.

The corridor of the North European Plain is at its narrowest between Poland's Baltic coast in the north and the beginning of the Carpathian Mountains in the south. This is where, from a Russian military perspective, the best defensive line could be placed or, from an attacker's viewpoint, the place at which its forces would be squeezed together before breaking out toward Russia.

The Poles have seen it both ways, as armies have swept east and west across it, frequently changing borders. If you take *The Times Atlas of European History* and flick through the pages quickly as if it were a flip book, you see Poland emerge circa 1000 CE, then continually change shape, disappear, and reappear until assuming its present form in the late twentieth century.

The location of Germany and Russia, coupled with the Poles' experience of these two countries, does not make either a natural ally for Warsaw. Like France, Poland wants to keep Germany locked inside the EU and NATO, while not-so-ancient fears of Russia have come to the fore with the crisis in Ukraine. Over the centuries, Poland has seen the Russian tide ebb and flow from and to them. After the low tide at the end of the Soviet (Russian) empire, there was only one direction it could subsequently flow.

Relations with Britain, as a counterweight to Germany within the EU, came easily despite the betrayal of 1939: Britain and France had signed a treaty guaranteeing to come to Poland's aid if Germany invaded. When the attack came, the response to the blitzkrieg was a "sitzkrieg"—both Allies sat behind the Maginot Line in France as Poland was swallowed up. Despite this, relations with the UK are strong, even if the main ally the newly liberated Poland sought out in 1989 was the United States.

The Americans embraced the Poles and vice versa: both had the Russians in mind. In 1999, Poland joined NATO, extending the Alliance's reach four hundred miles closer to Moscow. By then, several other former Warsaw Pact countries were also members of the Alliance, and in 1999 Moscow watched helplessly as NATO went to war with its ally, Serbia. In the 1990s, Russia was in no position to push back, but after the chaos of the Yeltsin years, Putin stepped in on the front foot and came out swinging.

The best-known quote attributed to Henry Kissinger originated in the 1970s, when he is reported to have asked: "If I want to phone Europe—who do I call?" The Poles have an updated question: "If the Russians threaten, do we call Brussels or Washington?" They know the answer.

The Balkan countries are also once again free of empire. Their mountainous terrain led to the emergence of so many small states in the region, and is one of the things that has kept them from integrating—despite the best efforts of the experiment of the Union of Southern Slavs, otherwise known as Yugoslavia.

With the wars of the 1990s behind them, most of the former Yugoslav countries are looking westward, but in Serbia, the pull of the east, with its Orthodox religion and Slavic peoples, remains strong. Russia, which has yet to forgive the Western nations for the bombing of Serbia in 1999 and the separation of Kosovo, is still attempting to coax Serbia into its orbit via the gravitational pull of language, ethnicity, religion, and energy deals.

Bismarck famously said that a major war would be sparked by "some damned fool thing in the Balkans"; and so it came to pass. The region is now an economic and diplomatic battleground with the EU, NATO, the Turks, and the Russians all vying for influence. Albania, Bulgaria, Croatia, and Romania have made their choice and are inside NATO—and, apart from Albania, are also in the EU, as is Slovenia.

The tensions extend into the north and Scandinavia. Denmark is already a NATO member, and the recent resurgence of Russia has caused a debate in Sweden over whether it is time to abandon the neutrality of two centuries and join the Alliance. In 2013, Russian jets staged a mock bombing run on Sweden in the middle of the night. The Swedish defense system appears to have been asleep, failing to scramble any jets, and it was the Danish air force that took to the skies to shepherd the Russians away. Despite that, the majority of Swedes remain against NATO membership, but the debate is ongoing, informed by Moscow's statement that it would be forced to "respond" if either Sweden or Finland were to join the Alliance.

The EU and NATO countries need to present a united front to these challenges: this will be impossible unless the key relationship in the EU remains intact—that between France and Germany.

As we've seen, France was best placed to take advantage of Europe's climate, trade routes, and natural borders. It is partially protected, except in one area—the northeast, at the point where the flatland of the North European Plain becomes what is now Germany. Before Germany existed as a single country this was not a problem. France was a considerable distance from Russia, far from the Mongol hordes, and had the Channel between itself and England, meaning that an attempt at a full-scale invasion and total occupation could probably be repulsed. In fact, France was the preeminent power on the Continent: it could even project its power as far as the gates of Moscow.

But then Germany united.

It had been doing so for some time. There had been the "idea" of Germany for centuries: the Eastern Frankish lands, which became the Holy Roman Empire in the tenth century, were sometimes called "the Germanies," comprising as they did up to five hundred Germanic mini-kingdoms. After it was dissolved in 1806, the German Confederation of thirty-nine statelets came together in 1815 at the Congress of Vienna. This in turn led to the North German Confederation, and then the unification of Germany in 1871 after the Franco-Prussian War, in which victorious German troops occupied Paris. Now France had a neighbor on its border that was geographically larger than itself, with a similar size of population but a better growth rate, and one that was more industrialized.

The unification was announced at the Palace of Versailles near Paris after the German victory. The weak spot in the French defense, the North European Plain, had been breached. It would be again, twice, in the following seventy years, after which France would use diplomacy instead of warfare to try to neutralize the threat from the east.

Germany had always had a bigger geographical problem than France. The flatlands of the North European Plain gave it two reasons to be fearful: to the west the Germans saw their long-unified and powerful neighbor France, and to the east the giant Russian Bear. Their ultimate fear was of a simultaneous attack by both powers across the flatland of the corridor. We can never know if it would have happened, but the fear of it had catastrophic consequences.

France feared Germany, Germany feared France, and when France joined both Russia and Britain in the Triple Entente of 1907, Germany feared all three. There was now also the added dimension that the British navy could, at a time of its choosing, blockade German access to the North Sea and the Atlantic. Germany's solution, twice, was to attack France first.

The dilemma of Germany's geographical position and belligerence became known as "the German Question." The answer, after the horrors of the Second World War, indeed after centuries of war, was the acceptance of the presence in the European lands of a single overwhelming power, the United States, which set up NATO and allowed for the eventual creation of the European Union. Exhausted by war, and with safety "guaranteed" by the American military, the Europeans embarked on an astonishing experiment. They were asked to trust one another.

What is now the EU was set up so that France and Germany could hug each other so tightly in a loving embrace that neither would be able to get an arm free with which to punch the other. It has worked brilliantly and created a huge geographical space now encompassing the biggest economy in the world.

It has worked particularly well for Germany, which rose from the ashes of 1945 and used to its advantage the geography it once feared. It became Europe's great manufacturer. Instead of sending armies across the flatlands, it sent goods with the prestigious tag MADE IN GERMANY, and these goods flowed down the Rhine and the Elbe, along the highways, and out into Europe and the world—north, south, west, and, increasingly since 1990, east.

However, what began in 1951 as the six-nation European Coal and Steel Community has become the twenty-eight-nation EU with an ideological core of "ever closer union." After the first major financial crisis to hit the Union, that ideology is on an uncertain footing and the ties that bind are fraying. There are signs within the EU of, as Robert Kaplan puts it, "the revenge of geography."

Ever-closer union led, for nineteen of the twenty-eight countries, to a single currency—the euro. All twenty-eight members, except for Denmark and the UK, are committed to joining it if and when they meet the criteria. What is clear now, and was clear to some at the time, is that at its launch in 1999 many countries that did join were simply not ready.

In 1999, many of the countries went into the newly defined relationship with eyes wide shut. They were all supposed to have levels of debt, unemployment, and inflation within certain limits. The problem was that some, notably Greece, were cooking the books. Most of the experts knew, but because the euro is not just a currency—it is also an ideology—the members turned a blind eye.

The eurozone countries agreed to be economically wedded, as the Greeks point out, "in sickness and in health," but when the economic crisis of 2008 hit, the wealthier countries had to bail out the poorer ones, and a bitter domestic row broke out. The partners are still throwing dishes at one another to this day.

The euro crisis and wider economic problems have revealed the cracks in the House of Europe (notably along the old fault line of the north-south divide). The dream of ever-closer union appears to be frozen, or possibly even in reverse. If it is, then the German question may return. Seen through the prism of seven decades of peace, this may seem alarmist, and Germany is among the most peaceful and democratic members of the European family; but seen through the prism of seven centuries of European warfare, it cannot be ruled out.

Germany is determined to remain a good European. Germans

know instinctively that if the Union fragments, the old fears of Germany will reappear, especially as it is now by far the most populous and wealthy European nation, with 80 million inhabitants and the world's fourth-biggest economy. A failed Union would also harm Germany economically: the world's third-largest exporter of goods does not want to see its closest market fragment into protectionism. This is why in the summer of 2015, after the fractious debate over Greece, Germany led the discussion about whether the eurozone countries should form a genuine fiscal union. This will require a level of pooling of sovereignty hitherto unseen in Europe, with a shared budget between member states. If it goes ahead it will bring into sharper relief the outlines of a "two-speed Europe," composed of "federalized" euro nations (still dominated by Germany) and the rest of the EU.

The German nation state, despite being less than 150 years old, is now Europe's indispensable power. In economic affairs it is unrivaled; it speaks quietly but carries a large euro-shaped stick, and the Continent listens. However, on global foreign policy it simply speaks quietly, sometimes not at all, and has an aversion to sticks.

The shadow of the Second World War still hangs over Germany. The Americans, and eventually the West Europeans, were willing to accept German rearmament due to the Soviet threat, but Germany rearmed almost reluctantly and has been loath to use its military strength. It played a walk-on part in Kosovo and Afghanistan, but chose to sit out the Libya conflict.

Its most serious diplomatic foray into a noneconomic crisis has been in Ukraine, which tells us a lot about where Germany is now looking. The Germans were involved in the machinations that overthrew Ukraine's President Yanukovych in 2014 and they were sharply critical of Russia's subsequent annexation of Crimea. However, mindful of the gas pipelines, Berlin was noticeably more restrained in its criticism and support for sanctions than, for example, the UK, which is far less reliant on Russian energy. Through the EU and NATO, Germany is anchored in Western Europe, but in stormy weather anchors can slip, and Berlin is geographically situated to shift the focus of its attention east if required and forge much closer ties with Moscow.

Watching all these continental machinations from the sidelines of the Atlantic is the UK, sometimes present on the territory of the continent, sometimes in "splendid isolation," always fully engaged in ensuring that no power greater than it will rise in Europe. This is as true now in the diplomatic chambers of the EU as it was on the battlefields of Agincourt, Waterloo, or Balaclava.

When it can, the UK inserts itself between the great Franco-German alliances in the EU; failing that, it seeks alliances among other, smaller member states to build enough votes to challenge policies with which it disagrees.

Geographically, the Brits are in a good place. Good farmland, decent rivers, excellent access to the seas and their fish stocks, close enough to the European continent to trade, and yet protected by dint of being an island race—there have been times when the UK gave thanks for its geography as wars and revolutions swept over its neighbors.

The British losses in, and experience of, the world wars are not to be underestimated, but they are dwarfed by what happened in continental Europe in the twentieth century and indeed before that. The British are at one remove from living with the historical collective memory of frequent invasions and border changes.

There is a theory that the relative security of the UK over the past few hundred years is why it has experienced more freedom and less despotism than the countries across the channel. The theory goes that there were fewer requirements for "strong men" or dictators, which, starting with the Magna Carta (1215) and then the Provisions of Oxford (1258), led to forms of democracy years ahead of other countries.

It is a good talking point, albeit one not provable. What is undeniable is that the water around the island; the trees upon it, which allowed a great navy to be built; and the economic conditions that sparked the Industrial Revolution all led to Great Britain controlling a global empire. Britain may be the biggest island in Europe, but it is not a large country. The expansion of its power across the globe in the eighteenth, nineteenth, and twentieth centuries is remarkable, even if its position has since declined.

Its location still grants it certain strategic advantages, one of which is the GIUK gap. This is a choke point in the world's sea-lanes—it is hardly as important as the Strait of Hormuz or the Strait of Malacca, but it has traditionally given the UK an advantage in the North Atlantic. The alternative route for north European navies (including Belgium, the Netherlands, and France) to access the Atlantic is through the English Channel, but this is narrow—only twenty miles across at the Strait of Dover—and very well defended. Any Russian naval ship coming from the Arctic also has to pass through the GIUK on its way to the Atlantic.

This strategic advantage has diminished in tandem with the reduced role and power of the Royal Navy, but in time of war it would again benefit the UK. The GIUK is one of many reasons why London flew into a panic in 2014 when, briefly, the vote on Scottish independence looked as if it might result in a yes. The loss of power in the North Sea and North Atlantic would have been a strategic blow to and a massive dent in the prestige of whatever was left of the UK.

What the British have now is a collective memory of greatness. That memory is what persuades many people on the island that if something in the world needs to be done, then Britain should be among the countries to do it. The British remain within Europe, and yet outside it; it is an issue still to be settled. Despite the UK Brexit vote in late June 2016, the rules of Britain's new relationship with Brussels, and indeed with Scotland, will take years to work out. The British led the way in what was both an anti-EU and anti-establishment soft revolution in Europe. The crash of 2008, then the immigration crisis, took the cork out of the bottle, and now the nation state genies are out and about to the horror of those who thought they could smother these potentially dark spirits under a blanket of pan-European prosperity.

The two main issues that caused the British to edge toward the EU exit door are related—they are sovereignty and immigration. Anti-EU opinion, backed by some EU waverers, is angered by the amount and type of laws enacted by the EU, which the UK, as part of the membership deal, has to abide by. Headlines are made about foreign criminals convicted of serious crimes in the UK who cannot be deported because of the European Convention on Human Rights.

At the same time the wave of economic immigrants and refugees arriving in the UK, from the Middle East and Africa, fuels anti-EU feeling as many migrants want to reach Britain, and it is believed are encouraged to so do by the EU countries through which they pass.

Prejudice against immigrants always rises during times of economic recession such as recently suffered in Europe, and the effects have been seen across the continent and have resulted in the rise of right-wing political parties, all of which militate against pan-nationalism and thus weaken the fabric of the EU. A stark example came in early

2016 when for the first time in half a century, Sweden began checking the documents of travelers from Denmark. This was a direct response to the waves of refugees and migrants flowing into northern Europe from the wider Middle East and the ISIS attacks on Paris in December 2015. The idea of the EU's "Schengen Area," a border-free area composed of twenty-six countries, has taken some heavy blows with different countries, at different times, reintroducing border controls on the grounds of security. Fearing a bottleneck, Denmark then began checking people crossing from Germany. This all has an economic cost, makes travel more difficult, and is both a physical and conceptual attack on "ever closer union." Some analysts have begun to speak of a "Fortress Europe" due to bids to reduce immigration levels; this misses that there is also a drift toward "Fortress Nation State."

Europe's traditional white population is graying. However, population projections, of an inverted pyramid, with older people at the top and few people to look after them or pay taxes, have not made a dent in the strength of anti-immigrant feeling in what was previously the indigenous population as it sees the world in which it grew up change rapidly.

This demographic change is in turn having an effect on the foreign policy of nation states, particularly toward the Middle East. On issues such as the Iraq War, or the Israeli-Palestinian conflict, for example, many European governments must, at the very least, take into account the feelings of their Muslim citizens when formulating policy.

The characters and domestic social norms of the European countries are also impacted. Debates about women's rights and the veiling of women, blasphemy laws, freedom of speech, and many other issues have all been influenced by the presence of large numbers of Muslims in Europe's urban areas. Voltaire's maxim that he would defend to the death the right of a person to say something, even if he found it offensive, was once taken as a given. Now, despite many people having been killed because what they said was insulting, the debate has shifted. It is not uncommon to hear the idea that perhaps insulting religion should be beyond the pale, possibly even made illegal.

Whereas previously liberals would be entirely behind Voltaire, there are now shades of relativism. The massacre of journalists at the French satirical magazine *Charlie Hebdo* in 2015 was followed by widespread condemnation and revulsion; however, sections of liberal condemnation were tinged with a "but perhaps the satirists went too far." This is something new for Europe in the modern age and is part of its culture wars, all of which loop back into attitudes toward the European political structures.

NATO is fraying at the edges at the same time as the European Union. Both can be patched up, but if not, then over time they may become either defunct or irrelevant. At this point we would return to a Europe of sovereign nation states, with each state seeking alliances in a balance of the power system. The Germans would again be fearing encirclement by the Russians and French, the French would again be fearing their bigger neighbor, and we would all be back at the beginning of the twentieth century.

For the French, this is a nightmare. They successfully helped tie Germany down inside the EU, only to find that, after German reunification, they became the junior partner in a twin-engine motor they had hoped to be driving. This poses a problem that Paris does not appear to be able to solve. Unless it quietly accepts that Berlin calls the European shots, it risks further weakening the Union. But if it accepts German leadership, then its own power is diminished.

France is capable of an independent foreign policy—indeed, with its force de frappe nuclear deterrent, its overseas territories, and its aircraft carrier–backed armed forces, it does just that—but it operates safe in the knowledge that its eastern flank is secure and it can afford to raise its eyes to the horizon.

Both France and Germany are currently working to keep the Union together and are discussing various ways of binding themselves together within the eurozone: they see each other now as natural partners. But only Germany has a plan B—Russia.

The end of the Cold War saw most of the continental powers reducing their military budgets and cutting back their armed forces. It has taken the shock of the Russian–Georgian war of 2008 and the annexation of Crimea by Russia in 2014 to focus attention on the possibility of the age-old problem of war in Europe.

Now the Russians regularly fly missions aimed at testing European air defense systems and are busy consolidating themselves in South Ossetia, Abkhazia, Crimea, Transnistria, and eastern Ukraine. They maintain their links with the ethnic Russians in the Baltics, and they still have their exclave of Kaliningrad on the Baltic Sea.

The Europeans have begun doing some serious recalculation on their military spending, but there isn't much money around, and they face difficult decisions. While they debate those decisions, the maps are being dusted off, and the diplomats and military strategists see that, while the threats of Charlemagne, Napoleon, Hitler, and the Soviets may have vanished, the North European Plain, the Carpathians, the Baltic, and the North Sea are still there.

In his book *Of Paradise and Power*, the historian Robert Kagan argues that Western Europeans live in paradise but shouldn't seek to operate by the rules of paradise once they move out into the world of power. Perhaps, as the euro crisis diminishes and we look around at paradise, it seems inconceivable that we could go backward; but history tells us how much things can change in just a few decades, and geography tells us that if humans do not constantly strive to overcome its "rules," its "rules" will overcome us.

This is what Helmut Kohl meant when he warned, upon leaving the chancellorship of Germany in 1998, that he was the last German leader to have lived through the Second World War and thus to have experienced the horrors it wrought. In 2012, he wrote an article for Germany's best-selling daily newspaper, *Bild*, and was clearly still haunted by the possibility that, because of the financial crisis, the current generation of leaders would not nurture the postwar experiment in European trust: "For those who didn't live through this themselves and who especially now in the crisis are asking what benefits Europe's unity brings, the answer despite the unprecedented European period of peace lasting more than 65 years and despite the problems and difficulties we must still overcome is: peace."

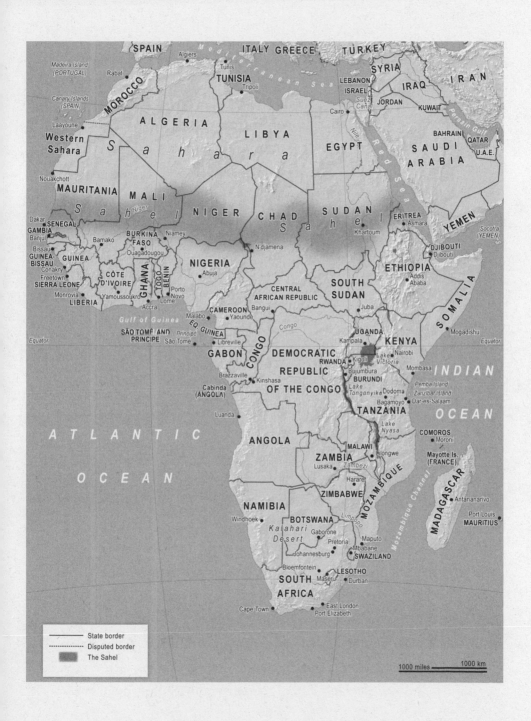

5

AFRICA

It always seems impossible until it is done.
—Nelson Mandela

Africa's coastline? Great beaches—really, really lovely beaches—but terrible natural harbors. Rivers? Amazing rivers, but most of them are worthless for actually transporting anything, given that every few miles you go over a waterfall. These are just two in a long list of problems that helps explain why Africa isn't technologically or politically as successful as Western Europe or North America.

There are lots of places that are unsuccessful, but few have been as unsuccessful as Africa, and that despite having a head start as the place where Homo sapiens originated approximately two hundred thousand years ago. As that most lucid of writers Jared Diamond put it in a brilliant *National Geographic* article in 2005, "It's the opposite of what one would expect from the runner first off the block." However, the first runners became separated from everyone else by the Sahara Desert and the Indian and Atlantic Oceans. Almost the entire continent developed in isolation from the Eurasian landmass, where ideas and technology were exchanged from east to west, and west to east, but not north to south.

Africa, being a huge continent, has always consisted of different regions, climates, and cultures, but what they all had in common was their isolation from one another and the outside world. That is less the case now, but the legacy remains.

The world's idea of African geography is flawed. Few people realize just how big it is. This is because most of us use the standard Mercator world map. This, as do other maps, depicts a sphere on a flat surface and thus distorts shapes. Africa is far, far longer than usually portrayed, which explains what an achievement it was to round the Cape of Good Hope, and is a reminder of the importance of the Suez Canal to world trade. Making it around the cape was a momentous achievement, but once it became unnecessary to do so, the sea journey from Western Europe to India was reduced by six thousand miles.

If you look at a world map and mentally glue Alaska onto California, then turn the United States on its head, it appears as if it would roughly fit into Africa with a few gaps here and there. In fact, Africa is three times larger than the United States. Look again at the standard Mercator map and you see that Greenland appears to be the same size as Africa, and yet Africa is actually fourteen times the size of Greenland! You could fit the United States, Greenland, India, China, Spain, France, Germany, and the UK into Africa and still have room for most of Eastern Europe. We know Africa is a massive landmass, but the maps rarely tell us how massive.

The geography of this immense continent can be explained in several ways, but the most basic is to think of Africa in terms of the top third and bottom two-thirds.

The top third begins on the Mediterranean coastlines of the

North African Arabic-speaking countries. The coastal plains quickly become the Sahara, the world's largest dry desert, which is almost as big as the United States. Directly below the Sahara is the Sahel region, a semiarid, rock-strewn, sandy strip of land measuring more than three thousand miles at its widest points and stretching from Gambia on the Atlantic coast through Niger, Chad, and right across to Eritrea on the Red Sea. The name Sahel comes from the Arabic *sahil*, which means "coast," and is how the people living in the region think of it—as the shoreline of the vast sand sea of the Sahara. It is another sort of shore, one where the influence of Islam diminishes. From the Sahel to the Mediterranean the vast majority of people are Muslims. South of it there is far more diversity in religion.

Indeed, south of the Sahel, in the bottom two-thirds of Africa, there is more diversity in most things. The land becomes more temperate, and green vegetation appears, which becomes jungle as we approach the Congo and the Central African Republic. Toward the east coast are the great lakes in Uganda and Tanzania, while across to the west more deserts appear in Angola and Namibia. By the time we reach the tip of South Africa the climate is again "Mediterranean," even though we have traveled almost five thousand miles from the northernmost point in Tunisia on the Mediterranean coast.

Given that Africa is where humans originated, we are all African. However, the rules of the race changed circa 8000 BCE when some of us, who'd wandered off to places such as the Middle East and around the Mediterranean region, lost the wanderlust, settled down, began farming, and eventually congregated in villages and towns.

But back south there were few plants willing to be domesticated, and even fewer animals. Much of the land consists of jungle, swamp, desert, or steep-sided plateau, none of which lend themselves to the growing of wheat or rice, or sustaining herds of sheep. Africa's rhinos, gazelles, and giraffes stubbornly refused to be beasts of burden—or as Jared Diamond puts it in a memorable passage, "History might have turned out differently if African armies, fed by barnyard-giraffe meat and backed by waves of cavalry mounted on huge rhinos, had swept into Europe to overrun its mutton-fed soldiers mounted on puny horses." But Africa's head start in our mutual story did allow it more time to develop something else that to this day holds it back: a virulent set of diseases, such as malaria and yellow fever, brought on by the heat and now complicated by crowded living conditions and poor health-care infrastructure. This is true of other regions—the subcontinent and South America, for example—but sub-Saharan Africa has been especially hard-hit, for example by HIV, and has a particular problem because of the prevalence of the mosquito and the tsetse fly.

Most of the continent's rivers also pose a problem, as they begin in highland and descend in abrupt drops that thwart navigation. For example, the mighty Zambezi may be Africa's fourth-longest river, running for 1,700 miles, and may be a stunning tourist attraction with its white-water rapids and the Victoria Falls, but as a trade route it is of little use. It flows through six countries, dropping from 4,900 feet to sea level when it reaches the Indian Ocean at Mozambique. Parts of it are navigable by shallow boats, but these parts do not interconnect, thus limiting the transportation of cargo.

Unlike in Europe, which has the Danube and the Rhine, this drawback has hindered contact and trade between regions—which in turn affects economic development and hinders the formation of large trading regions. The continent's great rivers—the Niger, the Congo, the Zambezi, the Nile, and others—don't connect, and this disconnection has a human factor. Whereas huge areas of Russia, China, and the United States speak a unifying language, which helps trade, in Africa thousands of languages exist and no one culture emerged to dominate areas of similar size. Europe, on the other hand, was small enough to have a lingua franca through which to communicate, and a landscape that encouraged interaction.

Even if technologically productive nation states had arisen, much of the continent would still have struggled to connect to the rest of the world because the bulk of the landmass is framed by the Indian and Atlantic Oceans and the Sahara Desert. The exchange of ideas and technology barely touched sub-Saharan Africa for thousands of years. Despite this, several African empires and city states did arise after about the sixth century CE: for example the Mali Empire (thirteenth to sixteenth century), and the city state of Great Zimbabwe (eleventh to fifteenth century), the latter in land around the Zambezi and Limpopo Rivers. However, these and others were isolated to relatively small regional blocs, and although the myriad cultures that did emerge across the continent may have been politically sophisticated, the physical landscape remained a barrier to technological development: by the time the outside world arrived in force, most had yet to develop writing, paper, gunpowder, or the wheel.

Traders from the Middle East and the Mediterranean had been doing business in the Sahara, after the introduction of camels, from approximately two thousand years ago, notably trading the vast resources of salt there; but it wasn't until the Arab conquests of the seventh century CE that the scene was set for a push southward. By the ninth century, they had crossed the Sahara, and by the eleventh were firmly established as far south as modern-day Nigeria. The Arabs were also coming down the east coast and establishing themselves in places such as Zanzibar and Dar es Salaam in what is now Tanzania.

When the Europeans finally made it down the west coast in the fifteenth century they found few natural harbors for their ships. Unlike Europe or North America, where the jagged coastlines give rise to deep natural harbors, much of the African coastline is smooth. And once they did make land they struggled to penetrate any farther inland than roughly one hundred miles, due to the difficulty of navigating the rivers as well as the challenges of the climate and disease.

Both the Arabs and then the Europeans brought with them new technology, which they mostly kept to themselves, and took away whatever they found of value, which was mainly natural resources and people.

Slavery existed long before the outside world returned to where it had originated. Traders in the Sahel region used thousands of slaves to transport vast quantities of the region's then most valuable commodity—salt—but the Arabs began the practice of subcontracting African slave–taking to willing tribal leaders who would deliver them to the coast. By the time of the peak of the Ottoman Empire in the fifteenth and sixteenth centuries, hundreds of thousands of Africans (mostly from the Sudan region) had been taken to Istanbul, Cairo, Damascus, and across the Arabian world. The Europeans followed suit, outdoing the Arabs and Turks in their appetite for, and mistreatment of, the people brought to the slave ships anchored off the west coast.

Back in the great capital cities of London, Paris, Brussels, and Lisbon, the Europeans then took maps of the contours of Africa's geography and drew lines on them—or, to take a more aggressive approach, lies. In between these lines they wrote words such as *Middle Congo* or *Upper Volta* and called them countries. These lines were more about how far each power's explorers, military forces, and businessmen had advanced on the map than what the people living between the lines felt themselves to be, or how they wanted to organize themselves. Many Africans are now partially the prisoners of the political geography the Europeans made, and of the natural barriers to progression with which nature endowed them. From this they are making a modern home and, in some cases, vibrant, connected economies.

There are now fifty-six countries in Africa. Since the "winds of change" of the independence movement blew through the mid-twentieth century, some of the words between the lines have been altered—for example, Rhodesia is now Zimbabwe—but the borders are, surprisingly, mostly intact. However, many encompass the same divisions they did when first drawn, and those formal divisions are some of the many legacies colonialism bequeathed the continent.

The ethnic conflicts within Sudan, Somalia, Kenya, Angola, the Democratic Republic of the Congo, Nigeria, Mali, and elsewhere are evidence that the European idea of geography did not fit the reality of Africa's demographics. There may have always been conflict: the Zulus and Xhosas had their differences long before they had ever set eyes on a European. But colonialism forced those differences to be resolved within an artificial structure—the European concept of a nation state. The modern civil wars are now partially a result of the colonialists' having told different nations that they were one nation in one state, and then after the colonialists were chased out, a dominant people emerged within the state who wanted to rule it all, thus ensuring violence.

Take, for example, Libya, an artificial construct only a few decades old, which at the first test fell apart into its previous incarnation as three distinct geographical regions. In the west it was, in Greek times, Tripolitania (from the Greek *tripolis*, "three cities," which eventually merged and became Tripoli). The area to the east, centered on the city of Benghazi but stretching down to the Chad border, was known in both Greek and Roman times as Cyrenaica. Below these two, in what is now the far southwest of the country, is the region of Fezzan.

Tripolitania was always orientated north and northwest, trading with its southern European neighbors. Cyrenaica always looked east to Egypt and the Arab lands. Even the sea current off the coast of the Benghazi region takes boats naturally eastward. Fezzan was traditionally a land of nomads who had little in common with the two coastal communities.

This is how the Greeks, Romans, and Turks all ruled the area—it is how the people had thought of themselves for centuries. The mere decades-old European idea of Libya will struggle to survive, and already one of the many Islamist groups in the east has declared an "emirate of Cyrenaica." While this may not come to pass, it is an example of how the concept of the region originated merely in lines drawn on maps by foreigners.

However, one of the biggest failures of European line drawing lies in the center of the continent, the giant black hole known as the Democratic Republic of the Congo—the DRC. Here is the land in which Joseph Conrad set his novella *Heart of Darkness* and it remains a place shrouded in the darkness of war. It is a prime example of how the imposition of artificial borders can lead to a weak and divided state, ravaged by internal conflict, and whose mineral wealth condemns it to being exploited by outsiders.

The DRC is an illustration of why the catchall term *developing world* is far too broad-brush a way to describe countries that are not part of the modern industrialized world. The DRC is not developing, nor does it show any signs of doing so. The DRC should never have been put together; it has fallen apart and is the most underreported war zone in the world, despite the fact that six million people have died there during wars that have been fought since the late 1990s.

The DRC is neither democratic nor a republic. It is the second-largest country in Africa with a population of approximately 75 million, although due to the situation there it is difficult to find accurate figures. It is bigger than Germany, France, and Spain combined and contains the Congo Rainforest, second only to the Amazon as the largest in the world.

The people are divided into more than two hundred ethnic groups, of which the largest is the Bantu. There are several hundred languages, but the widespread use of French bridges that gap to a degree. The French comes from the DRC's years as a Belgian colony (1908–60) and before that when King Leopold of the Belgians used it as his personal property from which to steal its natural resources to line his pockets. Belgian colonial rule made the British and French versions look positively benign and was ruthlessly brutal from start to finish, with few attempts to build any sort of infrastructure to help the inhabitants. When the Belgians left in 1960 they left behind little chance of the country holding together.

The civil wars began immediately and were later intensified by a blood-soaked walk-on role in the global Cold War. The government in the capital, Kinshasa, backed the rebel side in Angola's war, thus bringing itself to the attention of the United States, which was also supporting the rebel movement against the Soviet-backed Angolan government. Each side poured in hundreds of millions of dollars' worth of arms.

When the Cold War ended, both great powers had less interest in what by then was called Zaire, and the country staggered on, kept afloat by its natural resources. The Great Rift Valley curves into the DRC in its south and east and it has exposed huge quantities of cobalt, copper, diamonds, gold, silver, zinc, coal, manganese, and other minerals, especially in Katanga Province.

In King Leopold's day the world wanted the region's rubber for the expanding automobile industry; now China buys more than 50 percent of the DRC's exports, but still the population lives in poverty. In 2014, the United Nations' Human Development Index placed the DRC at number 186 out of 187 countries it measured. The bottom eighteen countries in that list are all in Africa.

Because it is so resource-rich and so large, everyone wants a bite out of the DRC, which, as it lacks a substantive central authority, cannot really bite back.

The region is also bordered by nine countries. They have all played a role in the DRC's agony, which is one reason why the Congo wars are also known as "Africa's world war." To the south is Angola, to the north the Republic of the Congo and the Central African Republic, to the east Uganda, Rwanda, Burundi, Tanzania, and Zambia. The roots of the wars go back decades, but the worst of times was triggered by the disaster that hit Rwanda in 1994 and swept westward in its aftermath.

After the genocide in Rwanda, the Tutsi survivors and moderate Hutus formed a Tutsi-led government. The killing machines of the Hutu militia, the Interahamwe, fled into eastern DRC but conducted border raids. They also joined with sections of the DRC army to kill the DRC's Tutsis, who live near the border region. In came the Rwandan and Ugandan armies, backed by Burundi and Eritrea. Allied with opposition militias, they attacked the Interahamwe and overthrew the DRC government. They also went on to control much of the country's natural wealth, with Rwanda in particular shipping back tons of coltan, which is used in the making of cell phones and computer chips. However, what had been the government forces did not give up and—with the involvement of Angola, Namibia, and Zimbabwe—continued the fight. The country became a vast battle-ground with more than twenty factions involved in the fighting.

The wars have killed, at a low estimate, tens of thousands of people and have resulted in the deaths of another six million due to disease and malnutrition. The UN estimates that almost 50 percent of the victims have been children under the age of five.

In recent years, the fighting has died down, but the DRC is home to the world's deadliest conflict since the Second World War and still requires the UN's largest peacekeeping mission to prevent full-scale war from breaking out again. Now the job is not to put Humpty Dumpty back together again, because the DRC was never whole. It is simply to keep the pieces apart until a way can be found to join them sensibly and peacefully. The European colonialists created an egg without a chicken, a logical absurdity repeated across the continent and one that continues to haunt it.

Burundi is another example that had ethnically rooted political tensions simmering throughout 2015 and worsening in 2016. Formerly part of German East Africa when it included what is now Tanzania, it was divided between Belgium and the UK after WWI and administered by Belgium from 1945 until independence in 1962. The Belgians used the Tutsi people to govern over the Hutus, and despite being just 15 percent of the population, they continue to dominate politics, economics, and the military. More than three hundred thousand people died in the civil war between 1993 and 2005. Levels of violence began to rise again in 2015 and 2016 after President Pierre

Nkurunziza interpreted the constitution as allowing him to run for a third term. This was not quite what President Obama had in mind when, during his Africa tour in July 2015, he criticized African leaders and mentioned Burundi before saying, "The continent will not advance if its leaders refuse to step down when their terms end . . . Sometimes you will hear leaders say 'I'm the only person who can hold this nation together.' If that's true then that leader has truly failed to build their nation." Those sentences encompassed both the colonial legacy of Africa and how its modern leaders have often been part of the problem rather than the solution to that legacy.

Africa has been equally cursed and blessed by its resources—blessed insofar as it has natural riches in abundance, but cursed because outsiders have long plundered them. In more recent times, the nation states have been able to claim a share of these riches, and foreign countries now invest rather than steal, but still the people are rarely the beneficiaries.

In addition to its natural mineral wealth, Africa is also blessed with abundant water—even though many of its rivers do not encourage trade, they are good for hydroelectricity. However, this, too, is a source of potential conflict.

The Nile, the longest river in the world (4,160 miles), affects ten countries considered to be in the proximity of its basin—Burundi, the DRC, Eritrea, Ethiopia, Kenya, Rwanda, Sudan, Tanzania, Uganda, and Egypt. As long ago as the fifth century BCE, the historian Herodotus said: "Egypt is the Nile, and the Nile is Egypt." It is still true, and so a threat to the supply to Egypt's seven-hundred-mile-long, fully navigable section of the Nile is for Cairo a concern—one over which it would be prepared to go to war.

Without the Nile, there would be no one there. It may be a huge country, but the vast majority of its 84 million population lives within a few miles of the Nile. Measured by the area in which people dwell, Egypt is one of the most densely populated countries in the world.

Egypt was, arguably, a nation state when most Europeans were living in mud huts, but it was never more than a regional power. It is protected by deserts on three sides and might have become a great power in the Mediterranean region but for one problem. There are hardly any trees in Egypt, and for most of history, if you didn't have trees you couldn't build a great navy with which to project your power. There has always been an Egyptian navy—it used to import cedar from Lebanon to build ships at huge expense—but it has never been a blue-water navy.

Modern Egypt now has the most powerful armed forces of all the Arab states, thanks to American military aid; but it remains contained by deserts, the sea, and its peace treaty with Israel. It will remain in the news as it struggles to cope with feeding 84 million people a day while battling an Islamist insurgency, especially in the Sinai, and guarding the Suez Canal, through which passes 8 percent of the world's entire trade every day. Some 2.5 percent of the world's oil passes this way daily; closing the canal would add about fifteen days' transit time to Europe and ten to the United States, with concurrent costs.

Despite having fought five wars with Israel, the country Egypt is most likely to come into conflict with next is Ethiopia, and the issue is the Nile. Two of the continent's oldest countries, with the largest armies, may come to blows over the region's major source of water.

The Blue Nile, which begins in Ethiopia, and the White Nile meet in the Sudanese capital, Khartoum, before flowing through the Nubian Desert and into Egypt. By this point the majority of the water is from the Blue Nile.

Ethiopia is sometimes called Africa's water tower, due to its high elevation, and has more than twenty dams fed by the rainfall in its highlands. In 2011, Addis Ababa announced a joint project with China to build a massive hydroelectric project on the Blue Nile near the Sudanese border called the Grand Ethiopian Renaissance Dam, scheduled to be finished by 2020. The dam will be used to create electricity, and the flow to Egypt should continue; but in theory the dam could also hold a year's worth of water, and completion of the project would give Ethiopia the potential to hold the water for its own use, thus drastically reducing the flow into Egypt.

As things stand, Egypt has a more powerful military, but that is slowly changing, and Ethiopia, a country of 96 million people, is a growing power. Cairo knows this, and also that, once the dam is built, destroying it would create a flooding catastrophe in both Ethiopia and Sudan. However, at the moment it does not have a casus belli to strike before completion, and despite the fact that a cabinet minister was recently caught on microphone recommending bombing, the next few years are more likely to see intense negotiations, with Egypt wanting cast-iron guarantees that the flow will never be stopped. Water wars are considered to be among the imminent conflicts this century, and this is one to watch.

Another hotly contested liquid is oil.

Nigeria is sub-Saharan Africa's largest producer of oil, and all of this high-quality oil is in the south. Nigerians in the north complain that the profits from that oil are not shared equitably across the country's regions. This in turn exacerbates the ethnic and religious tensions between the peoples from the Nigerian delta and those in the northeast.

By size, population, and natural resources, Nigeria is West Africa's most powerful country. It is the continent's most populous nation, with 177 million people, which, with its size and natural resources, makes it the leading regional power. It is formed from the territories of several ancient kingdoms that the British brought together as an administrative area. In 1898, they drew up a "British Protectorate on the River Niger" that in turn became Nigeria.

It may now be an independent regional powerhouse, but its people and resources have been mismanaged for decades. In colonial times the British preferred to stay in the southwestern area along the coast. Their "civilizing" mission rarely extended to the highlands of the center, nor up to the Muslim populations in the north, and this half of the country remains less developed than the south. Much of the money made from oil is spent paying off the movers and shakers in Nigeria's complex tribal system. The onshore oil industry in the delta is also being threatened by the Movement for the Emancipation of the Niger Delta, a fancy name for a group that does operate in a region devastated by the oil industry but that uses it as a cover for terrorism and extortion. The kidnapping of foreign oil workers is making it a less and less attractive place to do business. The offshore oil fields are mostly free of this activity and that is where the investment is heading.

The Islamist group Boko Haram, which wants to establish a caliphate in the Muslim areas, has used the sense of injustice engendered by underdevelopment to gain ground in the north. Boko Haram fighters are usually ethnically Kanuris from the northeast. They rarely operate outside of their home territory, not even venturing west to the Hausa region, and certainly not way down south to the coastal areas. This means that when the Nigerian military come looking for them, Boko Haram are operating on home ground. Much of the local population will not cooperate with the military, either for fear of reprisal or due to a shared resentment of the south.

The territory taken by Boko Haram does not yet endanger the existence of the state of Nigeria. The group does not even pose a threat to the capital, Abuja, despite its being situated halfway up the country; but they do pose a daily threat to people in the north and they damage Nigeria's reputation abroad as a place to do business.

Most of the villages they have captured are on the Mandara mountain range, which backs onto Cameroon. This means the national army is operating a long way from its bases and cannot surround a Boko Haram force. Cameroon's government does not welcome Boko Haram, but the countryside gives the fighters space to retreat to if required. The situation will not burn itself out for several years, during which time Boko Haram will try to form alliances with the jihadists up north in the Sahel region. Boko Haram has now changed its name to "Wilayat al Sudan al Gharbi," which loosely translates as "Islamic State's West African Province." However, its aims and methods have not altered, most people still call it by its former title, and the change appears to have been simply to capitalize on the name recognition and "cachet" of the words *Islamic State*.

The Americans and French have tracked the problem for several years and now operate surveillance drones in response to the growing threat of violence projecting out of the Sahel-Sahara region and connecting with northern Nigeria. The Americans use several bases, including the one in Djibouti, which is part of the US Africa Command, set up in 2007, and the French have access to concrete in various countries in what they call "Francophone Africa."

The dangers of the threat spreading across several countries has been a wake-up call. Nigeria, Cameroon, and Chad are all now involved militarily and coordinating with the Americans and the French.

Farther south, down the Atlantic coast, is sub-Saharan Africa's second-largest oil producer—Angola. The former Portuguese colony is one of the African nation states with natural geographical borders. It is framed by the Atlantic Ocean to the west, by jungle to the north, and by desert to the south, while the eastern regions are sparsely populated, rugged land that acts as a buffer zone with the DRC and Zambia.

The majority of the 22 million–strong population live in the western half, which is well watered and can sustain agriculture; and off the coast in the west lie most of Angola's oil fields. The rigs out in the Atlantic are owned mostly by American companies, but more than half of the output ends up in China. This makes Angola (dependent on the ebb and flow of sales) second only to Saudi Arabia as the biggest supplier of crude oil to the Middle Kingdom.

Angola is another country familiar with conflict. Its war for independence ended in 1975 when the Portuguese gave up, but it instantly morphed into a civil war between tribes disguised as a civil war over ideology. Russia and Cuba supported the "socialists," the United States and apartheid South Africa backed the "rebels." Most of the socialists of the MPLA (Popular Movement for the Liberation of Angola) were from the Mbundu tribe, while the opposition rebel fighters were mostly from two other main tribes, the Bakongo and the Ovimbundu. Their political disguise was as the FNLA (National Front for the Liberation of Angola) and UNITA (National Union for the Total Independence of Angola). Many of the civil wars of the 1960s and 1970s followed this template: if Russia backed a particular side, that side would suddenly remember that it had socialist principles, while its opponents would become anti-Communist.

The Mbundu had the geographical but not the numerical advantage. They held the capital, Luanda; had access to the oil fields and the main river, the Cuanza; and were backed by countries that could supply them with Russian arms and Cuban soldiers. They prevailed in 2002, and their top echelons immediately undermined their own somewhat questionable socialist credentials by joining the long list of colonial and African leaders who enriched themselves at the expense of the people.

This sorry history of domestic and foreign exploitation continues in the twenty-first century.

As we've seen, the Chinese are everywhere, they mean business, and they are now every bit as involved across the continent as the Europeans and Americans. About a third of China's oil imports come from Africa, which—along with the precious metals to be found in many African countries—means they have arrived, and will stay. European and American oil companies and big multinationals are still far more heavily involved in Africa, but China is quickly catching up. For example, in Liberia it is seeking iron ore, in the DRC and Zambia it's mining copper and, also in the DRC, cobalt. It has already helped develop the Kenyan port of Mombasa and is now embarking on much larger projects just as Kenya's oil assets are beginning to become commercially viable.

China's state-owned China Road and Bridge Corporation is building a $14 billion railroad project to connect Mombasa to the capital city of Nairobi. Analysts say the time taken for goods to travel between the two cities will be reduced from thirty-six hours to eight hours, with a corresponding cut of 60 percent in transport costs.

There are even plans to link Nairobi up to South Sudan, and across to Uganda and Rwanda. Kenya intends, with Chinese help, to be the economic powerhouse of the Eastern Seaboard.

Over the southern border, Tanzania is trying a rival bid to become East Africa's leader and has concluded billions of dollars' worth of deals with the Chinese on infrastructure projects. It has also signed a joint agreement with China and an Omani construction company to overhaul and extend the port of Bagamoyo, as the main port in Dar es Salaam is severely congested. It is planned that Bagamoyo will be able to handle 20 million cargo containers a year, which will make it the biggest port in Africa. Tanzania also has good transport links in the Southern Agricultural Growth Corridor of Tanzania and is connecting down into the fifteen-nation Southern African Development Community. This in turn links into the North-South Corridor, which connects the port of Durban to the copper regions of the DRC and Zambia with spurs linking the port of Dar es Salaam to Durban and Malawi.

Despite this, Tanzania looks as if it will be the second-tier power along the east coast. Kenya's economy is the powerhouse in the five-nation East African Community, accounting for approximately 40 percent of the region's GDP. It may have less arable land than Tanzania, but it uses what it has much more efficiently. Its industrial system is also more efficient, as is its system of getting goods to market—both domestic and international. If it can maintain political stability it looks destined to remain the dominant regional power in the near to medium term.

China's presence also stretches into Niger, with their National Petroleum Corporation investing in the small oil field in the Ténéré fields in the center of the country. And Chinese investment in Angola over the past decade exceeds $8 billion and is growing every year. The China Railway Engineering Corporation (CREC) has already spent almost $2 billion modernizing the Benguela railroad line, which links the DRC to the Angolan port of Lobito on the Atlantic coast eight hundred miles away. In this way travel the cobalt, copper, and manganese with which Katanga Province in the DRC is cursed and blessed.

In Luanda, the CREC is constructing a new international airport, and around the capital huge apartment buildings built to the Chinese model have sprung up to house some of the estimated 150,000 to 200,000 Chinese workers now in the country. Thousands of these workers are also trained in military skills and could provide a ready-made militia if China so required.

What Beijing wants in Angola is what it wants everywhere: the materials with which to make its products, and political stability to ensure the flow of those materials and products. So if President José Eduardo dos Santos, who has been in charge for thirty-six years, wants to pay Mariah Carey $1 million to sing at his birthday party in 2013, that's his affair. And if the Mbundu, to which dos Santos belongs, continue to dominate, that is theirs.

Chinese involvement is an attractive proposition for many African governments. Beijing and the big Chinese companies don't ask difficult questions about human rights, and they don't demand economic reform or even suggest that certain African leaders stop stealing their countries' wealth, as the IMF or World Bank might. For example, China is Sudan's biggest trading partner, which goes some way to explaining why China consistently protects Sudan at the UN Security Council and continued to back its President Omar al-Bashir even when there was an arrest warrant out for him issued by the International Criminal Court. Western criticism of this gets short shrift in Beijing, however; it is regarded as simply another power play aimed at stopping China from doing business, and hypocrisy, given the West's history in Africa. Lecturing the African leaders is going out of fashion due to the harsh realities of global economic competition and the threat of Islamism. When President Obama visited Kenya and Ethiopia in late July 2015, he made headlines in the Western media for criticizing homophobia and corruption in the former country, and human rights in the latter. In reality, the criticism was mild. Both countries are serious players in the African Union force fighting in Somalia and the US needs them onside in the global war on Islamist terror. Washington, DC, is also conscious that it now plays second fiddle to China in business terms across the continent.

All the Chinese want is the oil, the minerals, the precious metals, and the markets. This is an equitable government-to-government relationship, but we will see increasing tension between local populations and the Chinese workforces often brought in to assist with the big projects. This in turn may draw Beijing more into the local politics and require it to have some sort of minor military presence in various countries.

South Africa is China's largest trading partner in Africa. The two countries have a long political and economic history and are well placed to work together. Hundreds of Chinese companies, both state-owned and private, now operate in Durban, Johannesburg, Pretoria, Cape Town, and Port Elizabeth.

South Africa's economy is ranked second-largest on the continent, behind Nigeria. It is certainly the powerhouse in the south in terms of its economy (three times the size of Angola's), military, and population (53 million). South Africa is more developed than many

African nations, thanks to its location at the very southern tip of the continent with access to two oceans; its natural wealth of gold, silver, and coal; and a climate and land that allow for large-scale food production.

Because it is located so far south, and the coastal plain quickly rises into highland, South Africa is one of the very few African countries that do not suffer from the curse of malaria, as mosquitoes find it difficult to breed there. This allowed the European colonialists to push into its interior much farther and faster than in the malaria-riddled tropics, settle, and begin small-scale industrial activity that grew into what is now southern Africa's biggest economy.

For most of southern Africa, doing business with the outside world means doing business with Pretoria, Bloemfontein, and Cape Town. South Africa has used its natural wealth and location to tie its neighbors into its transport system, meaning there is a two-way rail and road conveyor belt stretching from the ports in East London, Cape Town, Port Elizabeth, and Durban; stretching north through Zimbabwe, Botswana, Zambia, Malawi, and Tanzania; reaching even into Katanga Province of the DRC and eastward into Mozambique. The new Chinese-built railway from Katanga to the Angolan coast has been laid to challenge this dominance and might take some traffic from the DRC, but South Africa looks destined to maintain its advantages.

During the apartheid years, the ANC (African National Congress) backed Angola's MPLA in its fight against Portuguese colonization. However, the passion of a shared struggle is turning into a cooler relationship now that each party controls its respective country and competes at a regional level. Angola has a long way to go to catch up with South Africa. This will not be a military confrontation:

South Africa's dominance is near total. It has large, well-equipped armed forces comprising one hundred thousand personnel, dozens of fighter jets and attack helicopters, as well as several modern submarines and frigates.

In the days of the British Empire, controlling South Africa meant controlling the Cape of Good Hope and thus the sea-lanes between the Atlantic and Indian Oceans. Modern navies can venture much farther out from the southern African coastline if they wish to pass by, but the cape is still a commanding piece of real estate on the world map and South Africa is a commanding presence in the whole of the bottom third of the continent.

There is a new scramble for Africa in this century, but this time it is two-pronged. There are the well-publicized outside interests, and meddling, in the competition for resources, but there is also the "scramble within" and South Africa intends to scramble fastest and farthest.

It dominates the fifteen-nation Southern African Development Community (SADC) and has managed to gain a permanent place at the International Conference on the Great Lakes Region, of which it is not even a member. The SADC is rivaled by the East African Community (EAC) comprising Burundi, Kenya, Rwanda, Uganda, and Tanzania. The latter is also a member of the SADC, and the other EAC members take a dim view of its flirtation with South Africa. For its part, South Africa appears to view Tanzania as its vehicle for gaining greater influence in the Great Lakes region and beyond.

The South African National Defense Force has a brigade in the DRC officially under the command of the UN, but it was sent there by its political masters to ensure that South Africa is not left out from the spoils of war in that mineral-rich country. This has brought it into competition with Uganda, Burundi, and Rwanda, which have their own ideas about who should be in charge in the DRC.

The Africa of the past was given no choice—its geography shaped it—and then the Europeans engineered most of today's borders. Now, with its booming populations and developing megacities, it has no choice but to embrace the modern globalized world to which it is so connected. In this, despite all the problems we have seen, it is making huge strides.

The same rivers that hampered trade are now harnessed for hydro-electric power. From the earth that struggled to sustain large-scale food production come minerals and oil, making some countries rich even if little of the wealth reaches the people. Nevertheless, in most, but not all, countries poverty has fallen as health-care and education levels have risen. Many countries are English-speaking, which in an English-language-dominated global economy is an advantage, and the continent has seen economic growth over most of the past decade.

On the downside, economic growth in many countries is dependent on global prices for minerals and energy. Countries whose national budgets are predicated on receiving $100 per barrel of oil, for example, have little to fall back on when prices drop to $80 or $60. Manufacturing-output levels are close to where they were in the 1970s. Corruption remains rampant across the continent, and in addition to the few "hot" conflicts (Somalia, Nigeria, Sudan, for example), there are several more economies that are merely frozen.

Nevertheless, every year more roads and railroads are being built connecting this incredibly diverse space. The vast distances of the oceans and deserts separating Africa from everywhere have been overcome by air travel, and industrial muscle has created harbors in places nature had not intended them to be.

In every decade since the 1960s, optimists have written about how Africa is on the brink of prevailing over the hand that history and nature have dealt it. Perhaps this time it is true. It needs to be. By some estimates, Sub-Saharan Africa currently holds 1.1 billion people—by 2050 that may just more than double, to 2.4 billion.

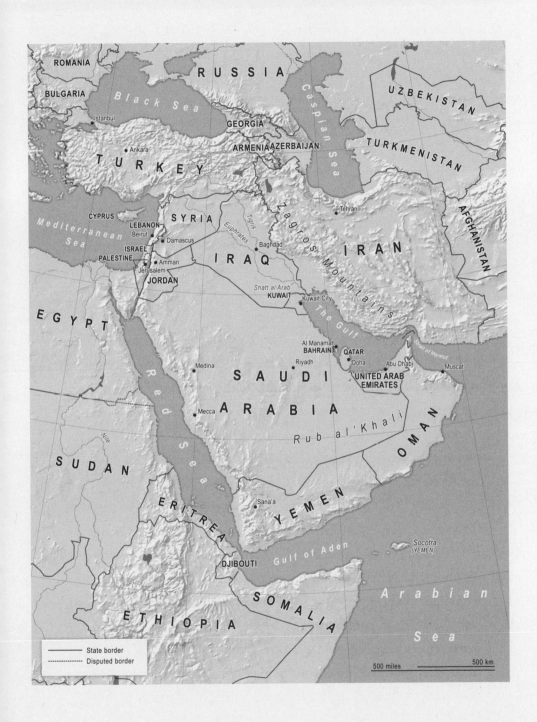

6

THE MIDDLE EAST

We've broken Sykes-Picot!
—Islamic State fighter, 2014

The Middle of what? East of where? The region's very name is based on a European view of the world, and it is a European view of the region that shaped it. The Europeans used ink to draw lines on maps: they were lines that did not exist in reality and created some of the most artificial borders the world has seen. An attempt is now being made to redraw them in blood.

One of the most important pieces of video to emerge from the Middle East in 2014 was overshadowed that year by footage of explosions and beheadings. It is a piece of slick propaganda by the Islamic State and shows a bulldozer wiping, or rather pushing, the Iraqi-Syrian border out of existence. The border is simply a high berm of sand. Move the sand, and the border no longer *physically* exists. This "line" still exists in theory. The next few years will determine whether the words of the Islamic State fighter quoted above are prophetic, or mere bravado: "We are destroying the borders and breaking the barriers. Thanks be to Allah."

After the First World War, there were fewer borders in the wider Middle East than currently exist, and those that did exist were usually determined by geography alone. The spaces within them were loosely subdivided and governed according to geography, ethnicity, and religion, but there was no attempt to create nation states.

The Greater Middle East extends across one thousand miles, west to east, from the Mediterranean Sea to the mountains of Iran. From north to south, if we start at the Black Sea and end on the shores of the Arabian Sea off Oman, it is two thousand miles long. The region includes vast deserts, oases, snow-covered mountains, long rivers, great cities, and coastal plains. And it has a great deal of natural wealth in the form that every industrialized and industrializing country around the world needs—oil and gas.

It also contains the fertile region known as Mesopotamia, the "land between the rivers" (Euphrates and Tigris). However, the most dominant feature is the vast Arabian Desert and scrubland in its center, which touches parts of Israel, Jordan, Syria, Iraq, Kuwait, Oman, Yemen, and most of Saudi Arabia, including the Rub al Khali or "Empty Quarter." This is the largest continuous sand desert in the world, incorporating an area the size of France. It is due to this feature that not only the majority of the inhabitants of the region live on its periphery, but also that, until European colonization, most of the people within it did not think in terms of nation states and legally fixed borders.

The notion that a man from a certain area could not travel across a region to see a relative from the same tribe unless he had a document, granted to him by a third man he didn't know in a faraway town, made little sense. The idea that the document was issued because a foreigner had said the area was now two regions and had made up names for them made no sense at all and was contrary to the way in which life had been lived for centuries.

The Ottoman Empire (1299–1922) was ruled from Istanbul. At its height, it stretched from the gates of Vienna, across Anatolia, and down through Arabia to the Indian Ocean. From west to east it took in what are now Algeria, Libya, Egypt, Israel/Palestine, Syria, Jordan, Iraq, and parts of Iran. It had never bothered to make up names for most of these regions; in 1867 it simply divided them into administrative areas known as Vilayets, which were usually based on where certain tribes lived, be they the Kurds in present-day northern Iraq, or the tribal federations in what is now part of Syria and part of Iraq.

When the Ottoman Empire began to collapse, the British and French had a different idea. In 1916, the British diplomat Colonel Sir Mark Sykes took a grease pencil and drew a crude line across a map of the Middle East. It ran from Haifa on the Mediterranean in what is now Israel to Kirkuk (now in Iraq) in the northeast. It became the basis of his secret agreement with his French counterpart François Georges-Picot to divide the region into two spheres of influence should the Triple Entente defeat the Ottoman Empire in the First World War. North of the line was to be under French control, south of it under British hegemony.

The term *Sykes-Picot* has become shorthand for the various decisions made in the first third of the twentieth century, which betrayed promises given to tribal leaders and which partially explains the unrest and extremism of today. This explanation can be overstated, though: there was violence and extremism before the Europeans arrived. Nevertheless, as we saw in Africa, arbitrarily creating "nation states" out of people unused to living together in one region is not a recipe for justice, equality, and stability.

Prior to Sykes-Picot (in its wider sense), there was no state of Syria, no Lebanon, nor were there Jordan, Iraq, Saudi Arabia, Kuwait, Israel, or Palestine. Modern maps show the borders and the names of nation states, but they are young and they are fragile.

Islam is the dominant religion of the Middle East but contains within it many different versions. The most important division within Islam is almost as old as the religion itself: the split between Sunni and Shia Muslims dates back to 632 CE, when the prophet Muhammad died, leading to a dispute over his succession.

The Sunni Muslims form the majority among Arabs, and indeed among the world's Muslim population, comprising perhaps 85 percent of the total, although within some of the Arab countries the percentages are less distinct. The name comes from al-Sunna, or "people of tradition." Upon the death of the prophet, those who would become Sunni argued that his successor should be chosen using Arab tribal traditions. They regard themselves as Orthodox Muslims.

The name *Shia* derives from *shiat Ali*, literally "the party of Ali," and refers to the son-in-law of the prophet Muhammad. Ali and his sons, Hassan and Hussein, were all assassinated and thus denied what the Shia feel was their birthright—to lead the Islamic community.

From this sprang several doctrinal disputes and cultural practices dividing the two main branches of Islam that have led to disputes and warfare, although there have also been long periods of peaceful coexistence.

There are also divisions within the division. For example, there are various branches of Sunni Islam that follow particular great scholars from the past, including the strict Hanbali tradition, named after the ninth-century Iraqi scholar Ahmad ibn Hanbal, favored by many Sunnis from Qatar and Saudi Arabia; this in turn has influenced the ultra-puritanical Salafi thought, which predominates among jihadists.

Shia Islam has three main divisions, the best known of which is probably the Twelvers, who adhere to the teaching of the twelve imams, but even that contains divisions. The Ismaili school disputes the lineage of the seventh imam, while the Zaidi school disputes that of the fifth imam. There are also several offshoots from mainstream Shia Islam, with the Alawites and Druze being considered so far away from traditional Islamic thought that many other Muslims, especially among the Sunni, do not even recognize them as being part of the religion.

The legacy of European colonialism left the Arabs grouped into nation states and ruled by leaders who tended to favor whichever branch of Islam (and tribe) from which they themselves came. These dictators then used the machinery of state to ensure their writ ruled over the entire area within the artificial lines drawn by the Europeans, regardless of whether this was historically appropriate and fair to the different tribes and religions that had been thrown together.

Iraq is a prime example of the ensuing conflicts and chaos. The more religious among the Shia never accepted that a Sunni-led government should have control over their holy cities such as Najaf and Karbala, where their martyrs Ali and Hussein are said to be buried. These communal feelings go back centuries; a few decades of being called "Iraqis" was never going to dilute such emotions.

As rulers of the Ottoman Empire the Turks saw a rugged, mountainous area dominated by Kurds, then, as the mountains fell away into the flatlands leading toward Baghdad and west to what is now

Syria, they saw a place where the majority of people were Sunni Arabs. Finally, after the two great rivers of the Tigris and the Euphrates merged and ran down to the Shatt al-Arab waterway, the marshlands, and the city of Basra, they saw more Arabs, most of whom were Shia. They ruled this space accordingly, dividing it into three administrative regions: Mosul, Baghdad, and Basra.

In antiquity, the regions very roughly corresponding to the above were known as Assyria, Babylonia, and Sumer. When the Persians controlled the space they divided it in a similar way, as did Alexander the Great, and later the Umayyad dynasty. The British looked at the same area and divided the three into one, a logical impossibility Christians can resolve through the Holy Trinity, but which in Iraq has resulted in an "unholy" mess.

Many analysts say that only a strong man could unite these three areas into one country, and Iraq had one strong man after another. But in reality the people were never unified; they were only frozen with fear. In the one place that the dictators could not see, people's minds, few bought into the propaganda of the state, which wallpapered over the systematic persecution of the Kurds, the domination by Saddam Hussein's Sunni Muslim clan from his hometown of Tikrit, and the mass slaughter of the Shia after their failed uprising in 1991.

The Kurds were the first to leave. The smallest minorities in a dictatorship will sometimes pretend to believe the propaganda that their rights are protected because they lack the strength to do anything about the reality. For example, Iraq's Christian minority, and its handful of Jews, felt they might be safer keeping quiet in a secular dictatorship, such as Saddam's, than risk change and what they feared might follow, and indeed has followed. However, the Kurds were geographically defined and, crucially, numerous enough to be able to react when the reality of dictatorship became too much.

Iraq's five million Kurds are concentrated in the north and northeastern provinces of Erbil, Sulaymaniyah, and Dahuk and their surrounding areas. It is a giant crescent of mostly hills and mountains, which meant the Kurds retained their distinct identity despite repeated cultural and military attacks against them, such as the al-Anfal campaign of 1988, which included aerial gas attacks against villages. During the eight-stage campaign, Saddam's forces took no prisoners and killed all males between the ages of fifteen and fifty whom they came across. Up to one hundred thousand Kurds were murdered and 90 percent of their villages wiped off the map.

When in 1990 Saddam Hussein overreached into Kuwait, the Kurds went on to seize their chance to make history and turn Kurdistan into the reality they had been promised after the First World War in the Treaty of Sèvres (1920), but never granted. At the tail end of the Gulf War conflict, the Kurds rose up, the Allied forces declared a "safe zone" into which Iraqi forces were not allowed, and a de facto Kurdistan began to take shape. The 2003 invasion of Iraq by the United States cemented what appears to be a fact—Baghdad will not again rule the Kurds.

Kurdistan is not a sovereign-recognized state but it has many of the trappings of one, and current events in the Middle East only add to the probability that there will be a Kurdistan in name and in international law. The questions are: What shape will it be? And how will Syria, Turkey, and Iran react if their Kurdish regions attempt to be part of it and try to create a contiguous Kurdistan with access to the Mediterranean?

Although not a recognized state, there is an identifiable "Kurdistan" region. Crossing borders as it does, this is an area of potential trouble should the Kurdish regions attempt to establish an independent country.

There will be another problem: unity among the Kurds. Iraqi Kurdistan has long been divided between two rival families. Syria's Kurds are trying to create a statelet they call Rojava. They see it as part of a future, greater Kurdistan, but in the event of its creation, questions would arise as to who would have how much power, and where. If Kurdistan does become an internationally recognized state, then the shape of Iraq will change. That assumes there will be an Iraq. There may not be.

The Hashemite Kingdom, as Jordan is also known, is another place that was carved out of the desert by the British, who in 1918 had one large piece of territory to administer and several problems to solve.

Various Arabian tribes had helped the British against the Ottomans during the First World War, but there were two in particular that London promised to reward at the war's end. Unfortunately, both were promised the same thing—control of the Arabian Peninsula. Given that the Saudi and Hashemite tribes frequently fought each other, this was a little awkward. So London dusted off the maps, drew some lines, and said the head of the Saudi family could rule over one region and the head of the Hashemites could rule the other, although each would "need" a British diplomat to keep an eye on things. The Saudi leader eventually landed on a name for his territory, calling it after himself, hence we know the area as Saudi Arabia—the rough equivalent would be calling the UK "Windsorland."

The British, sticklers for administration, named the other area Transjordan, which was shorthand for "the other side of the Jordan River." A dusty little town called Amman became the capital of Transjordan, and when the British went home in 1948 the country's name changed to Jordan. But the Hashemites were not from the Amman area: they were originally part of the powerful Qureshi tribe from the Mecca region, and the original inhabitants were mostly Bedouin. The majority of the population is now Palestinian: when the Israelis occupied the West Bank in 1967, many Palestinians fled to Jordan, which was the only Arab state to grant them citizenship. We now have a situation where the majority of Jordan's 6.5 million citizens are Palestinian, many of whom do not regard themselves as loyal subjects of the current Hashemite ruler, King Abdullah. Added to this problem are the one million Iraqi and Syrian refugees the country has also taken in who are putting a huge strain on its extremely limited resources.

Such changes to a country's demographics can cause serious problems, and nowhere more so than in Lebanon.

Until the twentieth century, the Arabs in the region saw the area between the Lebanese mountains and the sea as simply a province of the region of Syria. The French, into whose grasp it fell after the First World War, saw things differently.

The French had long allied themselves with the region's Arab Christians and by way of thanks made up a country for them in a place in which they appeared in the 1920s to be the dominant population. As there was no other obvious name for this country the French named it after the nearby mountains, and thus Lebanon was born. This geographical fancy held until the late 1950s. By then the birthrate among Lebanon's Shia and Sunni Muslims was growing faster than that of the Christians, while the Muslim population had been swollen by Palestinians fleeing the 1948 Arab–Israeli War in neighboring Israel/Palestine. There has been only one official census in Lebanon (in 1932), because demographics is such a sensitive issue and the political system is partially based on population sizes.

There have long been bouts of fighting between the various confessional groups in the area, and what some historians call the first Lebanese civil war broke out in 1958 between the Maronite Christians and the Muslims, who by this time probably slightly outnumbered the Christians. They are now in a clear majority but there are still no official figures, and academic studies citing numbers are fiercely contested.

Some parts of the capital, Beirut, are exclusively Shia Muslim, as is most of the south of the country. This is where the Shia Hezbollah group (backed by Shia-dominated Iran) is dominant. Another Shia stronghold is the Bekaa Valley, which Hezbollah has used as a staging post for its forages into Syria to support government forces there. Other towns are overwhelmingly Sunni Muslim. For example, Tripoli, in the north, is thought to be 80 percent Sunni, but it also has a sizable Alawite minority, and given the Sunni-Alawite tensions next door in Syria, this has led to sporadic bouts of fighting.

Lebanon appears to be a unified state only from the perspective of seeing it on a map. It takes just a few minutes after arriving at Beirut Airport to discover it is far from that. The drive from the airport to the center takes you past the exclusively Shia southern suburbs, which are partially policed by the Hezbollah militia, probably the most efficient fighting force in the country. The Lebanese army exists on paper, but in the event of another civil war, such as that of 1975–90, it would fall apart, as soldiers in most units would simply go back to their hometowns and join the local militias.

That is, in part, what happened to the Syrian armed forces once the civil war there really took hold toward the end of 2011.

Syria is another multi-faith, multi-confessional, multi-tribal state that fell apart at the first time of asking. Typical of the region, the country is majority Sunni Muslim—about 70 percent—but has substantial minorities of other faiths. Until 2011 many communities lived side by side in the towns, cities, and countryside, but there were still distinct areas in which a particular group dominated. As in Iraq, locals would always tell you, "We are one people, there are no divisions between us." However, as in Iraq, your name, place of birth, or place of habitation usually meant your background could be easily identified, and, as in Iraq, it didn't take much to pull the one people apart into many.

When the French ruled the region they followed the British example of divide and rule. At that time, the Alawites were known as Nusayris. Many Sunnis do not count them as Muslims, and such was the hostility toward them that they rebranded themselves as Alawites, as in "followers of Ali" to reinforce their Islamic credentials.

They were a backward hill people, at the bottom of the social strata in Syrian society. The French took them and put them into the police force and military, from where, over the years, they established themselves as a major power in the land.

Fundamentally, everyone was aware of the tension of having leaders from a small minority of the population ruling the majority. The Assad clan, from which President Bashar al-Assad comes, is Alawite, which comprises approximately 12 percent of the population. The family has ruled the country since Bashar's father, Hafez, took power in a coup d'état in 1970. In 1982, Hafez crushed a Muslim Brotherhood Sunni uprising in Hama, killing perhaps thirty thousand people over several days. The Brotherhood never forgave or forgot, and when the nationwide uprising began in 2011 there were scores to be settled. In some respects the ensuing civil war was simply Hama, part two.

The final shape and makeup of Syria is now in question, but there is one scenario in which, if Damascus falls (although that is far from probable), the Alawites retreat to their ancient coastal and hill strongholds and form a mini-statelet such as existed in the 1920s and 1930s. It is theoretically possible, but hundreds of thousands of Sunni Muslims would remain in the region, and were a new Sunni-dominated government to be formed in Damascus, one of its priorities would be to secure a route to the Syrian coast and defeat the last pockets of resistance.

In the near future, Syria looks as if it is destined to be ruled as a number of fiefdoms with various warlords holding sway. At the time of this writing, President al-Assad is simply the most powerful warlord of many. Lebanon's most recent civil war lasted for fifteen years, and at times it remains perilously close to another one. Syria may suffer a similar fate.

It is doubtful that whoever eventually "wins" would look kindly upon a Kurdish statelet within what are nominally the borders of Syria. Not only would the Syrian Sunni majority oppose losing territory, but the Turks would be horrified at having a Syrian Kurdish state on its borders. There would inevitably be moves to join it up to some of the Kurdish-dominated regions inside Turkey itself.

In July and August of 2015, when the Turks finally cracked down on the Islamic State forces in Northern Syria, they also took the opportunity to deliver several painful blows to Kurdish forces as well, even at the risk of reigniting the civil war inside Turkey between the Kurds and the state.

Syria has also become, like Lebanon, a place used by outside powers to further their own aims. Russia, Iran, and Lebanese Hezbollah support the Syrian government forces. The Arab countries support the opposition, but different states support different opposition groups: the Saudis and Qataris, for example, are both vying for influence but each backs a different proxy to achieve it.

It will require skill, courage, and an element so often lacking—compromise—to hold many of these regions together as a single governable space. Especially as Sunni jihadist fighters are trying to pull them apart in order to widen their "caliphate."

Groups such as al-Qaeda and, more recently, the Islamic State have garnered what support they have partially because of the humiliation caused by colonialism and then the failure of pan-Arab nationalism—and to an extent the Arab nation state. Arab leaders have failed to deliver prosperity or freedom, and the siren call of Islamism, which promises to solve all problems, has proved attractive to many in a region marked by a toxic mix of piety, unemployment, and repression. The Islamists hark back to a golden age when Islam ruled an empire and was at the cutting edge of technology, art, medicine, and govern-ment. They have helped bring to the surface the ancient suspicions of "the other" throughout the Middle East.

The Islamic State grew out of the "al-Qaeda in Iraq" franchise group in the late 2000s, which nominally was directed by the rem-nants of the al-Qaeda leadership. By the time the Syrian civil war was in full flow the group had split from al-Qaeda and renamed itself. At first it was known by the outside world as ISIL (Islamic State of Iraq and the Levant) but as the Arabic word for the Levant is *al-Sham*, gradually it became ISIS. In the summer of 2014 the group began call-ing itself the Islamic State, having proclaimed such an entity in large parts of Iraq and Syria.

It quickly became the "go to" jihadist group, drawing thousands of foreign Muslims to the cause, partially due to its pious romanti-cism and partially for its brutality. Its main attraction, though, was its success in creating a caliphate; where al-Qaeda murdered people and captured headlines, the IS murdered people and captured territory.

The IS also seized upon an area that is increasingly important in the Internet age—psychological space. It built on the pioneer-ing work of al-Qaeda in social media and took it to new heights of sophistication and brutality. By 2015, the IS was ahead of any govern-ment in levels of public messaging, using jihadists brought up on the sometimes brutalizing effects of the Internet and its obsession with violence and sex. They are Generation Jackass Jihadis and they are ahead of the deadly game.

By the summer of 2015 many Arabs across the Middle East, including most of the regional media, were calling the Islamic State by another name, one which encapsulated how repulsive many ordi-nary people felt the organization to be—DAESH.

It is an acronym of sorts for the Arabic *Dawlat al-Islamiya f'al-Iraq wa al-Shams*, but the reason people came up with the name is because the Islamic State members hate the term. It sounds similar to the word *daes*—one who is underhanded and sows dissent. More important, it rhymes with negative words such as *fahish*—"sinner"—and best of all, for those who despise the organization's particular brand of Islam, is that it rhymes with and sounds a bit like *jahesh*—"stupid ass." This is worse than being called a donkey, because in Arab culture one of the few things more stupid than a donkey is an ass.

In 2015, the war raged back and forth across parts of Iraq with the Islamic State losing the town of Tikrit, but taking Ramadi, which the government then had to fight for yet again.

In the battle for Tikrit the US Air Force found itself in the odd position of flying reconnaissance missions and limited air strikes, which assisted Iranian Revolutionary Guard commanders who had been brought in to oversee the Iraqi assault on the town.

The IS wanted Tikrit partially to guard against the Iraqi government trying to retake Mosul to the north, but more important to them was Ramadi. It is in Anbar province, which is an overwhelmingly Sunni region of Iraq and links through to the Syrian border. Holding the territory strengthened their claim to be a "state."

August 2015 marked the first anniversary of the American-led bombing missions against the Islamic State in both Iraq and Syria. There have been thousands of air strikes with many of the US planes flying from the *USS George H. W. Bush* and *USS Carl Vinson* aircraft carriers in the Gulf. The F-22 Raptor stealth jet fighter was also introduced to the fight in 2015, attacking the Islamic State's oil facilities from a base in the United Arab Emirates, and other planes have flown out of Kuwait. The US pilots, who flew the majority of the missions, suffered from not having American Special Forces forward air controllers calling in the coordinates for the strikes. As targets were frequently in the urban areas, the "rules of engagement" meant many planes returned to their bases without firing their weapons.

Since late summer 2015 the Islamic State has been steadily losing territory. Significant losses included the Syrian town of Kobane, recaptured by Kurdish fighters, and in January 2016 the major Iraqi city of Ramadi was retaken by the Iraqi army. At the same time, IS has come under enormous pressure from an increase in air strikes. The Russians have become even more involved, striking both FSA and IS targets in Syria following the alleged IS attack on one of its passenger airliners in Egypt. The French responded to the terror attacks on Paris in November 2015 with massive air strikes on IS, and then asked the UK for assistance. The British parliament voted to extend its air strikes in Iraq to include Syria. The result has seen Islamic State's "caliphate" shrink in size, some of its leaders and many rank and file killed. However, hundreds of fighters then headed to Libya to set up another base, possibly as a backup in the event they are routed in Syria and Iraq. By the spring of 2016 Libya was clearly another front in a long battle.

With the Russian, the British, the Americans, the French, and others all now heavily committed, thousands of "drone" missions have been flown as well, some from within the Continental United States. Drones are a clear modern example of technology overcoming some of the restrictions of geography but at the same time serving to underline geography's importance. The United States houses its growing fleet of drones on at least ten bases around the world. This allows it to hit targets via a joystick operated by a person sitting in an air-conditioned office in Nevada, or transfer control to an operative near the target. But it also means the United States needs to keep good relations with whichever country it receives permission from to house the regional drone HQ. This is a reminder of the conceptual map of US power required to fully understand geopolitics today. For example, the signal sent from Nevada may need to travel through an underwater cable to Germany and then be sent up to a satellite belonging to a third country that sells bandwidth to the Pentagon.

Drone strikes are also subject to rules of engagement, but have been used to devastating effect against individual targets. They made a huge contribution to the situation the Islamic State found itself in during 2015 and 2016, when it had lost several thousand square miles of territory in Iraq even though it still controlled large swaths of the Sunni-dominated regions of the country.

Sunni Islamist fighters from across the globe, drawn like moths to the light of a billion pixels, have taken advantage of the three-way split between the Kurds, Sunni, and Shia in Iraq. They offer the Sunni Arabs a heady mix of the promise of restoring them to their "rightful" place as the dominant force in the region, and the reestablishment of the caliphate in which their version of all true believers (Sunni Muslims) live under one ruler.

However, it is the very fanaticism of their beliefs and practices that explains why they cannot achieve their utopian fantasies.

First, only some of the Sunni Iraqi tribes will support the jihadist aims, and even then only to achieve their own ends—which do not include a return to the sixth century. Once they get what they want, they will then turn on the jihadists, especially the foreign ones. Second, the jihadists have demonstrated that there is no mercy for anyone who opposes them and that being a non-Sunni is akin to a death sentence. So, all non-Sunni Muslims and all the minorities in

Iraq—Christians, Chaldeans, Yazidis, and others—are against them, as are dozens of Western and Muslim countries.

The non-jihadist Iraqi Sunnis are in a difficult position. In the event of either a fragmented or a legally federalized Iraq, they are stuck in the middle, surrounded by sand in an area that is known as the Sunni Triangle, with its points roughly located just east of Baghdad, west of Ramadi, and north of Tikrit. Sunnis living here often have more in common with their related tribes in Syria than they do with the Kurds in the north or the Shia of the south.

There is not enough economic diversity within the triangle to sustain a Sunni entity. History bequeathed oil to "Iraq," but the de facto division of the country means the oil is mostly in the Kurdish and Shia areas; and if there is no strong, unified Iraq then the oil money flows back to where the oil is found. The Kurdish lands cannot be brought under their control, the cities south of Baghdad such as Najaf and Karbala are overwhelmingly Shia, and the ports of Basra and Umm Qasr are far away from the Sunni territory. This dilemma leaves the Sunnis fighting for an equal share in a country they once ruled, sometimes toying with the idea of separation, but knowing that their future would probably be self-rule over not very much.

In the event of a split, the Shia are geographically best placed to take advantage. The region they dominate has oil fields; thirty-five miles of coastline; the Shatt al-Arab waterway; ports; access to the outside world; and a religious, economic, and military ally next door in the form of Iran.

The jihadist fantasy is global domination by Salafi Islam. In their more lucid, yet still wild, moments, they plan, and fight, for a more limited aim—a caliphate throughout the Middle East. One of the jihadists' battle cries is "From Mosul to Jerusalem!" meaning that they hope to control the area from Mosul in Iraq right across to Beirut in Lebanon, Amman in Jordan, and Jerusalem in Israel. However, the real size of the Islamic State's geographical caliphate is limited by its capabilities.

This is not to underestimate the problem or the scale of what may be the Arab version of Europe's Thirty Years' War (1618–48). It is not just a Middle Eastern problem. Many of the international jihadists who survive will return home to Europe, North America, Indonesia, the Caucasus, and Bangladesh, where they are unlikely to settle for a quiet life. The intelligence services in London believe there are far more British Muslims fighting in the Middle East for jihadist groups than there are serving in the British army. The radicalization program undertaken by the Islamists began several decades before the deradicalization initiatives now under way in European countries.

Most countries in the region face their own version of this generational struggle to a greater or lesser degree. Saudi Arabia, for example, has taken on al-Qaeda cells over the past decade, but having mostly taken them apart, it now faces renewed challenges from the next generation of jihadists. It has another problem in the south, on the border with Yemen, which itself is blighted with violence, separatist movements, and a strong jihadist element.

There is also a simmering Islamist movement in Jordan, especially in the town of Zarqa, in the northeast toward the Syrian and Iraqi borders, which is home to some of the several thousand supporters of groups such as al-Qaeda and the Islamic State. The authorities are fearful of a jihadist group in Iraq or Syria reaching the now fragile borders in strength and crossing into Jordan. The British-trained Jordanian army is thought to be one of the most robust in the Middle East, but it might struggle to cope if local Islamists and foreign fighters took to the streets in guerrilla warfare. If the Palestinian Jordanians declined to defend the country, it is not unrealistic to believe that it would descend into the sort of chaos we now see in Syria. This is the last thing the Hashemite rulers want—and it's the last thing the Israelis want as well.

The battle for the future of the Arab Middle East has, to an extent, taken the spotlight off the Israeli-Arab struggle. The fixation with Israel/Palestine does sometimes return, but the magnitude of what is going on elsewhere has finally enabled at least some observers to understand that the problems of the region do not come down to the existence of Israel. That was a lie peddled by the Arab dictators as they sought to deflect attention from their own brutality, and it was bought by many people across the area and the dictators' useful idiots in the West. Nevertheless, the Israeli/Palestinian joint tragedy continues, and such is the obsession with this tiny piece of land that it may again come to be considered by some the most pressing conflict in the world.

The Ottomans had regarded the area west of the Jordan River to the Mediterranean coast as a part of the region of Syria. They called it Filistina. After the First World War, under the British Mandate, this became Palestine.

For millennia the Jews had lived in what used to be called Israel, but the ravages of history had dispersed them across the globe. Israel remained for them the "promised land," and Jerusalem, in particular, was sacred ground. However, by 1948 Arab Muslims and Christians had been a clear majority in the land for more than a thousand years.

In the twentieth century, with the introduction of the Mandate for Palestine, the Jewish movement to join their minority coreligionists grew, and, propelled by the pogroms in Eastern Europe, more and more Jews began to settle there. The British looked favorably on the creation of a "Jewish homeland" in Palestine and allowed Jews to move there and buy land from the Arabs. After the Second World War and the Holocaust, Jews tried to get to Palestine in even greater numbers. Tensions between Jews and non-Jews reached the boiling point, and an exhausted Britain handed over the problem to the United Nations in 1948, which voted to partition the region into two countries. The Jews agreed, the Arabs said no. The outcome was war, which created the first wave of Palestinian refugees fleeing the area and Jewish refugees coming in from across the Middle East.

The Golan Heights, the West Bank, and Gaza remain contested territory following the Six-Day War in 1967.

Jordan occupied the West Bank region, including East Jerusalem. Egypt occupied Gaza, considering it to be an extension of its territory. Neither was minded to give the people living there citizenship or statehood as Palestinians, nor was there any significant movement by the inhabitants calling for the creation of a Palestinian state. Syria meanwhile considered the whole area to be part of greater Syria and the people living there Syrians.

To this day Egypt, Syria, and Jordan are suspicious of Palestinian independence, and if Israel vanished and were replaced by Palestine, all three might make claims to parts of the territory. In this century, however, there is a fierce sense of nationhood among the Palestinians, and any Arab dictatorship seeking to take a chunk out of a Palestinian state of whatever shape or size would be met with massive opposition. The Palestinians are very aware that most of the Arab countries, to which some of them fled in the twentieth century, refuse to give them citizenship; they insist that the status of their children and grandchildren remains "refugee," and work to ensure that they do not integrate into the country.

During the Six-Day War of 1967, the Israelis won control of all of Jerusalem, the West Bank, and Gaza. In 2005, they left Gaza, but hundreds of thousands of settlers remain in the West Bank.

Israel regards Jerusalem as its eternal, indivisible capital. The Jewish religion says the rock upon which Abraham prepared to sacrifice Isaac is there, and that it stands directly above the Holy of Holies, King Solomon's Temple. For the Palestinians, Jerusalem has a religious resonance that runs deep throughout the Muslim world: the city is regarded as the third most holy place in Islam because the prophet Muhammad is said to have ascended to heaven from that same rock, which is on the site of what is now the "Farthest Mosque" (Al-Aqsa). Militarily, the city is of only moderate strategic geographical importance—it has no real industry to speak of, no river, and no airport—but it is of overwhelming significance in cultural and religious terms: the ideological need for the place is of more importance than its location. Control of, and access to, Jerusalem is not an issue upon which a compromise solution can be easily achieved.

In comparison, the Gaza Strip was easier for the Israelis to give up (although it was still difficult). Whether the people living there have gained much by the Israeli departure, however, is open to debate.

The Gaza Strip is by far the worse off of the two current Palestinian "entities." It is only 25 miles long and 7.5 miles wide. Crammed into this space are 1.8 million people. It is in effect a "city state," albeit a horribly impoverished one. Due to the conflict with Israel, its citizens are penned in on three sides by a security barrier created by Israel and Egypt and by the sea to their west. They can build only to within a certain distance of the border with Israel because the Israelis are trying to limit the ability of rocket fire from Gaza to reach deep into Israel. The last decade has seen an asymmetric arms race gain pace, with militants in Gaza seeking rockets that can fire farther, and Israel developing its antimissile defense system.

Because of its urban density, Gaza makes good fighting ground for its defenders but it is a nightmare for its civilians, who have little or no shelter from war and no link to the West Bank, although the distance between the two is only twenty-five miles at its narrowest point. Until a peace deal is agreed upon, there is nowhere for the Gazans to go, and little for them to do inside the Strip.

The West Bank is almost seven times the size of Gaza but is landlocked. Much of it comprises a mountain ridge that runs north to south. From a military perspective, this gives an advantage to whoever controls the high ground of the coastal plain on the western side of the ridge and the Jordan Rift Valley to its east. Leaving to one side the ideology of Jewish settlers, who claim the biblical right to live in what they call Judea and Samaria, from a military perspective the Israeli view is that a non-Israeli force cannot be allowed to control these heights, as heavy weapons could be fired onto the coastal plain, where 70 percent of Israel's population lives. The plain also includes its most important road systems, many of its successful high-tech companies, the international airport, and most of its heavy industry.

This is one reason for the demand for "security" by the Israeli side and its insistence that, even if there is an independent Palestinian state, that state cannot have an army with heavy weapons on the ridge, and that Israel must also maintain control of the border with Jordan. Because Israel is so small it has no real "strategic depth," nowhere to fall back to if its defenses are breached, and so militarily it concentrates on trying to ensure that no one can get near it. Furthermore, the distance from the West Bank border to Tel Aviv is approximately ten miles at its narrowest; from the West Bank ridge, any half-decent military could cut Israel in two. Likewise, in the case of the West Bank, Israel prevents any group from becoming powerful enough to threaten its existence.

Under current conditions, Israel faces threats to its security and to the lives of its citizens by terrorist attacks and rocket fire from its immediate neighbors, but not a threat to its very existence. Egypt, to the southwest, is not a threat. There is a peace treaty that currently suits both sides, and the partially demilitarized Sinai Peninsula acts as a buffer between them. East of this, across the Red Sea at Aqaba in Jordan, the desert also protects Israel, as does its peace treaty with Amman. To the north there is a potential menace from Lebanon but it is a relatively small one, in the form of cross-border raids and/or limited shelling. However, if and when Hezbollah in Lebanon use their larger and longer-range rockets to reach deep into Israel, the response will be massive.

The more serious potential threat comes from Lebanon's bigger neighbor, Syria. Historically, Damascus wants and needs direct access to the coast. It has always regarded Lebanon as part of Syria (as indeed it was) and remains bitter about its troops having been forced to leave in 2005. If that route to the sea is blocked, the alternative is to cross the Golan Heights and descend to the hilly region around the Sea of Galilee en route to the Mediterranean. But the Heights were seized by Israel after Syria attacked it in the 1967 war, and it would take an enormous onslaught by a Syrian army to break through to the coastal plain leading to the major Israeli population centers. This cannot be discounted at some future point, but in the medium term it remains extremely unlikely, and—as long as the Syrian civil war continues—impossible.

That leaves the question of Iran—a more serious consideration, as it raises the issue of nuclear weapons.

Iran is a non-Arabic, majority Farsi-speaking giant. It is bigger than France, Germany, and the UK combined, but while the populations of those countries amount to 200 million people, Iran has only 78 million. With limited habitable space, most live in the mountains; the great deserts and salt plains of the interior of Iran are no place for human habitation. Just driving through them can subdue the human spirit, and living in them is a struggle few undertake.

There are two huge mountain ranges in Iran: the Zagros and the Elburz. The Zagros runs from the north, nine hundred miles down along Iran's borders with Turkey and Iraq, ending almost at the Strait of Hormuz in the Gulf. In the southern half of the range there is a plain to the west where the Shatt al-Arab divides Iran and Iraq. This is also where the major Iranian oil fields are, the others being in the north and center. Together they are thought to comprise the world's third-largest reserves. Despite this, Iran remains relatively poor due to mismanagement, corruption, mountainous topography that hinders transport connections, and economic sanctions that have, in part, prevented certain sections of industry from modernizing.

The Elburz range also begins in the north, but along the border with Armenia. It runs the whole length of the Caspian Sea's south shore and on to the border with Turkmenistan before descending as it reaches Afghanistan. This is the mountain range you can see from the capital, Tehran, towering above the city to its north. It provides spectacular views, and also a better-kept secret than the Iranian nuclear project: the skiing conditions are excellent for several months each year.

Iran is defended by this geography, with mountains on three sides, swampland and water on the fourth. The Mongols were the last force to make any progress through the territory, in 1219–21, and since then attackers have ground themselves into dust trying to make headway across the mountains. By the time of the Second Gulf War in 2003, even the United States, the greatest fighting force the world has seen, thought better than to take a right turn once it had entered

Iraq from the south, knowing that even with its superior firepower, Iran was not a country to invade. In fact, the US military had a catch-phrase at the time: "We do deserts, not mountains."

In 1980, when the Iran-Iraq War broke out, the Iraqis used six divisions to cross the Shatt al-Arab in an attempt to annex the Iranian province of Khuzestan. They never even made it off the swamp-ridden plains, let alone entered the foothills of the Zagros. The war dragged on for eight years, taking at least a million lives.

The mountainous terrain of Iran means that it is difficult to create an interconnected economy and that it has many minority groups each with keenly defined characteristics. Khuzestan, for example, is ethnically majority Arab, and elsewhere there are Kurds, Azeri, Turkmen, and Georgians, among others. At most, 60 percent of the country speaks Farsi, the language of the dominant Persian majority. As a result of this diversity, Iran has traditionally centralized power and used force and a fearsome intelligence network to maintain internal stability. Tehran knows that no one is about to invade Iran, but also that hostile powers can use its minorities to try and stir dissent and thus endanger its Islamic revolution.

Iran also has a nuclear industry that many countries, particularly Israel, believe is being used to prepare for the construction of nuclear weapons, increasing tensions in the region. The Israelis feel threatened by the prospect of Iranian nuclear weapons. It is not just Iran's potential to rival their own arsenal and wipe out Israel with just one bomb: if Iran were to get the bomb, then the Arab countries would probably panic and attempt to get their own as well. The Saudis, for example, fear that the ayatollahs want to dominate the region, bring all the Shia Arabs under their guidance, and even have designs on controlling the holy cities of Mecca and Medina. A nuclear-armed

Iran would be the regional superpower par excellence, and to counter this danger the Saudis would probably try to buy nuclear weapons from Pakistan (with whom they have close ties). Egypt and Turkey might follow suit.

This means that the threat of an Israeli air strike on Iran's nuclear facilities is a constant presence, but there are many restraining factors. One is that, in a straight line, it is one thousand miles from Israel to Iran. The Israeli air force would need to cross two sovereign borders, those of Jordan and Iraq; the latter would certainly tell Iran that the attack was coming. Another is that any other route requires refueling capabilities that may be beyond Israel, and that (if flying the northern route) also overfly sovereign territory. A final reason is that Iran holds what might be a trump card—the ability to close the Strait of Hormuz in the Gulf through which passes each day, depending on sales, about 20 percent of the world's oil needs. At its narrowest point, the Strait, which is regarded as the most strategic in the world, is only twenty-one miles across. The industrialized world fears the effect of Hormuz being closed possibly for months on end, with ensuing spiraling prices. This is one reason why so many countries pressure Israel not to act.

In the 2000s, the Iranians feared encirclement by the Americans. The US navy was in the Gulf, and American troops were in Iraq and Afghanistan. With the military drawdowns in both countries, Iranian fears have now faded, and Iran is left in the dominant position with a direct line to its allies in Shia-dominated Iraq. The south of Iraq is also a bridge for Iran to its Alawite allies in Damascus, and then to its Shia allies in the form of Hezbollah in Lebanon on the Mediterranean coast.

In the sixth to the fourth centuries BCE the Persian Empire

stretched all the way from Egypt to India. Modern-day Iran has no such imperial designs, but it does seek to expand its influence, and the obvious direction is across the flatlands to its west—the Arab world and its Shia minorities. It has made ground in Iraq since the US invasion delivered a Shia-majority government. This has alarmed Sunni-dominated Saudi Arabia and helped fuel the Middle East's version of the Cold War with the Saudi–Iranian relationship at its core. Saudi Arabia may be bigger than Iran, and it may be many times richer than Iran due to its well-developed oil and gas industries, but its population is much smaller (28 million Saudis as opposed to 78 million Iranians) and militarily it is not confident about its ability to take on its Persian neighbor if this cold war ever turns hot and their forces confront each other directly. Each side has ambitions to be the dominant power in the region, and each regards themselves as the champions of their respective versions of Islam. When Iraq was under the heel of Saddam, a powerful buffer separated Saudi Arabia and Iran; with that buffer gone, the two countries now glare at each other across the Gulf. The American-led deal on Iran's nuclear facilities that was concluded in the summer of 2015 has in no way reassured the Gulf States that the threat to them from Iran has diminished. Western media reporting concentrated on the Israeli reaction to the deal, but the Arab media across the entire region was wholly against it, with some newspapers comparing it to the Munich Agreement of 1938. One leading Saudi columnist called for the kingdom to begin building a bomb to be ready for when Iran does the same.

This was the background to the shocking events of early 2016 when Saudi Arabia (a majority Sunni country) executed forty-seven prisoners in a single day, among them the country's most senior Shia sheikh—Nimr al-Nimr. This was a calculated move by the ruling Sunni royal family to show the world, including America, that nuclear deal or no nuclear deal—the Saudis were going to face down Iran. Demonstrations broke out across the Shia Muslim world, the Saudi embassy in Tehran was duly ransacked and set on fire, diplomatic relations were broken between the two countries, and the scene was set for the continuation of the bitter Sunni/Shia civil war.

Northwest of Iran is a country that is both European and Asian. Turkey lies on the borders of the Arab lands but is not Arabic, and although most of its landmass is part of the wider Middle East region, it tries to distance itself from the conflicts taking place there.

The Turks have never been truly recognized as part of Europe by their neighbors to the north and northwest. If Turkey *is* European, then Europe's borders are on the far side of the vast Anatolian Plain, meaning they stop at Syria, Iraq, and Iran. This is a concept few people accept. If it is *not* part of Europe, then where is it? Its greatest city, Istanbul, was the 2010 European Capital of Culture, it competes in the Eurovision Song Contest and the UEFA European Championship, and it applied for membership in what is now the European Union in the 1970s; and yet, less than 5 percent of its territory is in Europe. Most geographers regard the small area of Turkey that is west of the Bosporus as being in Europe, and the rest of the country, south and southeast of the Bosporus, as being in the Middle East (in its widest sense).

That is one reason why it has never been accepted into the EU. Other factors are its record on human rights, especially when it comes to the Kurds, and its economy. Its population is 75 million, and European countries fear that given the disparity in living standards, EU membership would result in a mass influx of labor. What may also be a factor, albeit unspoken within the EU, is that Turkey is a majority Muslim country (98 percent). The EU is neither a secular nor a Christian organization, but there has been a difficult debate about "values." For each argument for Turkey's EU membership there is an argument against it, and in the past decade the prospects for Turkey joining have diminished. This has led the country to reflect on what other choices there may be.

In the 1920s, for one man at least, there was no choice. His name was Mustafa Kemal and he was the only Turkish general to emerge from the First World War with an enhanced reputation. After the victorious powers carved up Turkey, he rose to become president on a platform of resisting the terms imposed by the Allies, but at the same time modernizing Turkey and making it part of Europe. Western legal codes and the Gregorian calendar were introduced and Islamic public institutions banned. The wearing of the fez was forbidden, the Latin alphabet replaced Arabic script, and he even granted the vote to women (two years ahead of Spain and fifteen years ahead of France). In 1934, when Turks embraced legally binding surnames, Kemal was given the name Atatürk—"Father of the Turks." He died in 1938, but subsequent Turkish leaders continued working to bring Turkey into the West European fold, and those who didn't found themselves on the wrong end of a coup d'état by a military determined to complete Atatürk's legacy.

By the late 1980s, however, the continued rejection by Europe and the stubborn refusal of many ordinary Turks to become less religious resulted in a generation of politicians who began to think the unthinkable—that perhaps Turkey needed a plan B. President Turgut

Özal, a religious man, came to office in 1989 and began the change. He encouraged Turks to again see Turkey as the great land bridge between Europe, Asia, and the Middle East, and a country that could again be a great power in all three regions. The current president, Recep Tayyip Erdoğan, has similar ambitions, perhaps even greater ones, but has faced similar hurdles in achieving them. These are in part geographical.

Politically, the Arab countries remain suspicious that Erdoğan wants to re-create the Ottoman Empire economically and they resist close ties. The Iranians see Turkey as their most powerful military and economic competitor in their own backyard. Relations, never warm, have cooled due to their being on opposite sides in support for factions involved in the Syrian civil war. Turkey's strong support for the Muslim Brotherhood government in Egypt was a policy that backfired when the Egyptian military staged its second coup and took power. Relations between Cairo and Ankara are now icy.

Worse still are relations between Ankara and Moscow. The Turks and Russians have been at odds for five hundred years but over the past century have mostly learned to rub along without too much friction. The Syrian civil war has changed that with Russia backing President Assad, and Turkey working hard to help overthrow the Assad regime and replace it with a Sunni Muslim–led government. Things came to a head in late 2015 after the Russians intervened in Syria militarily. The Turks shot down a Russian Su-24 fighter jet that strayed into its airspace. A bitter war of words followed, there was even the vague threat of it turning into a shooting match, but both sides settled for vitriol and economic sanctions. This fierce row was not just about Syria and the Russian jet—it was about Turkey and

Russia vying for influence in the Black Sea, the Caspian Sea, and among the Turkic peoples in countries such as Turkmenistan. They both know that as Turkey continues to grow it will seek to rival Russia in the "'stans" and neither is minded to back down on issues of sovereignty and "honor."

The Turkish elite have learned that scoring Islamist points by picking fights with Israel results in Israel cooperating with Cyprus and Greece to create a trilateral energy alliance to exploit the gas fields off their respective coasts. The Egyptian government's dim view of Turkey is contributing to Cairo's interest in being a major customer for this new energy source. Meanwhile, Turkey, which could have benefited from Israeli energy, remains largely reliant on its old foe Russia for its energy needs while simultaneously working with Russia to develop new pipelines to deliver energy to EU countries.

The Americans, alarmed at the new cold war between Turkey and Israel, two of its allies, are working to bring them together again. The United States wants a better relationship between them so as to strengthen NATO's position in the eastern Mediterranean. In NATO terms, Turkey is a key country because it controls the entrance to and exit from the Black Sea through the narrow gap of the Bosporus Strait. If it closes the strait, which is less than a mile across at its narrowest point, the Russian Black Sea Fleet cannot break out into the Mediterranean and then the Atlantic. Even getting through the Bosporus takes you only into the Sea of Marmara; you still have to navigate through the Dardanelles Strait to get to the Aegean Sea en route to the Mediterranean.

Given its landmass, Turkey is not often thought of as a sea power, but it borders three seas, and its control of these waters has always made it a force to be reckoned with; it is also a trade and transportation bridge linking Europe with the Middle East, the Caucasus, and on up to the central Asian countries, with which it shares history and, in some regions, ethnic ties.

Turkey is determined to be at the crossroads of history even if the traffic can at times be hazardous. The web page of the Turkish Foreign Ministry emphasizes this in the section "Synopsis of the Turkish Foreign Policy": "The Afro-Eurasian geography where Turkey is situated at the epicenter is an area where such opportunities and risks interact in the most intensive way." It also says: "Turkey is determined to become a full member of the European Union as part of its bicentennial effort to reach the highest level of contemporary civilization."

That looks unlikely in the short to medium term. Until a few years ago, Turkey was held up as an example of how a Middle Eastern country, other than Israel, could embrace democracy. That example has taken a few knocks recently with the ongoing Kurdish problem, the difficulties facing some of the tiny Christian communities, and the tacit support for Islamist groups in their fight against the Syrian government. President Erdoğan's remarks on Jews, race, and gender equality, taken with the creeping Islamization of Turkey, have set alarm bells ringing. However, compared with the majority of Arab states, Turkey is far more developed and recognizable as a democracy. Erdoğan may be undoing some of Atatürk's work, but the grandchildren of the Father of the Turks live more freely than anyone in the Arab Middle East.

Because the Arab states have not experienced a similar opening-up and have suffered from colonialism, they were not ready to turn the Arab uprisings (the wave of protests that started in 2010) into a real Arab Spring. Instead, they soured into perpetual rioting and civil war.

The Arab Spring is a misnomer, invented by the media; it clouds our understanding of what is happening. Too many reporters rushed to interview the young liberals who were standing in city squares with placards written in English, and mistook them for the voice of the people and the direction of history. Some journalists had done the same during the Green Revolution, describing the young students of north Tehran as the "Youth of Iran," thus ignoring the other young Iranians who were joining the reactionary Basij militia and Revolutionary Guard.

In 1989 in Eastern Europe there was one form of totalitarianism: Communism. In the majority of people's minds there was only one direction in which to go: toward democracy, which was thriving on the other side of the Iron Curtain. East and West shared a historical memory of periods of democracy and civil society. The Arab world of 2011 enjoyed none of those things and faced in many different directions. There were, and are, the directions of democracy, liberal democracy (which differs from the former), nationalism, the cult of the strong leader, and the direction in which many people had been facing all along—Islam in its various guises, including Islamism.

In the Middle East, power does indeed flow from the barrel of a gun. Some good citizens of Misrata in Libya may want to develop a liberal democratic party, some might even want to campaign for gay rights; but their choice will be limited if the local de facto power shoots liberal democrats and gays. Iraq is a case in point: a democracy in name only, far from liberal, and a place where people are routinely murdered for being homosexual.

The second phase of the Arab uprising is well into its stride. This is the complex internal struggle within societies where religious beliefs, social mores, tribal links, and guns are currently far more powerful forces than "Western" ideals of equality, freedom of expression, and universal suffrage. The Arab countries are beset by prejudices, indeed hatreds, of which average Westerners know so little that they tend not to believe them even if they are laid out in print before their eyes. We are aware of our own prejudices, which are legion, but often seem to turn a blind eye to those in the Middle East.

The routine expression of hatred for others is so common in the Arab world that it barely draws comment other than from the region's often Western-educated liberal minority who have limited access to the platform of mass media. Anti-Semitic cartoons that echo the Nazi *Der Stürmer* propaganda newspaper are common. Week in, week out, shock-jock imams are given space on prime-time TV shows.

Western apologists for this sort of behavior are sometimes hamstrung by a fear of being described as one of Edward Said's "Orientalists." They betray their own liberal values by denying their universality. Others, in their naïveté, say that these incitements to murder are not widespread and must be seen in the context of the Arabic language, which can be given to flights of rhetoric. This signals their lack of understanding of the "Arab street," the role of the mainstream Arab media, and a refusal to understand that when people who are full of hatred say something, they mean it.

When Hosni Mubarak was ousted as president of Egypt, it was indeed people power that toppled him, but what the outside world failed to see was that the military had been waiting for years for an opportunity to be rid of him and his son Gamal, and that the theater of the street provided the cover they needed. It was only when the Muslim Brotherhood called its supporters out that there was enough cover. There were only three institutions in Egypt: Mubarak's National Democratic Party, the military, and the Brotherhood. The latter two destroyed the former, the Brotherhood then won an election, began turning Egypt into an Islamist state, and paid the price by itself being overthrown by the real power in the land—the military.

The Islamists remain the second power, albeit now underground. When the anti-Mubarak demonstrations were at their height, the gatherings in Cairo attracted several hundred thousand people. After Mubarak's fall, when the radical Muslim Brotherhood preacher Yusuf al-Qaradawi returned from exile in Qatar, at least a million people came out to greet him, but few in the Western media called this the "voice of the people." The liberals never had a chance. Nor do they now. This is not because the people of the region are radical; it is because if you are hungry and frightened, and you are offered either bread and security or the concept of democracy, the choice is not difficult.

In impoverished societies with few accountable institutions, power rests with gangs disguised as "militia" and "political parties." While they fight for power, sometimes cheered on by naive Western sympathizers, many innocent people die. It looks as if it will be that way in Libya, Syria, Yemen, Iraq, and possibly other countries for years to come.

The Americans are keen to scale down their political and military investment in the region due to a reduction in their energy-import requirements; if they do withdraw, then China, and to a lesser extent India, may have to get involved in equal proportion to the loss of interest. The Chinese are already major players in Saudi Arabia, Iraq, and Iran. That scenario is on a global level and will be determined in the chancelleries of the capitals of the great powers. On the ground the game will be played with people's imaginations, wants, hopes, and needs, and with their lives.

Sykes-Picot is breaking; putting it back together, even in a different shape, will be a long and bloody affair.

7

INDIA AND PAKISTAN

India is not a nation, nor a country. It is a subcontinent of nationalities.
—Muhammad Ali Jinnah

India and Pakistan can agree on one thing: neither wants the other one around. This is somewhat problematic, given that they share a 1,900-mile-long border. Each country fairly bristles with antagonism and nuclear weapons, so how they manage this unwanted relationship is a matter of life and death on a scale of tens of millions.

India has a population approaching 1.3 billion people, while Pakistan's is 182 million. Impoverished, volatile, and splintering, Pakistan appears to define itself by its opposition to India, while India, despite obsessing about Pakistan, defines itself in many ways, including that of being an emerging world power with a growing economy and an expanding middle class. From this vantage point it looks across at Pakistan and sees how it outperforms it on almost all economic and democratic indicators.

They have fought four major wars and many skirmishes. Emotions run hot. An oft-quoted remark by a Pakistani officer that Pakistan would make India bleed by a thousand cuts was addressed in late 2014 by military analyst Dr. Amarjit Singh writing in the *Indian Defence Review*: "Whatever others may believe, my opinion is simply that it is better for India to brave a costly nuclear attack by Pakistan, and get it over with even at the cost of tens of millions of deaths, than suffer ignominy and pain day in and day out through a thousand cuts and wasted energy in unrealized potential." That may not reflect official government policy, but it is an indication of the depth of feeling at many levels in both societies. Modern Pakistan and India were born in fire; next time the fire could kill them.

The two are tied together within the geography of the Indian subcontinent, which creates a natural frame. The Bay of Bengal, the Indian Ocean, and the Arabian Sea are respectively to the southeast, south, and southwest, the Hindu Kush to the northwest, and the Himalayas to the north. Moving clockwise, the plateau of the Baluchistan Desert climbs steadily before becoming the mountains of the North-West Frontier, which rise even higher to become the Hindu Kush. A right turn east connects to the Karakoram Range, which then leads to the Himalayas. They sweep right along the border with China all the way to Burma. From there, as India curves around Bangladesh, the terrain descends south to the Bay of Bengal.

The interior of the frame contains what are modern-day India, Pakistan, Bangladesh, Nepal, and Bhutan. The latter two are impoverished landlocked nations dominated by their giant neighbors, China and India. Bangladesh's problem is not that it lacks access to the sea but that the sea has too much access to Bangladesh: flooding from the waters of the Bay of Bengal constantly afflicts the low-lying territory. Its other geographical problem is that it is almost entirely surrounded by India: the 2,545-mile-long frontier, agreed to in 1974, wrapped India around Bangladesh, leaving it only a short border with Burma as an alternative land route to the outside world.

Bangladesh is volatile and contains Islamist militants who trouble India, but none of these three smaller countries within the subcontinent can ever rise to threaten its undisputed master. Nor would Pakistan be considered a threat to India had it not mastered the technology of developing nuclear weapons in the decades following the partition of the region in 1947.

The area within our frame, despite being relatively flat, has always been too large and diverse to have strong central rule. Even the British colonial overlords, with their famed bureaucracy and connecting rail system, allowed regional autonomy and indeed used it to play local leaders off against one another. The linguistic and cultural diversity is partially due to the differences in climate—for example, the freezing north of the Himalayas in contrast to the jungles of the south—but it is also because of the subcontinent's rivers and religions.

Various civilizations have grown up along these rivers, such as the Ganges, the Brahmaputra, and the Indus. To this day the population centers are dotted along their banks, and the regions, so different from one another—for example the Punjab, with its Sikh majority, and the Tamil speakers of Tamil Nadu—are based on these geographical divides.

Different powers have invaded the subcontinent over the centuries, but none have ever truly conquered it. Even now, New Delhi does not truly control India and, as we shall see, to an even greater extent Islamabad does not control Pakistan. The Muslims had the greatest success in uniting the subcontinent under one leadership, but even Islam never overcame the linguistic, religious, and cultural differences.

The first Muslim invasion was as early as the seventh century CE, when the Arabs of the Umayyad Caliphate made it as far as the Punjab in what is now Pakistan. From then until the eighteenth century various foreign invasions brought Islam to the subcontinent; however, east of the Indus River Valley a majority of the Hindu population resisted conversion, thus sowing the seeds for the eventual partition of India.

The British came and went, and when they went the center could not hold, and things fell apart. In truth, there was no real center, the region has always been divided by the ancient disparities of the languages of the Punjab and Gujarat, the mountains and the deserts, and Islam and Hinduism. By 1947, the forces of postcolonial nationalism and religious separatism broke the subcontinent into two, and later three, major pieces: India, Pakistan, and Bangladesh. The British, exhausted by two world wars, and aware that the days of empire were coming to a close, did not cover themselves in glory in the manner of their leaving.

On June 3, 1947, the announcement was made in the House of Commons: the British would withdraw—India was to be partitioned into the two independent dominions of India and Pakistan. Seventy-three days later, on August 15, they were all but gone.

An extraordinary movement of people followed as millions of Muslims fled the new borders of India, heading west to Pakistan, with millions of Hindus and Sikhs coming the other way. Columns of people thirty thousand strong were on the roads as whole communities moved. Trains packed full of refugees crisscrossed the subcontinent, disgorging people into cities and making the return journey filled with those heading in the other direction.

It was carnage. Riots broke out across both countries as Muslims,

Hindus, Sikhs, and others turned on one another in panic and fear. The British government washed its hands and refused pleas from the new Indian and Pakistani leaders for the few troops still in the country to help maintain order. Estimates of the death toll vary, but at least a million people died and 15 million were displaced. The Muslim-majority areas in the west—the Indus Valley region west of the Thar Desert and the Ganges River basin—became West Pakistan, while those to the east of Calcutta became East Pakistan.

What did Pakistan get out of this? Much less than India. It inherited India's most troublesome border, the North-West Frontier with Afghanistan, and it was a state split into two noncontiguous regions with little to hold it together, as one thousand miles of Indian territory separated West Pakistan from East Pakistan. Alaska and the rest of the United States have managed the problem of noncontiguous distance without difficulty, but they are culturally, linguistically, and economically linked and operating in a stable environment. The only connection between the two parts of Pakistan was Islam. They never really came together, so it was no surprise when they were torn apart; in 1971, East Pakistan rebelled against the dominance of West Pakistan, India intervened and, after much bloodshed, East Pakistan seceded, becoming Bangladesh.

However, back in 1947, twenty-five years after the end of the Ottoman Empire, Jinnah and the other leaders of the new Pakistan, amid much fanfare and promises of a bright future, claimed they had created a united Muslim homeland.

Pakistan is geographically, economically, demographically, and militarily weaker than India. Its national identity is also not as strong. India, despite its size, cultural diversity, and secessionist movements, has built a solid secular democracy with a unified sense of Indian identity. Pakistan is an Islamic state with a history of dictatorship and populations whose loyalty is often more to their cultural region than to the state.

Secular democracy has served India well, but the 1947 division did give it a head start. Within the new borders of India was the vast majority of the subcontinent's industry, most of the taxable income base, and the majority of the major cities. For example, Calcutta, with its port and banking sector, went to India, thus depriving East Pakistan of this major income provider and connection to the outside world.

Pakistan received just 17 percent of the financial reserves that had been controlled by the pre-partition government. It was left with an agricultural base, no money to spend on development, a volatile western frontier, and a state divided within itself in multiple ways.

The name *Pakistan* gives us clues about these divisions; *pak* means "pure" and *stan* means "land" in Urdu, so it is the land of the pure, but it is also an acronym. *P* is for Punjab, *A* is for Afghania (the Pashtun area by the Afghan border), *K* for Kashmir, *S* for Sindh, and *T* stands for "tan," as in Baluchistan.

From these five distinct regions, each with their own language, one state was formed, but not a nation. Pakistan tries hard to create a sense of unity, but it remains rare for a Punjabi to marry a Baluchi, or a Sindh to marry a Pashtun. The Punjabis comprise 60 percent of the population, the Sindhs 14 percent, the Pashtuns 13.5 percent, and the Baluchis 4.5 percent. Religious tensions are ever present—not only in the antagonism sometimes shown to the country's Christian and Hindu minorities, but also between the majority Sunni and the minority Shia Muslims. In Pakistan there are several nations within one state.

The regions that make up Pakistan all have their own distinct identities and languages, which often hinders a sense of national unity.

The official language is Urdu, which is the mother tongue of the Muslims of India who fled in 1947, most of whom settled in Punjab. This does not endear the language to the rest of the country. The Sindh region has long chafed at what it feels to have Punjabi dominance, and many Sindhs think they are treated as second-class citizens. The Pashtuns of the North-West Frontier have never accepted the rule of outsiders: parts of the frontier region are named the Federally Administered Tribal Areas, but in reality they have never been administered from Islamabad. Kashmir remains divided between

Pakistan and India, and although a majority of Kashmiris want independence, the one thing India and Pakistan can agree on is that they cannot have it. Baluchistan also has an independence movement that periodically rises up against the state.

Baluchistan is of crucial importance: while it may contain only a small minority of Pakistan's population, without it there is no Pakistan. It comprises almost 45 percent of the country and holds much of its natural gas and mineral wealth. Another source of income beckons with the proposed overland routes to bring Iranian and Caspian Sea oil up through Pakistan to China. The jewel in this particular crown is the coastal city of Gwadar. Many analysts believe this strategic asset was the Soviet Union's long-term target when it invaded Afghanistan in 1979: Gwadar would have fulfilled Moscow's long-held dream of a warm-water port. The Chinese have also been attracted by this jewel and invested billions of dollars in the region. A deep-water port was inaugurated in 2007 and the two countries are now working to link it to China. In the long run, China would like to use Pakistan as a land route for its energy needs. This would allow it to bypass the Strait of Malacca, which as we saw in chapter two is a choke point that could strangle Chinese economic growth.

Massive Chinese investment in building a land route would make Pakistan very happy, and this is one of the reasons Pakistan will always seek to crush any secessionist movements that arise in the province. However, until more of the wealth Baluchistan creates is returned home and used for its own development, the area is destined to remain restive and occasionally violent.

In late 2015, China signed a forty-year lease on 2,300 acres of land to develop a massive "special economic zone" and an international airport in the port area. The Chinese will build a road from the port to the airport and then onward toward China—all part of a $46 billion investment to create the China-Pakistan Economic Corridor linking China to the Arabian Sea. Because both sides know that Baluchistan is likely to remain volatile, a security force of up to twenty-five thousand men is being formed to protect the zone.

Islam, cricket, the intelligence services, the military, and fear of India are what hold Pakistan together. None of these will be enough to prevent it from being pulled apart if the forces of separatism grow stronger. In effect, Pakistan has been in a state of civil war for more than a decade, following periodic and ill-judged wars with its giant neighbor, India.

The first was in 1947, shortly after partition, and was fought over Kashmir, which in 1948 ended up divided along the Line of Control (also known as Asia's Berlin Wall); however, both India and Pakistan continue to claim sovereignty.

Nearly twenty years later, Pakistan miscalculated the strength of the Indian military because of India's poor performance in the 1962 India-China war. Tensions between India and China had risen due to the Chinese invasion of Tibet, which in turn had led India to give refuge to the Dalai Lama. During this brief conflict the Chinese military showed their superiority and pushed forward almost into the state of Assam near the Indian heartland. The Pakistan military watched with glee, then, overestimating their own prowess, went to war with India in 1965 and lost.

In 1984, Pakistan and India fought skirmishes at an altitude of twenty-two thousand feet on the Siachen Glacier, thought to be the highest battle in history. More fighting broke out in 1985, 1987, and 1995. Pakistan continued to train militants to infiltrate across the Line of Control and another battle broke out over Kashmir in 1999.

By then both countries were armed with nuclear weapons, and for several weeks the unspoken threat of an escalation to nuclear war hovered over the conflict before American diplomacy kicked in and the two sides were talked down. They came close to war again in 2001, and gunfire still breaks out sporadically along the border.

Militarily, India and Pakistan are pitted against each other. Both sides say their posture is defensive, but neither believes the other and so they continue to amass troops on the border, locked together in a potential dance of death.

The relationship between India and Pakistan will never be friendly, but were it not for the thorn of Kashmir in both sides it could potentially be cordial. As it is, India is content to see Pakistan divided within itself and will work to maintain that situation, and Pakistan will seek to undermine India, with elements within the state even supporting terrorist attacks inside India such as the Mumbai massacre of 2008.

The Kashmir issue is partially one of national pride, but it is also strategic. Full control of Kashmir would give India a window into central Asia and a border with Afghanistan. It would also deny Pakistan a border with China and thus diminish the usefulness of a Chinese-Pakistani relationship. The Pakistani government likes to trumpet that its friendship with China is "taller than the mountains and deeper than the oceans." This is not true, but it is useful in sometimes making the Americans nervous about cutting Pakistan off from the massive financial aid it receives from Washington. China, well aware of this, is quite happy to chip away at American influence. It is already Pakistan's biggest military supplier, and in 2015 signed a multibillion-dollar deal with Islamabad to sell Pakistan eight submarines and six patrol ships.

If Pakistan had full control of Kashmir it would strengthen Islamabad's foreign policy options and deny India opportunities. It would also help Pakistan's water security. The Indus River originates in Himalayan Tibet, but passes through the Indian-controlled part of Kashmir before entering Pakistan and then running the length of the country and emptying into the Arabian Sea at Karachi.

The Indus and its tributaries provide water to two-thirds of the country: without it the cotton industry and many other mainstays of Pakistan's struggling economy would collapse. By a treaty that has been honored through all of their wars, India and Pakistan agreed to share the waters; but both populations are growing at an alarming rate, and global warming could diminish the water flow. Annexing all of Kashmir would secure Pakistan's water supply. Given the stakes, neither side will let go; and until they agree on Kashmir the key to unlocking the hostility between them cannot be found. Kashmir looks destined to remain a place where a sporadic proxy war between Pakistani-trained fighters and the Indian army is conducted—a conflict that threatens to spill over into full-scale war with the inherent danger of the use of nuclear weapons.

Both countries will also continue to fight another proxy war—in Afghanistan—especially now that most NATO forces have left.

Pakistan lacks internal "strategic depth"—somewhere to fall back to in the event of being overrun from the east—from India. The Pakistan-India border includes swampland in the south, the Thar Desert, and the mountains of the north; all are extremely difficult territory for an army to cross. It can be done, and both sides have battle plans of how to fight there. The Indian army plan involves blockading the port of Karachi and its fuel storage depots by land and sea, but an easier invasion route is between the south and the north—it lies in the center, in the more hospitable Punjab, and in Punjab is Pakistan's capital, Islamabad.

The distance from the Indian border to Islamabad is less than 250 miles, most of it flat ground. In the event of a massive, overwhelming, conventional attack, the Indian army could be in the capital within a few days. That they profess no desire to do so is not the point: from Pakistan's point of view they might, and the geographical possibility is enough for Pakistan to require a plan A and a plan B to counter the risk.

Plan A is to halt an Indian advance in the Punjab and possibly counterattack across the border and cut off the Indian Highway 1A, which is a vital supply route for the Indian military. The Indian army is more than one million strong, twice the size of Pakistan's, but if it can't be supplied, it can't fight. Plan B is to fall back across the Afghan border if necessary, and that requires a sympathetic government in Kabul. Hence, geography has dictated that Pakistan will involve itself in Afghanistan, as will India.

To thwart each other, each side seeks to mold the government of Afghanistan to its liking—or, to put it another way, each side wants Kabul to be an enemy of its enemy.

When the Soviets invaded Afghanistan in 1979, India gave diplomatic support to Moscow, but Pakistan was quick to help the Americans and Saudis to arm, train, and pay for the mujahideen to fight the Red Army. Once the Soviets were beaten, Pakistan's intelligence service, the ISI, helped to create, and then back, the Afghan Taliban, which duly took over the country.

Pakistan had a natural "in" with the Afghan Taliban. Most are Pashtun, the same ethnicity as the majority of the Pakistanis of the North-West Frontier. They have never thought of themselves as two peoples and consider the border between them as a Western invention, which in some ways it is.

The main ethnic groups in the Afghan-Pakistani area did not fit into the border that was imposed in 1893 by the Durand Line; many of these groups continue to identify more with their tribes beyond the borders than with the rest of the nation.

The Afghan-Pakistani border is known as the Durand Line. Sir Mortimer Durand, the foreign secretary of the colonial government of India, drew it in 1893 and the then ruler of Afghanistan agreed to it. However, in 1949, the Afghan government "annulled" the agreement, believing it to be an artificial relic of the colonial era. Since then, Pakistan has tried to persuade Afghanistan to change its mind, Afghanistan refuses, and the Pashtuns on each side of the mountains try to carry on as they have for centuries by ignoring the border and maintaining their ancient connections.

Central to this area, sometimes called Pashtunistan, is the Pakistani city of Peshawar, a sort of urban Taliban military-industrial complex. Knockoff Kalashnikovs, bomb-making technology, and fighters flow out from the city, and support from within sections of the state flows in.

It is also a staging post for ISI officers en route to Afghanistan with funds and instructions for the Talibanesque groups across the border. Pakistan has been involved militarily in Afghanistan for decades now, but it has overreached itself, and the tiger it was riding has bitten it.

In 2001 the Pakistani-created Taliban had been hosting the foreign fighters of al-Qaeda for several years. Then, on 9/11, al-Qaeda struck the United States on its home soil in an operation put together in Afghanistan. In response, US military power ran the Taliban and al-Qaeda out of town. Afghan Northern Alliance anti-Taliban forces moved down to take over the country and a NATO stabilization force followed.

Across the border on the day after 9/11, the Americans had begun breathing diplomatic fire on the Pakistanis, demanding their participation in the "War on Terror" and an end to their support for terrorism. The then secretary of state, Colin Powell, had phoned President Musharraf and demanded he come out of a meeting to take the call, in which he told him: "You are either with us or against us."

It has never been confirmed by the American side, but Musharraf has written that the call was followed up by Powell's deputy, Richard Armitage, ringing the head of the ISI and telling him "that if we chose the terrorists, then we should be prepared to be bombed back to the Stone Age." Pakistan cooperated, and that was that. Except— they hadn't fully cooperated, and that wasn't that.

Islamabad was forced to act, and did; but not everyone in the Pakistani system was on board. The government banned several militant groups and tried to rein in religious groups it deemed extremist. By 2004 it was involved militarily against groups in the North-West

Frontier and privately accepted the American policy of drone strikes on its territory while publicly decrying them.

These were tough decisions. The Pakistan military and the ISI had to turn on the very Taliban leaders they had trained and formed friendships with in the 1990s. The Taliban groups reacted with fury, seizing complete control of several regions in the tribal areas. Musharraf was the target of three failed assassination attempts, his would-be successor, Benazir Bhutto, was murdered, and amid the chaos of bombing campaigns and military offensives, up to fifty thousand Pakistani civilians have been killed.

The American-NATO operation in Afghanistan, and the Pakistani measures across the border, had helped scatter the Arab, Chechen, and other foreign fighters of al-Qaeda to the corners of the earth, where their leadership was hunted down and killed; but the Taliban had nowhere to go—they were Afghans and Pakistanis—and, as they told these new technologically advanced foreign invaders from America and Europe, "You may have the watches—but we have the time." They would wait out the foreigners no matter what was thrown at them, and in this they would be helped by elements in Pakistan.

Within a couple of years it became clear: the Taliban had not been defeated; they had melted into where they came from—the Pashtun population—and were now emerging again at times and places of their choosing.

The Americans came up with a "hammer and anvil" strategy. They would hammer the Afghan Taliban against the anvil of the Pakistani operation on the other side of the border. The "anvil" in the tribal areas turned out instead to be a sponge that soaked up whatever was thrown at it, including any Afghan Taliban retreating from the American hammer.

In 2006, the British decided they would stabilize Helmand Province in the south, where the Afghan government's remit did not run far outside of the provincial capital, Lashkar Gah. This was Afghan Pashtun heartland territory. The British went in with good intentions; they knew their history, but it seems they just ignored it—the reason why remains a mystery. The then British defense secretary John Reid is wrongly quoted, and blamed, for having said that summer that he "hoped not a shot will be fired in anger." In fact, he said, "We're in the south to help and protect the Afghan people to reconstruct their economy and democracy. We would be perfectly happy to leave in three years' time without firing one shot."

That may have been a fine aspiration, but was it ever feasible? That summer, after he gave a briefing at the Foreign Office in London, I had an exchange with the defense secretary, as follows:

"Don't worry, Tim. We're not going after the Taliban, we're there to protect people."

"Don't worry, Secretary of State, the Taliban are going to come after you."

It was an amicable exchange, conducted before more than 450 British soldiers had been killed, but to this day I don't know if the British government was softening up public opinion ahead of the deployment of troops while privately predicting it would be tough going, or whether it was being inexplicably naive about what lay ahead.

So the Taliban bled the British, bled the Americans, bled NATO, waited NATO out, and after thirteen years NATO went away.

During this whole period, members of the highest levels of Pakistan's establishment were playing a double game. America might have its strategy, but Pakistan knew what the Taliban knew: that one day the Americans would go away, and when they left, Pakistan's foreign policy would still require a Pakistan-friendly government in Afghanistan. Factions within the Pakistan military and government had continued to give help to the Taliban, gambling that after NATO's retreat the southern half of Afghanistan at the very least would revert to Taliban dominance, thus ensuring that Kabul would need to talk to Islamabad.

Pakistan's perfidy was laid bare when the Americans eventually found al-Qaeda's leader, Osama bin Laden, hiding in plain sight of the government in Abbottabad, a military garrison town. By that point, such was the Americans' lack of trust in their Pakistani "allies" that they failed to tell Islamabad in advance about the Special Forces team that flew in to kill bin Laden. This was a breach of sovereignty that humiliated the military and government of Pakistan, as did the argument that went: "If you didn't know he was there you were incompetent, if you did you were complicit."

The Pakistani government had always denied playing the double game that resulted in the deaths of huge numbers of Afghans and Pakistanis, as well as relatively small numbers of Americans. After the Abbottabad mission, Islamabad continued the denials, but now there were fewer people who believed them. If elements of the Pakistani establishment were prepared to give succor to America's most wanted man, even though he was by then of limited value to them, it was obvious they would support groups that furthered their ambitions to influence events in Afghanistan. The problem was that those groups now had their counterparts in Pakistan and they wanted to influence events there. The biter was bitten.

The Pakistani Taliban is a natural outgrowth of the Afghan version. Both are predominantly Pashtun and neither will accept domination from any non-Pashtun power, be it the British army of the nineteenth century or the Punjabi-dominated Pakistani army of the twenty-first century.

This was always understood and accepted by Islamabad. The Pakistani government pretended it ruled the entire country, and the Pashtun of the North-West Frontier pretended they were loyal to the Pakistani state. This relationship worked until September 11, 2001.

The years since then have been exceptionally hard on Pakistan. The civilian death toll is enormous and foreign investment has dwindled away, making ordinary life even harder. The army, forced to go up against what was a de facto ally, has lost up to five thousand men and the civil war has endangered the fragile unity of the state.

Things became so bad that the Pakistani military and government ended up having to give the United States military intelligence and coordinates allowing the United States to conduct drone strikes against Pakistani Taliban targets in the North-West Frontier. At the same time, when the strikes became apparent, Islamabad had to pretend to condemn them and describe them as a violation of Pakistani sovereignty due to the hundreds of civilian deaths attributed to mistakes by the United States.

The drones were mostly flown out of a base in Afghanistan, but some are thought to have been launched from a secret base inside Pakistan. Wherever they came from, there were a lot of them. Drone strikes in Afghanistan and Pakistan massively increased during the Obama presidency from the numbers fired during George Bush's tenure.

By the spring of 2015 things had got even tougher. NATO had left Afghanistan and the Americans announced an end to combat missions, leaving behind only a residual force. Officially, this is to conduct Special Forces operations and training missions; unofficially it is to try to ensure that Kabul does not fall to the Taliban. Without NATO harrying the Taliban on the Afghan side of the border, Pakistan's job of beating the Pakistani Taliban has become even harder. Washington continues to press Islamabad, and this leaves several possible scenarios:

- The full weight of the Pakistani military falls upon the North-West Frontier and defeats the Taliban.
- The Taliban campaign continues to hasten the fracturing of Pakistan until it becomes a failed state.
- The Americans lose interest, the pressure on Islamabad relents, and the government compromises with the Taliban. The situation returns to normal, with the North-West Frontier left alone but Pakistan continuing to push its agenda in Afghanistan.

Of these scenarios the least likely is the first. No foreign force has ever defeated the tribes of the North-West Frontier, and a Pakistani army containing Punjabis, Sindhis, Baluchis, and Kashmiris (and some Pashtun) is considered a foreign force once it moves into the tribal areas.

Scenario two is possible but, after being deaf to years of wake-up calls, the Taliban's 2014 massacre of 132 schoolchildren in Peshawar does seem to have jolted enough of the Pakistani establishment to make it realize that the movement it helped to create might now destroy it.

This makes scenario three the most likely. The Americans have limited interest in Afghanistan so long as the Taliban quietly promise not to host an international jihadist group again. The Pakistanis will maintain enough links with the Afghan Talibs to ensure that governments in Kabul will listen to Islamabad and not cozy up to India, and once the pressure is off they can do a deal with the Pakistani Taliban.

None of this would have been necessary if the Afghan Taliban, in part created by the Pakistani ISI, had not been stupid enough to host the Arabs of bin Laden's al-Qaeda and then after 9/11 had not fallen back upon the Pashtun culture of honoring guests, thus refusing to give them up when the Americans came calling. In the event, after a decade and a half of fighting the situation remains so bad that the US government has had to reverse policy and keep thousands more troops than it had planned in Afghanistan. In June 2016 NATO agreed to hold on to its broad geographic layout of bases in the country, a move that signaled that although they will no longer go on the offensive, the alliance knows it needs to be there for several more years.

As for India, it can multitask—indeed it has to, given that it has more to think about than only Pakistan, even if it is the number-one foreign policy priority for New Delhi. Having a hostile nuclear-armed state next door is bound to focus the mind, but India also has to concentrate on managing 1.3 billion people while simultaneously emerging as a potential world power.

Its relationship with China would dominate its foreign policy but for one thing—the Himalayas. Without the world's tallest mountain range between them, what is a lukewarm relationship would probably be frosty. A glance at the map indicates two huge countries cheek by jowl, but a closer look shows they are walled off from each other along what the CIA's *World Factbook* lists as 1,652 miles of border.

There are issues that cause friction, chief among them Tibet, the highest region on earth. As previously discussed, China wanted Tibet, both to prevent India from having it, and—almost as bad in Beijing's view—to prevent an independent Tibet allowing India to base military forces there, thus giving them the commanding heights.

India's response to the Chinese annexation of Tibet was to give a home to the Dalai Lama and the Tibetan independence movement in Dharamsala in the state of Himachal Pradesh. This is a long-term insurance policy, paid for by India but without the expectation that it will ever be cashed in. As things stand, Tibetan independence looks impossible; but if the impossible were to occur, even in several decades' time, India would be in a position to remind a Tibetan government who their friends were during the years of exile.

The Chinese understand that this scenario is extremely unlikely, but remain irritated by Dharamsala. Their response is seen in Nepal, where Beijing ensures it has influence with the Maoist movement there.

India does not want to see a Maoist-dominated Nepal ultimately controlled by China, but knows that Beijing's money and trade is buying influence there. China may care little for Maoism these days; it cares enough about Tibet to signal to India that it, too, can afford the payments on a long-term insurance policy. Any "interference" in Tibet can be met with "interference" in Nepal. The more India has to concentrate on the smaller states in its neighborhood, the less it can concentrate on China.

Another issue between them is the northeastern Indian state of Arunachal Pradesh, which China claims as "south Tibet." As China's confidence grows, so does the amount of territory there it says is Chinese. Until recently, China claimed only the Tawang area in the extreme west of the state. However, in the early 2000s, Beijing decided that all of Arunachal Pradesh was Chinese, which was news to the Indians, who have exercised sovereignty over it since 1955. The Chinese claim is partly geographical and partly psychological. Arunachal Pradesh borders China, Bhutan, and Burma, making it strategically useful, but the issue is also valuable to China as a reminder to Tibet that independence is a nonstarter.

That is a message India also has to send periodically to several of its own regions. There are numerous separatist movements, some more active than others, some dormant, but none that look set to achieve their aims. For example, the Sikh movement to create a state for Sikhs from part of both Indian and Pakistani Punjab has for the moment gone quiet, but it could flare up again. The state of Assam has several competing movements, including the Bodo-speaking peoples, who want a state for themselves, and the Muslim United Liberation Tigers of Assam, who want a separate country created within Assam for Muslims.

There is even a movement to create an independent Christian state in Nagaland, where 75 percent of the population is Baptist; however, the prospect of the Naga National Council achieving its aims is as remote as the land it seeks to control, and that looks to be true of all of the separatist movements.

Despite these and other groups seeking independence, with a Sikh population of 21 million people and a Muslim minority of 150 million, India retains a strong sense of itself and unity within diversity. This will help as it emerges further onto the world stage.

The world has so marveled at China's stunning rise to power that its neighbor is often overlooked, but India may yet rival China as an economic powerhouse this century. It is the world's seventh-largest country, with the second-largest population. It has borders with six countries (seven if you include Afghanistan). It has nine thousand miles of internal navigable waterways, reliable water supplies, and huge areas of arable land; is a major coal producer; has useful quantities of oil and gas, even if it will always be an importer of all three; and its subsidization of fuel and heating costs is a drain on its finances.

Despite its natural riches, India has not matched China's growth, and because China is now moving out into the world, the two countries may bump up against each other—not along their land border, but at sea.

For thousands of years the regions of what are now modern-day China and India could ignore each other because of their terrain. Expansion into each other's territory through the Himalayas was impossible and, besides, each had more than enough arable land.

Now, though, the rise of technology means each requires vast amounts of energy; geography has not bequeathed them such riches, and so both countries have been forced to expand their horizons and venture out into the oceans, and it is there that they have encountered each other.

Twenty-five years ago, India embarked on a "look east" policy, partially as a block to what it could see would be the imminent rise of China. It has "taken care of business" by dramatically increasing trade with China (mostly imports) while simultaneously forging strategic relationships in what China regards as its own backyard.

India has strengthened its ties with Burma, the Philippines, and Thailand, but more important, it is working with Vietnam and Japan to check China's increasing domination of the South China Sea.

In this it has a new ally, albeit one it keeps at arm's length—the United States. For decades, India was suspicious that the Americans were the new British, but with a different accent and more money. In the twenty-first century a more confident India, in an increasingly multipolar world, has found reason to cooperate with the United States. When President Obama attended the 2015 Indian Republic Day military parade, New Delhi took care to show off its shiny new US-supplied C-130 Hercules and C-17 Globemaster transport aircraft as well as its Russian-supplied tanks. The two giant democracies are slowly moving closer together.

India has a large, well-equipped modern navy that includes an aircraft carrier, but it will not be able to compete with the massive blue-water navy that China is planning. Instead, India is aligning itself with other interested parties so together they can at least shadow, if not dominate, the Chinese navy as it sails the China seas, through the Strait of Malacca, past the Bay of Bengal, and around the tip of India into the Arabian Sea toward the friendly port China has built at Gwadar in Pakistan.

With India, it always comes back to Pakistan, and with Pakistan, to India.

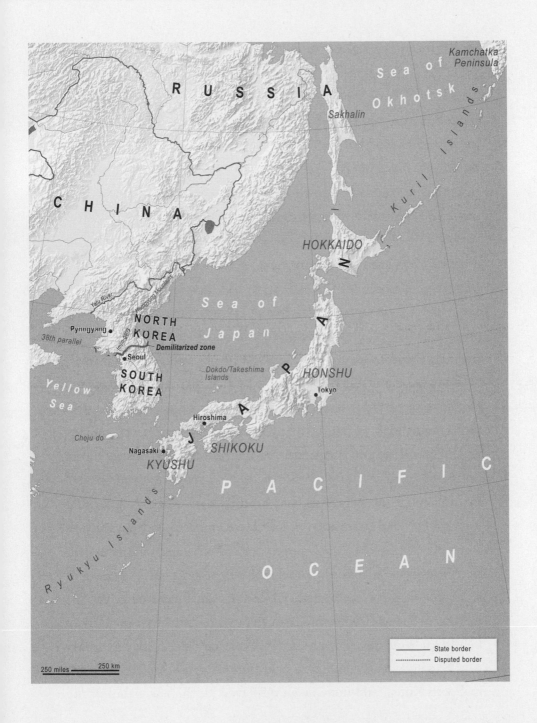

RUSSIA

Kamchatka
Peninsula

Sea of

Okhotsk

Sakhalin

Kuril Islands

CHINA

HOKKAIDO

Sea of

Yalu River

Hamgyong Mountains

Japan

NORTH
KOREA

Pynngyang •

38th parallel

Imjin-an

Demilitarized zone

• Seoul

SOUTH
KOREA

Yellow
Sea

Dokdo/Takeshima
Islands

HONSHU

• Tokyo

Cheju do

Hiroshima •

Nagasaki •

KYUSHU

SHIKOKU

Ryukyu Islands

PACIFIC

OCEAN

	State border
	Disputed border

250 miles   250 km

8

KOREA AND JAPAN

I . . . began to phrase a little pun about Kim Jong-il being the
"Oh Dear Leader," but it died on my lips.
—Christopher Hitchens,
Love, Poverty and War: Journeys and Essays

How do you solve a problem like Korea? You don't, you just manage it—after all, there's a lot of other stuff going on around the world that needs immediate attention.

The whole of the region from Malaysia up to the Russian port of Vladivostok eyes the North/South Korea problem nervously. All the neighbors know it has the potential to blow up in their faces, dragging in other countries and damaging their economies. The Chinese don't want to fight on behalf of North Korea, but nor do they want a united Korea containing American bases close to their border. The Americans don't really want to fight for the South Koreans, but nor can they afford to be seen as giving up on a friend. The Japanese, with their long history of involvement in the Korean Peninsula, must be seen to tread lightly, knowing that whatever happens will probably involve them.

The solution is compromise, but there is limited appetite for that in South Korea, and none at all displayed by the leadership of the

North. The way forward is not at all clear; it seems as if it is always just out of sight over the horizon.

For several years, the United States and Cuba have danced quietly around each other, dropping hints that they would like to tango without tangling, leading to the partial breakthrough toward reestablishing diplomatic relations in 2015. North Korea, on the other hand, glares at any requests from would-be suitors to take the floor, occasionally pulling faces.

North Korea is a poverty-stricken country of an estimated 25 million people, led by a basket case of a morally corrupt, bankrupt Communist monarchy, and supported by China, partly out of a fear of millions of refugees flooding north across the Yalu River. The United States, anxious that a military withdrawal would send out the wrong signal and embolden North Korean adventurism, continues to station almost thirty thousand troops in South Korea, and the South, with mixed feelings about risking its prosperity, continues to do little to advance reunification.

All the actors in this East Asian drama know that if they try to force an answer to the question at the wrong time, they risk making things worse. A lot worse. It is not unreasonable to fear that you would end up with two capital cities in smoking ruins, a civil war, a humanitarian catastrophe, missiles landing in and around Tokyo, and another Chinese-American military face-off on a divided peninsula in which one side has nuclear weapons. If North Korea implodes, it might well also explode, projecting instability across the borders in the form of war, terrorism, and/or a flood of refugees, and so the actors are stuck, leaving the solution to the next generation of leaders, and then the next one.

If world leaders even speak openly about preparing for the day when North Korea collapses, they risk hastening that day; and as no one has planned for it—best keep quiet. Catch-22.

North Korea continues to play the crazed, powerful weakling to good effect. Its foreign policy consists, essentially, of being suspicious of everyone except the Chinese, and even Beijing is not to be fully trusted despite supplying 84.12 percent of North Korea's imports and buying 84.48 percent of its exports, according to 2014 figures by the Observatory of Economic Complexity. North Korea puts a lot of effort into playing all outsiders against one another, including the Chinese, in order to block a united front against it.

To its captive population it says it is a strong, munificent, magnificent state standing up against all the odds and against the evil foreigners, calling itself the Democratic People's Republic of Korea (DPRK). It has a unique political philosophy of *Juche*, which blends fierce nationalism with Communism and national self-reliance.

In reality, it is the least democratic state in the world: it is not run for the people and it is not a republic. It is a dynasty shared by one family and one party. It also checks off every box in the dictatorship test: arbitrary arrest, torture, show trials, internment camps, censorship, rule of fear, corruption, and a litany of horrors on a scale without parallel in the twenty-first century. Satellite images and witness testimony suggest that at least 150,000 political prisoners are held in giant work and "reeducation" camps. North Korea is a stain on the world's conscience, and yet few people know the full scale of the horrors taking place there.

News stories about purged members of the elite being executed with an anti-aircraft gun, or fed to a pack of starving dogs, have never been confirmed. However, true or not, there is little doubt about the litany of horrors perpetrated by the dictatorship upon the people. Total state control has resulted in beatings, torture, prison camps, and extrajudicial murder.

Such is the self-imposed isolation of the country, and the state's almost total control of knowledge, that we can only guess at what the people may feel about their country, system, and leaders and whether they support the regime. Analyzing what is going on politically, and why, is akin to looking through an opaque window while wearing sunglasses. A former ambassador to Pyongyang once told me: "It's like you are on one side of the glass, and you try to prize it open, but there's nothing to get a grip on to peer inside."

The founding story of Korea is that it was created in 2333 BCE by heavenly design. The Lord of Heaven sent his son Hwanung down to earth, where he descended to the Paektu Mountain and married a woman who used to be a bear, and their son, Dangun, went on to engage in an early example of nation building.

The earliest recorded version of this creation legend dates from the thirteenth century. It may in some ways explain why a Communist state has a leadership that is passed down through one family and given divine status. For example, Kim Jong-il was described by the Pyongyang propaganda machine as "Dear Leader, who is a perfect incarnation of the appearance that a leader should have," "Guiding Sun Ray," "Shining Star of Paektu Mountain," "World Leader of the twenty-first century," and "Great Man who descended from heaven," as well as "Eternal Bosom of Hot Love." His father had very similar titles, as does his son, Kim Jong-Un.

How does the general population feel about such statements? Even the experts are left guessing. When you look at footage of the mass hysteria of North Koreans mourning Kim Jong-il, who died in 2011, it's interesting to note that after the first few rows of sobbing, shrieking people, the level of grief appears to diminish. Is this because those at the front know the camera is on them and thus for their own safety they must do what is required? Or have the party faithful been put at the front? Or are they ordinary people who are genuinely grief-stricken, a North Korean magnification of the sort of emotional outbursts we saw in the UK after the death of Princess Diana?

Nevertheless, the DPRK is still pulling off the crazy-dangerous, weak-dangerous act. It's quite a trick, and its roots lie partially in Korea's location and history, trapped as it is between the giants of China and Japan.

The name the Hermit Kingdom was earned by Korea in the eighteenth century after it attempted to isolate itself following centuries of being a target for domination, occupation, and plunder, or occasionally simply a route on the way to somewhere else. If you come from the north, then once you are over the Yalu River there are few major natural defensive lines all the way down to the sea, and if you can land from the sea, the reverse is true. The Mongols came and went, as did the Chinese Ming dynasty, the Manchurians, and the Japanese several times. So for a while the country preferred not to engage with the outside world, cutting many of its trade links in the hope that it would be left alone.

It was not successful. In the twentieth century the Japanese were back, annexing the whole country in 1910, and later set about destroying its culture. The Korean language was banned, as was the teaching of Korean history, and worship at Shinto shrines became compulsory. The decades of repression have left a legacy that even today impacts on relations between Japan and both the Korean states.

The defeat of Japan in 1945 left Korea divided along the 38th parallel. North of it was a Communist regime overseen first by the Soviets and later by Communist China, south of the line was a pro-American dictatorship called the Republic of Korea (ROK). This was the very beginning of the Cold War era, when every inch of land was contested, with each side looking to establish influence or control around the world, unwilling to let the other maintain a sole presence.

The choice of the 38th parallel as the line of division was unfortunate in many ways and, according to historian Don Oberdorfer, arbitrary. He says that Washington was so focused on the Japanese surrender on August 10 that it had no real strategy for Korea. With Soviet troops on the move in the north of the peninsula and the White House convening an all-night emergency meeting, two junior officers, armed only with a *National Geographic* map, chose the 38th parallel as a place to suggest to the Soviets they halt, on the grounds that it was halfway down the country.

No Koreans were present, nor any Korea experts. If they had been, they could have told President Truman and his secretary of state James Byrnes that the line was the same one that the Russians and Japanese had discussed for spheres of influence half a century earlier, following the Russo-Japanese War of 1904–5. Moscow, not knowing that the Americans were making up policy on the fly, could be forgiven for thinking this was the United States's de facto recognition of that suggestion and therefore acceptance of division and a Communist north. The deal was done, the nation divided, and the die cast.

The Soviets pulled their troops out of the north in 1948 and the Americans followed suit in the south in 1949. In June 1950, an emboldened North Korean military fatally underestimated America's Cold War geopolitical strategy and crossed the 38th parallel, intent on reuniting the peninsula under one Communist government. The Northern forces raced down the country almost to the tip of the southern coast, sounding the alarm bells in Washington.

The North Korean leadership, and its Chinese backers, had correctly worked out that, in a strictly military sense, Korea was not vital to the United States; but what they failed to understand was that the Americans knew that if they didn't stand up for their South Korean ally, their other allies around the world would lose confidence in them. If America's allies, at the height of the Cold War, began to hedge their bets or go over to the Communist side, then its entire global strategy would be in trouble. There are parallels here with the United States's policy in modern East Asia and Eastern Europe. Countries such as Poland, the Baltic States, Japan, and the Philippines need to be confident that America has their back when it comes to their relations with Russia and China.

In September 1950, the United States, leading a United Nations force, surged into Korea, pushing the Northern troops back across the 38th parallel and then up almost to the Yalu River and the border with China.

Now it was Beijing's turn to make a decision. It was one thing to have US forces on the peninsula, quite another when they were north of the parallel—indeed north of the mountains above Hamhung—and within striking distance of China itself. Chinese troops poured across the Yalu, and thirty-six months of fierce fighting ensued with massive casualties on all sides before they ground to a halt along the current border and agreed to a truce, but not a treaty. There they were, stuck on the 38th parallel, and stuck they remain.

The geography of the peninsula is fairly uncomplicated and a reminder of how artificial the division is between North and South. The real (broad-brush) split is west to east. The west of the peninsula is much flatter than the east and is where the majority of people live. The east has the Hamgyong mountain range in the north and lower ranges in the south. The demilitarized zone (DMZ), which cuts the peninsula in half, in parts follows the path of the Imjin/Han River, but this was never a natural barrier between two entities, just a river within a unified geographical space all too frequently entered by foreigners.

The two Koreas are still technically at war, and given the hair-trigger tensions between them, a major conflict is never more than a few artillery rounds away.

Japan, the United States, and South Korea all worry about North Korea's nuclear weapons, but South Korea in particular has another threat hanging over it. North Korea's ability to successfully miniaturize its nuclear technology and create warheads that could be launched is uncertain, but it is definitely capable, as it already showed in 1950, of a surprise, first-strike, conventional attack.

A major concern for South Korea is how close Seoul and the surrounding urban areas are to the border with North Korea. Seoul's position makes it vulnerable to surprise attacks from its neighbor, whose capital is much farther away and partially protected by mountainous terrain.

South Korea's capital, the megacity of Seoul, lies just thirty-five miles south of the 38th parallel and the DMZ. Almost half of South

Korea's 50 million people live in the greater Seoul region, which is home to much of its industry and financial centers, and it is all within range of North Korean artillery.

In the hills above the 148-mile-long DMZ, the North Korean military has an estimated ten thousand artillery pieces. They are well dug in, some in fortified bunkers and caves. Not all of them could reach the center of Seoul, but some could, and all are able to reach the greater Seoul region. There's little doubt that within two or three days the combined might of the South Korean and US air forces would have destroyed many of them, but by that time Seoul would be in flames. Imagine the effect of just one salvo of shells from ten thousand artillery weapons landing in urban and semi-urban areas, then multiply it dozens of times.

Two experts on North Korea, Victor Cha and David Kang, writing for *Foreign Policy* magazine, estimated that the DPRK forces could fire up to five hundred thousand rounds toward the city in the first hour of a conflict. That seems a very high estimate, but even if you divide it by five the results would still be devastating. The South Korean government would find itself fighting a major war while simultaneously trying to manage the chaos of millions of people fleeing south, even as it tried to reinforce the border with troops stationed below the capital.

The hills above the DMZ are not high and there is a lot of flat ground between them and Seoul. In a surprise attack, the North Korean army could push forward quite quickly, aided by special forces who would enter via underground tunnels that the South Koreans believe have already been built. North Korea's battle plans are thought to include submarines landing shock troops south of Seoul, and to activate sleeper cells placed in the South's population. It is estimated to have one hundred thousand personnel it regards as Special Forces.

The North has also already proved it can reach Tokyo with ballistic missiles by firing several of them over the Sea of Japan and into the Pacific, a route that takes them directly over Japanese territory. Its armed forces are more than a million strong, one of the biggest armies in the world, and even if large numbers of them are not highly trained they would be useful to Pyongyang as cannon fodder while it sought to widen the conflict.

The Americans would be fighting alongside the South, the Chinese military would be on full alert and approaching the Yalu, and the Russians and Japanese would be looking on nervously.

It is not in anyone's interest for there to be another major war in Korea, as both sides would be devastated, but that has not prevented wars in the past. In 1950, when North Korea crossed the 38th parallel, it had not foreseen a three-year war with up to four million deaths, ending in a stalemate. A full-scale conflict now might be even more catastrophic. The ROK's economy is eighty times stronger than the North's, its population is twice the size, and the combined South Korean and US armed forces would almost certainly overwhelm North Korea eventually, assuming China did not decide to join in again.

And then what? There has been limited serious planning for such an eventuality. The South is thought to have done some computer modeling on what might be required, but it is generally accepted that the situation would be chaotic. The problems that would be created by Korea imploding or exploding would be multiplied if it happened as a result of warfare. Many countries would be affected and they would have decisions to make. Even if China did not want to intervene during the fighting, it might decide it had to cross the border and secure the North to retain the buffer zone between it and the US forces. It might decide that a unified Korea, allied to the United States, which is allied to Japan, would be too much of a potential threat to allow.

———

The United States would have to decide how far across the DMZ it would push and whether it should seek to secure all of North Korea's sites containing nuclear and other weapons of mass destruction maté-riel. China would have similar concerns, especially as some of the nuclear facilities are only thirty-five miles from its border.

On the political front, Japan would have to decide if it wanted a powerful, united Korea across the Sea of Japan. Given the brittle relations between Tokyo and Seoul, Japan has reasons to be nervous about such a thing, but as it has far greater concerns about China it would be likely to come down on the side of supporting reunifica-tion, despite the probable scenario that it would be asked to assist financially due to its long occupation of the peninsula in the last century. Besides, it knows what Seoul knows: most of the economic costs of reunification will be borne by South Korea, and they will dwarf those of German reunification. East Germany may have been lagging far behind West Germany, but it had a history of devel-opment, an industrial base, and an educated population. Develop-ing the north of Korea would be building from ground zero, and the costs would hold back the economy of a united peninsula for a decade. After that, the benefits of the rich natural resources of the north, such as coal, zinc, copper, and iron, and the modernization program would be expected to kick in, but there are mixed feelings about risking the prosperity of one of the world's most advanced nations in the meantime.

Those decisions are for the future. For now, each side continues to prepare for a war; as with Pakistan and India, they are locked in a mutual embrace of fear and suspicion.

South Korea is now a vibrant, integrated member of the nations of the world, with a foreign policy to match. With open water to its west, east, and south, and with few natural resources, it has taken care to build a modern navy in the past three decades, one that is capable of getting into the Sea of Japan and the East China Sea to safeguard the ROK's interests. Like Japan, it is dependent on foreign sources for its energy needs, and so keeps a close eye on the sea-lanes of the whole region. It has spent time hedging its bets, investing diplomatic capital in closer relations with Russia and China, much to Pyongyang's annoyance.

A miscalculation by either side could lead to a war that, as well as having devastating effects on the people of the peninsula, could wreck the economies of the region, with massive ramifications for the US economy. What started with the United States defending its Cold War stance against Russia has developed into an issue of strategic importance to its economy and that of several other countries.

South Korea still has issues with Tokyo, relating back to the Japanese occupation, and even when it is at its best, which is rare, the relationship is only cordial. In early 2015, when the Americans, South Koreans, and Japanese got down to the details of an agreement to share military intelligence they had each gathered on North Korea, Seoul said it would pass along only a limited amount of secret information to Tokyo via Washington. It will not deal directly with the Japanese.

The two countries still have a territorial dispute over what South Korea calls the Dokdo (solitary) Islands and the Japanese know as the Takeshima (bamboo) islands. The South Koreans currently control the rocky outcrops, which are in good fishing grounds, and there may be gas reserves in the region. Despite this thorn in their sides, and the still-fresh memories of occupation, both have reasons to cooperate and leave behind their troubled past.

Japan's history is very different to that of Korea, and the reason for this is partly due to its geography.

The Japanese are an island race, with the majority of the 127 million population living mostly on the four large islands that face Korea and Russia across the Sea of Japan, and a minority inhabiting some of the 6,848 smaller islands. The largest of the main islands is Honshu, which includes the biggest megacity in the world, Tokyo, and its 39 million people.

At its closest point, Japan is 120 miles from the Eurasian landmass, which is among the reasons why it has never been successfully invaded. The Chinese are some five hundred miles away across the East China Sea; and although there is Russian territory much closer, the Russian forces are usually far away because of the extremely inhospitable climate and sparse population located across the Sea of Okhotsk.

In the 1300s, the Mongols tried to invade Japan after sweeping through China, Manchuria, and down through Korea. On the first occasion they were beaten back and on the second a storm wrecked their fleet. The seas in the Korea Strait were whipped up by what the Japanese said was a "Divine Wind," which they called a *kamikaze*.

So the threat from the west and northwest was limited, and to the southeast and east there was nothing but the Pacific. This last perspective is why the Japanese gave themselves the name Nippon, or "sun origin": looking east there was nothing between them and the horizon, and each morning, rising on that horizon, was the sun. Apart from sporadic invasions of Korea they mostly kept to themselves until the modern world arrived, and when it did, after first pushing it away, they went out to meet it.

Opinions differ about when the islands became Japan, but there is a famous letter sent from what we know as Japan to the Emperor of China in 617 CE in which a Japanese leading nobleman writes: "Here I the emperor of the country where the sun rises send a letter to the emperor of the country where the sun sets. Are you healthy?" History records that the Chinese emperor took a dim view of such perceived impertinence. His empire was vast, while the main Japanese islands were still only loosely united, a situation that would not change until approximately the sixteenth century.

The territory of the Japanese islands makes up a country that is bigger than the two Koreas combined, or, in European terms, bigger than France or Germany. However, three-quarters of the land is not conducive to human habitation, especially in the mountainous regions, and only 13 percent is suitable for intensive cultivation. This leaves the Japanese living in close proximity to one another along the coastal plains and in restricted inland areas, where some stepped rice fields can exist in the hills. Its mountains mean that Japan has plenty of water, but the lack of flatland also means that its rivers are unsuited to navigation and therefore trade, a problem exacerbated by the fact that few of the rivers join one another.

So the Japanese became a maritime people, connecting and trading along the coasts of their myriad islands, making forays into Korea, and then after centuries of isolation pushing out to dominate the whole region.

By the beginning of the twentieth century Japan was an industrial power with the third-largest navy in the world, and in 1905 it defeated the Russians in a war fought on land and at sea. However, the very same island-nation geography that had allowed it to remain isolated was now giving it no choice but to engage with the world. The problem was that it chose to engage militarily.

Japan had few of the natural resources required to become an industrialized nation. It had limited and poor-quality supplies of coal, very little oil, scant quantities of natural gas, limited supplies of rubber, and a shortage of many metals. This is as true now as it was one hundred years ago, although offshore gas fields are being explored along with those of underwater precious metals. Nevertheless, it remains the world's largest importer of natural gas, and the third-largest importer of oil.

It was the thirst for these products, notably iron and oil, that caused Japan to rampage across the far-less developed Southeast Asia in the 1930s and early '40s. It had already occupied Taiwan in 1895 and followed this up with the annexation of Korea in 1910. Japan occupied Manchuria in 1931, then conducted a full-scale invasion of China in 1937. As each domino fell, the expanding empire and the growing Japanese population required more oil, more coal, more metal, more rubber, and more food.

With the European powers preoccupied with war in Europe, Japan went on to invade northern Indochina. Eventually the Americans, who by then were supplying most of Japan's oil needs, gave them an ultimatum—withdrawal or an oil embargo. The Japanese responded with the attack on Pearl Harbor and then swept on across Southeast Asia, taking Burma, Singapore, and the Philippines, among other territory.

This was a massive overstretch, not just taking on the United States, but grabbing the very resources, rubber, for example, that the United States required for its own industry. The giant of the twentieth century mobilized for total war. Japan's geography then played a role in its greatest catastrophes—Hiroshima and Nagasaki.

The Americans had fought their way across the Pacific, island to island, at great cost. By the time they took Okinawa, which sits in the Ryukyu island chain between Taiwan and Japan, they were faced with a still-fanatical enemy prepared to defend the approaches and four main islands from amphibious invasion. Massive US losses were predicted. If the terrain had been easier the Americans' choice may have been different—they might have fought their way to Tokyo—but they chose the nuclear option, unleashing upon Japan, and the collective conscience of the world, the terror of a new age.

After the radioactive dust had settled on a complete Japanese surrender, the Americans helped them rebuild, partially as a hedge against Communist China. The new Japan showed its old inventiveness and within three decades became a global economic powerhouse.

However, its previous belligerence and militarism was not entirely gone: it had just been buried beneath the rubble of Hiroshima and Nagasaki and a shattered national psyche. Japan's postwar constitution did not allow for it to have an army, air force, or navy, only "Self-Defense Forces," which for decades were a pale shadow of the prewar military. The postwar agreement imposed by the United States limited Japan's defense spending to 1 percent of the GDP and left tens of thousands of American forces on Japanese territory, thirty-two thousand of whom are still there.

But by the early 1980s, the faint stirrings of nationalism could again be detected. There were sections of the older generation who had never accepted the enormity of Japan's war crimes, and sections of the younger who were not prepared to accept guilt for the sins of their fathers. Many of the children of the Land of the Rising Sun wanted their "natural" place under the sun of the postwar world.

A flexible view of the constitution became the norm, and slowly the Japanese Self-Defense Forces were turned into a modern fighting unit. This happened as the rise of China was becoming increasingly apparent, and so the Americans, realizing they were going to need military allies in the Pacific region, were prepared to accept a remilitarized Japan.

In the present century, Japan has altered its defense policy to allow its forces to fight alongside allies abroad, and changes to the constitution are expected to follow to put this on a more solid legal footing. Its 2013 Security Strategy document was the first in which it named a potential enemy, saying: "China has taken actions that can be regarded as attempts to change the status quo by coercion."

The wording of Chapter II, Article 9, of the Japanese constitution makes it difficult for Tokyo to use its military abroad. Prime Minister Abe's coalition government has a flexible view of Article 9 and intends to persuade a sometimes-skeptical public that Japan now needs to play a more adventurous role in the region, especially in supporting its allies as part of "collective defense."

———

The 2015 defense budget was its biggest to date, with the yen mostly going to naval and air equipment, including six US-made F-35A stealth fighters. In the spring of 2015, Tokyo also unveiled what it called a "helicopter-carrying destroyer." It didn't take a military expert to notice that the vessel was as big as the Japanese aircraft carriers of the Second World War, which are forbidden by the surrender terms of 1945. The ship can be adapted for fixed-wing aircraft, but the defense minister issued a statement saying that he was "not thinking of using it as an aircraft carrier." This is akin to buying a motorcycle, then saying that because you are not going to use it as a motorcycle, it is a bicycle. The Japanese now have an aircraft carrier.

The money spent on that and other shiny new gear is a clear statement of intent, as is much of its positioning. The military infrastructure at Okinawa, which guards the approaches to the main islands, will be upgraded. This will also allow Japan greater flexibility to patrol its Air Defense Zone, part of which overlaps with China's equivalent zone after an expansion was announced by Beijing in 2013.

Both zones cover the islands called the Senkaku or Diaoyu (in Japanese and Chinese, respectively), which Japan controls but that are claimed by China, too. They also form part of the Ryukyu island chain, which is particularly sensitive as any hostile power must pass the islands on the way to the Japanese heartlands; they give Japan a lot of territorial sea space, and they might contain exploitable underwater gas and oil fields. Thus Tokyo intends to hold on to them by all means necessary.

China's expanded Air Defense Identification Zone in the East China Sea covers territory claimed by China, Japan, Taiwan, and South Korea. When Beijing said that any plane flying through the zone must identity itself or "face defensive measures," Japan, South Korea, and the United States responded by flying through it without doing so. There was no hostile response from China, but this is an issue that can be turned into an ultimatum at a time of Beijing's choosing.

Japan also claims sovereignty over the Kuril Islands in its far north, off Hokkaido, which it lost to the Soviet Union in the Second World War and that are still under Russian control. Russia prefers not to discuss the matter, but the debate is not in the same league as Japan's disputes with China. There are only approximately nineteen thousand inhabitants of the Kuril Islands, and although the islands sit in fertile fishing grounds, the territory is not one of particular strategic importance. The issue ensures that Russia and Japan maintain a frosty relationship, but within that frost they have pretty much frozen the question of the islands.

It is China that keeps Japanese leaders awake at night and keeps them close to the United States, diplomatically and militarily. Many Japanese, especially on Okinawa, resent the US military presence, but the might of China, added to the decline in the Japanese population, is likely to ensure that the postwar US-Japan relationship continues, albeit on a more equal basis. Japanese statisticians fear that the population will shrink to under 100 million by the middle of the century. If the current birth rate continues, it is even possible that by 2110 the population will have fallen below the 50 million it was in 1910. Japanese governments are trying a variety of measures to reverse the decline. A recent example is using millions of dollars of taxpayers' money to fund a matchmaking service for young couples. Subsidized *konkatsu* parties are arranged for single men and women to meet, eat, drink, and—eventually—have babies. Immigration is another possible solution, but Japan remains a relatively insular society and immigration is not favored by the population. Given that increasingly assertive China has a population of 1.4 billion, Japan, itself a remilitarizing power with a quietly hawkish outlook, is going to require friends in the neighborhood.

So the Americans are staying in both Korea and Japan. There is now a triangular relationship among them, as underlined by the intelligence agreement noted earlier. Japan and South Korea have plenty to argue about, but will agree that their shared anxiety about China and North Korea will overcome this.

Even if they do go on to solve a problem like Korea, the issue of China will still be there, and this means the US 7th Fleet will remain in Tokyo Bay and US Marines will remain in Okinawa, guarding the paths in and out of the Pacific and the China seas. The waters can be expected to be rough.

Caribbean Sea

ATLANTIC

OCEAN

Caracas

VENEZUELA

Georgetown
Paramaribo

Bogotá

GUYANA

Cayenne

COLOMBIA

SURINAM

FRENCH GUIANA
(FRANCE)

Galápagos Islands
(ECUADOR)

Quito

ECUADOR

A
N
D
E
S

Amazon

Amazon Rainforest

B R A Z I L

Lima

P
E
R
U

A
N
D
E
S

C
e
r
r
a
d
o

Lake Titicaca

La Paz

BOLIVIA

Brasília

Sucre

PACIFIC

Atacama Desert

PARAGUAY

São Paulo

Rio de Janeiro

Acunción

OCEAN

A
N
D
E
S

Paraná

CHILE

Aconcagua

URUGUAY

Santiago

Buenos
Aires

Montevideo

ARGENTINA

Rio de la Plata

Vaca
Muerta

ATLANTIC

A
N
D
E
S

OCEAN

Falkland Islands
(UK)

South Georgia
(UK)

Tierra del
Fuego

Cape Horn

State border

Amazon rainforest

1000 miles   1000 km

9

LATIN AMERICA

Latin America is very fond of the word "hope." We like to be
called the "continent of hope" . . . This hope is like a promise of heaven,
an IOU whose payment is always put off. It is put off until the next
legislative campaign, until next year, until the next century.
—Pablo Neruda, Chilean poet and Nobel Laureate

Latin America, particularly its south, is proof that you can bring the Old World's knowledge and technology to the new, but if geography is against you, then you will have limited success, especially if you get the politics wrong. Just as the geography of the United States helped it become a great power, so that of the twenty countries to the south ensures that none will rise to seriously challenge the North American giant this century nor come together to do so collectively.

The limitations of Latin America's geography were compounded right from the beginning in the formation of its nation states. In the United States, once the land had been taken from its original inhabitants, much of it was sold or given away to small landholders; by contrast, in Latin America the Old World culture of powerful landowners and serfs was imposed, which led to inequality. On top of this, the European settlers introduced another geographical problem that to this day holds many countries back from developing their full potential: they stayed near the coasts, especially (as we saw in Africa) in regions where the interior was infested by mosquitoes and disease. Most of the countries' biggest cities, often the capitals, were therefore near the coasts, and all roads from the interior were developed to connect to the capitals but not to one another.

In some cases, for example in Peru and Argentina, the metropolitan area of the capital city contains more than 30 percent of the country's population. The colonialists concentrated on getting the wealth out of each region, to the coast and on to foreign markets. Even after independence the predominantly European coastal elites failed to invest in the interior, and what population centers there are inland remain poorly connected with one another.

At the beginning of this decade it was fashionable among many business leaders, professors, and media analysts to argue passionately that we were at the dawn of the "Latin American decade." It has not come to pass, and although the region has as yet unfulfilled potential, it will constantly be fighting against the hand it was dealt by nature and history.

Mexico is growing into a regional power, but it will always have the desert wastelands in its north, its mountains to the east and west, and its jungles in the south, all physically limiting its economic growth. Brazil has made its appearance on the world stage, but its internal regions will remain isolated from one another; and Argentina and Chile, despite their wealth of natural resources, will still be far farther away from New York and Washington than are Paris and London.

Two hundred years after the beginning of the struggle for independence, the Latin American countries lag far behind the North Americans and the Europeans. Their total population (including the

Caribbean) is 600 million people, and yet their combined GDP is equivalent to that of France and the UK, which together comprise 120 million people. They have come a long way since colonialism and slavery. There is still a long way to go.

Latin America begins at the Mexican border with the United States and stretches southward seven thousand miles through Central America, and then South America, before ending at Tierra del Fuego on Cape Horn, where the world's two great oceans, the Pacific and the Atlantic, meet. At its widest point, west to east, from Brazil across to Peru, it is 3,200 miles. On the western side is the Pacific, on the other the Gulf of Mexico, the Caribbean Sea, and the Atlantic. None of the coastlines have many natural deep harbors, thus limiting trade.

Central America is hill country with deep valleys, and at its narrowest point is only 120 miles across. Then, running parallel to the Pacific, for 4,500 miles, is the longest continuous mountain chain in the world—the Andes. They are snow-capped along their entire length and mostly impassable, thus cutting off many regions in the west of the continent from the east. The highest point in the Western Hemisphere is here—the 22,843-foot Aconcagua Mountain—and the waters tumbling down from the mountain range are a source of hydroelectric power for the Andean nations of Chile, Peru, Ecuador, Colombia, and Venezuela. Finally, the land descends, forests and glaciers appear, we are into the Chilean archipelago, and then—land's end. The eastern side of Latin America is dominated by Brazil and the Amazon River, the second longest in the world after the Nile.

One of the few things the countries have in common is language based on Latin. Spanish is the language of almost all of them, but in Brazil it is Portuguese, and in French Guiana—French. But this linguistic connection disguises the differences in a continent that has five different climatological regions. The relative flatland east of the Andes and temperate climate of the lower third of South America, known as the Southern Cone, are in stark contrast to the mountains and jungle farther north and enable agricultural and construction costs to be reduced, thus making them some of the most profitable regions on the entire continent—whereas Brazil, as we shall see, even has difficulty moving goods around its own domestic market.

Academics and journalists are fond of writing that the continent is "at a crossroads"—as in about to embark at last on its great future. I would argue that geographically speaking, it is less at a crossroads than at the bottom of the world; there's a lot going on all over this vast space, but the problem is much of it is going on a long way from anywhere other than itself. That may be considered a Northern Hemispheric view, but it is also a view of where the major economic, military, and diplomatic powers are situated.

Despite its remoteness from history's major population centers, there have been people living south of what is now the Mexico-US border for approximately fifteen thousand years. They are thought to have originated from Russia and crossed the Bering Strait on foot at a time when it was still land. The present-day inhabitants are a mixture of Europeans, Africans, indigenous tribes, and the Mestizo population, who are of European and Native American descent.

This mix can be traced back to the Treaty of Tordesillas between Spain and Portugal in 1494, one of the early examples of European colonialists drawing lines on maps of faraway places about which they knew little—or, in this case, nothing. As they set off westward to explore the oceans, the two great European sea powers agreed that any land discovered outside Europe would be shared between them. The pope agreed. The rest is a very unfortunate history in which the vast majority of the occupants of the lands now called South America were wiped out.

The independence movements began in the early 1800s, led by Simón Bolívar of Venezuela and José de San Martín of Argentina. Bolivar in particular is etched in the collective consciousness of South America: Bolivia is named in his honor, and the left-leaning countries of the continent are loosely tied in a "Bolivarian" ideology against the United States. This is a fluctuating set of anticolonialist/ pro-socialist ideas that often stray into nationalism as and when it suits the politicians who espouse them.

In the nineteenth century, many of the newly independent countries broke apart, either through civil conflict or cross-border wars, but by the end of that century the borders of the various states were mostly set. The three richest nations—Brazil, Argentina, and Chile— then set off on a ruinously expensive naval arms race, which held back the development of all three. There remain border disputes throughout the continent, but the growth of democracy means that most are either frozen or there are attempts to work them out diplomatically.

Particularly bitter is the relationship between Bolivia and Chile, which dates back to the 1879 War of the Pacific in which Bolivia lost a large chunk of its territory, including 250 miles of coastline, and has been landlocked ever since. It has never recovered from this blow, which partially explains why it is among the poorest Latin American countries. This in turn has exacerbated the severe divide between the mostly European lowlands population and the mostly indigenous peoples of the highlands.

Time has not healed the wounds between them, nor those between the two countries. Despite the fact that Bolivia has the third-largest reserves of natural gas in South America it will not sell any to Chile, which is in need of a reliable supplier. Two Bolivian presidents who toyed with the idea were thrown out of office and the current president, Evo Morales, has a "gas to Chile" policy consisting of a "gas for coastline" deal, which is dismissed by Chile despite its need for energy. National pride and geographical need on both sides trump diplomatic compromise.

Another border dispute dating back to the nineteenth century is indicated by the borders of the British territory of Belize and neighboring Guatemala. They are straight lines, such as we have seen in Africa and the Middle East, and they were drawn by the British. Guatemala claims Belize as part of its sovereign territory but, unlike Bolivia, is unwilling to push the issue. Chile and Argentina argue over the Beagle Channel water route, Venezuela claims half of Guiana, and Ecuador has historical claims on Peru. This last example is one of the more serious land disputes in the continent and has led to three border wars over the past seventy-five years, the most recent being in 1995; but again, the growth of democracy has eased tensions.

The second half of the twentieth century saw Central and South America become a proxy battlefield of the Cold War with accompanying coups d'état, military dictatorships, and massive human rights abuses, for example, in Nicaragua. The end of the Cold War allowed many nations to move toward democracy and, compared to the twentieth century, relations between them are now relatively stable.

The Latin Americans, or at least those south of Panama, mostly reside on, or near, the western and eastern coasts, with the interior and the freezing cold far south very sparsely populated. South America is in effect a demographically hollow continent and its coastline is often referred to as the "populated rim." This is less true of Central America and especially Mexico, where the populations are more equally distributed; but Mexico in particular has difficult terrain, which limits its ambitions and foreign policies.

In its far north, Mexico has a two-thousand-mile-long border with the United States, almost all of which is desert. The land here is so harsh that most of it is uninhabited. This acts as a buffer zone between it and its giant northern neighbor—but a buffer that is more advantageous to the Americans than the Mexicans due to the disparity in their technology. Militarily, only US forces could stage a major invasion across it; any force coming the other way would be destroyed. As a barrier to illegal entry into the United States it is useful, but porous—a problem with which successive US administrations will have to deal.

All Mexicans know that before the 1846–48 war with the United States the land that is now Texas, California, New Mexico, and Arizona was part of Mexico. The conflict led to half of Mexico's territory being ceded to the United States. However, there is no serious political movement to regain the region and no pressing border dispute between the two countries. Throughout most of the twentieth century they squabbled over a small piece of land after the Rio Grande changed course in the 1850s, but in 1967 both sides agreed the area was legally part of Mexico.

By the middle of the twenty-first century, Hispanics are likely to be the largest ethnic group in the four American states listed above and many will be of Mexican origin. There may eventually be Spanish-speaking political movements on both sides of the US-Mexico border calling for reunification, but tempering this would be the fact that many US Latinos will not have Mexican heritage, and that Mexico is unlikely to have anything approaching the living standards of the United States. The Mexican government struggles to control even its own territory—it will not be in a position to take on any more in the foreseeable future. Mexico is destined to live in the United States's shadow and as such will always play the subservient role in bilateral relations. It lacks a navy capable of securing the Gulf of Mexico or pushing out into the Atlantic, and so relies on the US navy to ensure the sea-lanes remain open and safe.

Private companies from both nations have set up factories just south of the border to cut costs in labor and transport, but the region is hostile to human existence and will remain the buffer land across which many of the poor of Latin America will continue to cross as they seek entry, legal or illegal, to the Promised Land to the north.

Mexico's major mountain ranges, the Sierra Madres, dominate the west and east of the country and between them is a plateau. In the south, in the Valley of Mexico, is the capital—Mexico City—one of the world's megacapital cities with a population of around 20 million people.

On the western slopes of the highlands and in the valleys the soil is poor, and the rivers of limited assistance in moving goods to market. On the eastern slopes the land is more fertile, but the rugged terrain still prevents Mexico from developing as it would like. To the south lie the borders with Belize and Guatemala. Mexico has little interest in expanding southward because the land quickly rises to become the sort of mountainous terrain it is difficult to conquer or control. Extending into either country would not enlarge the limited amount of profitable land Mexico already has. It has no ideological territorial ambitions and instead concentrates on trying to develop its limited oil-producing industry and attracting more investment into its factories. Besides, Mexico has enough internal problems to cope with, without getting into any foreign adventures—perhaps none greater than its role in satisfying the Americans' voracious appetite for drugs.

The Mexican border has always been a haven for smugglers, but never more so than in the last twenty years. This is a direct result of the US government's policy in Colombia, 1,500 miles away to the south.

It was President Nixon in the 1970s who first declared a "War on Drugs," which, like a "War on Terror," is a somewhat nebulous concept in which victory cannot be achieved. However, it wasn't until the early 1990s that Washington took the war directly to the Colombian drug cartels with overt assistance to the Colombian government. It also had success in closing down many of the air and sea drug routes from Colombia into the United States.

The cartels responded by creating a land route—up through Central America and Mexico, and into the American Southwest. This in turn led the Mexican drug gangs to get in on the action by facilitating the routes and manufacturing their own produce. The route partially follows the Pan-American Highway, which runs south to north up the continent. Originally designed to move goods in each direction to a variety of countries, it is now also used to move drugs north to the United States. The multibillion-dollar business sparked local turf wars, with the winners using their new power and money to infiltrate and corrupt the Mexican police and military and get inside the political and business elites.

In this there are parallels with the heroin trade in Afghanistan. Many of the Afghan farmers growing the poppy crop responded to NATO's attempts to destroy their traditional way of making a living by either taking up arms or supporting the Taliban. It may be the government's policy to wage a War on Drugs, but this does not mean that the orders are carried out at a regional level, which the Afghan drug lords have penetrated. So it is in Mexico.

Throughout history, successive governments in Mexico City have never had a firm grip on the country. Now its opponents, the drug cartels, have paramilitary wings which are as well armed as the forces of the state, often better paid, more motivated, and in several regions are regarded as a source of employment by some members of the public. The vast sums of money made by the gangs now swill around the country, much of it being washed through what appear on the surface to be legitimate businesses.

The overland supply land route is firmly established, and the demand in the United States shows few signs of diminishing. All Mexican governments try to keep on the right side of their powerful neighbor and have responded to American pressure by waging their own War on Drugs. Here lies a conundrum. Mexico makes its living by supplying consumer goods to America, and as long as Americans consume drugs, Mexicans will supply them—after all, the idea here is to make things that are cheap to produce and sell them at prices higher than those in legal trade. Without drugs the country would be even poorer than it is, as a vast amount of foreign money would be cut off. With drugs it is even more violent than it would be. The same is true of some of the countries to Mexico's south.

Mexico is now in the grip of what is almost a civil war. The cartels try to control territory through intimidation; the government tries to pretend it is in charge of the rule of law; and hundreds of civilians, caught in the middle, are being killed. Among the most horrific recent manifestations of this was the presumed murder of forty-three student teachers by a cartel in 2014, an act which traumatized the country, galvanized the authorities, but ultimately looks to be "just" another terrible milestone in what will be a long struggle.

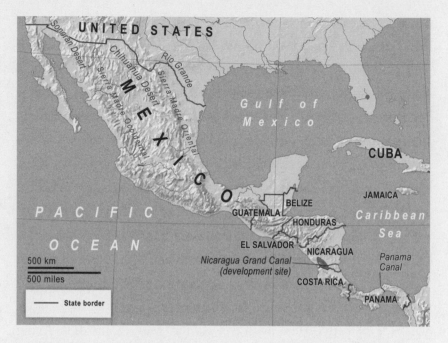

Central America could see many changes in the regions that are receiving Chinese investment, such as the development of the Nicaragua Grand Canal.

Central America has little going for it by way of geography but for one thing. It is thin. So far, the only country to gain advantage from this has been Panama, but with the arrival of new money from China that may be about to change.

Modern technology means the Chinese can see from a glance at a satellite photograph the trade opportunities this thin stretch of land might bring. In 1513, the Spanish explorer Vasco Núñez de Balboa had to sail across the Atlantic, land in what is now Panama, then trek through jungles and over mountains before seeing another vast ocean—the Pacific. The advantages of linking them were obvious, but it was another 401 years before technology caught up with geography. In 1914, the newly built, fifty-mile-long, American-controlled Panama Canal opened, thus saving ships an eight-thousand-mile

240

journey from the Atlantic to the Pacific Ocean and leading to economic growth in the canal region.

Since 1999, the canal has been controlled by Panama, but is regarded as a neutral international waterway that is safeguarded by the US and Panama navies. And therein, for the Chinese, lies a problem.

Panama and the United States are friends—in fact, such good friends that in 2014 Venezuela cut ties with Panama, calling it a "US lackey." The effect of the rhetoric of the increasingly embattled country's Bolivarian revolutionary era is tempered by the knowledge that the United States is Venezuela's most important commercial partner and that Venezuela supplies 12 percent of US oil imports. The energy trade between them is likely to fall as the effects of the US shale revolution kick in, but Beijing will be a willing importer of Venezuelan oil, and is working on how to get it to China without relying on the route through Panama.

China, as we saw in chapter two, has designs on being a global power, and to achieve this aim it will need to keep sea-lanes open for its commerce and its navy. The Panama Canal may well be a neutral passageway, but at the end of the day, passage through it is dependent on American goodwill. So, why not build your own canal up the road in Nicaragua? After all, what's $50 billion to a growing superpower?

The Nicaragua Grand Canal project is funded by a Hong Kong businessman named Wang Jing, who has made a lot of money in telecommunications but has no experience in engineering, let alone masterminding one of the most ambitious construction projects in the history of the world. Mr. Wang is adamant that the Chinese government not be involved in the project. Given the nature of China's business culture and the participation of its government in all aspects of life, this is unusual.

The $50-billion cost estimate for the project, which is due for completion in the early 2020s, is four times the size of the entire Nicaraguan economy and forms part of the substantial investment in Latin America from China, which is slowly but steadily supplanting the United States as the region's main trading partner. Exactly who is financially backing Mr. Wang is unclear, but Nicaragua's President Daniel Ortega signed on to the plan with alacrity and with scarcely a glance at the thirty thousand people who may be required to move from their lands because of the project.

The former revolutionary socialist Sandinista firebrand now finds himself accused of being on the side of big business. The canal will split the country in two and six municipalities will find themselves divided. There will be only one bridge across the canal along its entire length. Ortega must know he risks sowing the seeds of dissent, but argues that the project will bring tens of thousands of jobs and much-needed investment and revenue to the second-poorest country in the Western Hemisphere. In the fall of 2016 the project was not going well. Mr. Wang lost an estimated 85 percent of his fortune in the Chinese stock market crash of September 2015. Most construction work was delayed, but all sides insisted the project would succeed.

If that is so, then the Nicaraguan canal will be longer than the Panama and, crucially, will be significantly wider and deeper, thus allowing much bigger tankers and container ships through, not to mention large Chinese naval vessels. It will run directly east to west, whereas the Panama Canal actually runs north to south. The middle section will be dredged out of Lake Nicaragua, which has led environmentalists to warn that Latin America's largest freshwater lake may become contaminated.

Given that the Panama Canal a few hundred miles to the south is being widened, skeptics ask why the Nicaraguan version is necessary.

China will have control of a canal able to take bigger ships, which will help guarantee the economies of scale only China is capable of. There are questions about the future profitability of the Nicaraguan canal—it may take decades to make money—but this is a project that appears to be more about the national interests of China than about commercial profit.

Gouging a link between two oceans out of a nation state is just the most visible sign of China's investment in Latin America. We've grown used to seeing the Chinese as major players in Africa, but for twenty years now they have been quietly moving in south of the Rio Grande.

As well as investing in construction projects, China is lending huge sums of money to Latin American governments, notably those in Argentina, Venezuela, and Ecuador. In return, China will be expecting support in the United Nations for its regional claims back home, including the issue of Taiwan.

Beijing is also buying. The Latin American states have been picked off one by one by the United States, which prefers bilateral trade deals to doing business with the region as a whole, as they have to do with the EU. The Chinese are doing the same thing but at least offer an alternative, thus reducing the region's dependency on the United States as its market. For example, China has now replaced the United States as Brazil's main trading partner, and may do the same with several other Latin American countries.

The Latin American countries do not have a natural affinity with the United States. Relations are dominated by America's starting position, laid out in the Monroe Doctrine of 1823 (as we have seen in chapter three) during President Monroe's State of the Union address. The doctrine warned off the European colonialists and said, in as many words, that Latin America was the United States' backyard and sphere of influence. It has been orchestrating events there ever since and many Latin Americans believe the results have not always been positive.

Eight decades after Monroe's Doctrine, along came another president with "Monroe reloaded." In a speech in 1904, Theodore Roosevelt said: "In the Western Hemisphere the adherence of the United States to the Monroe Doctrine may force the United States, however reluctantly, in flagrant cases of such wrongdoing or impotence, to the exercise of an international police power." In other words, the United States could militarily intervene whenever it chose to in the Western Hemisphere. Not including the funding of revolutions, the arming of groups, and the provision of military trainers, the United States used force in Latin America almost fifty times between 1890 and the end of the Cold War.

After that, overt interference dropped off rapidly and, in 2001, the United States was a signatory to the thirty-four-nation Inter-American Democratic Charter drafted by the Organization of American States, which proclaims that "The peoples of the Americas have a right to democracy and their governments have an obligation to promote and defend it." Since then the United States has concentrated on binding the Latin American countries to itself economically by building up existing trade pacts like the North American Free Trade Association, and introducing others such as the Central American Free Trade Agreement.

The lack of warmth thus engendered in south/north historic and economic relationships meant that when the Chinese came knocking, doors quickly opened. Beijing now sells or donates arms to Uruguay, Colombia, Chile, Mexico, and Peru, and offers them military exchanges. It is trying to build a military relationship with Venezuela, which it hopes will outlast the Bolivarian revolution if and when it collapses. The arms supplies to Latin America are relatively small-scale but complement China's efforts at soft power. Its sole hospital ship, *Peace Ark*, visited the region in 2011. It is only a three-hundred-bed vessel, dwarfed by the American one-thousand-bed version that also visits, but it was a signal of intent and a reminder that China increasingly "gets" soft power.

However, with or without Chinese trade, the countries of Latin America are inescapably locked into a geographical region—which means that the United States will always be a major player.

Brazil, which makes up fully one-third of the land of South America, is the best example. It is almost as big as the United States, and its twenty-seven federal states equal an area bigger than the twenty-eight EU countries combined; but unlike them it lacks the infrastructure to be as rich. A third of Brazil is jungle, where it is painfully expensive, and in some areas illegal, to carve out land fit for modern human habitation. The destruction of the Amazon rainforest is a long-term ecological problem for the whole world, but it is also a medium-term problem for Brazil: the government allows slash-and-burn farmers to cut down the jungle and then use the land for agriculture. But the soil is so poor that within a few years crop-growing is untenable. The farmers move on to cut down more rainforest, and once the rainforest is cut it does not grow back. The climate and soil work against the development of agriculture.

The Amazon River may be navigable in parts, but its banks are muddy and the surrounding land makes it difficult to build on. This problem, too, seriously limits the amount of profitable land available. Just below the Amazon region, in the highlands, is the savannah and, by contrast, it is a success story. Twenty-five years ago this area was considered unfit for agriculture, but Brazilian technology has turned it into one of the world's largest producer of soybeans, which—together with the growth in grain production—means the country is becoming a major agricultural producer.

To the south of the savannah are the traditional Brazilian agricultural lands. We are now in the Southern Cone of South America, which Brazil shares with Argentina, Uruguay, and Chile. The relatively small Brazilian section is where the first Portuguese colonialists lived, and it was to be three hundred years before the population could push out from this heartland and significantly populate the rest of the country. To this day most people still live close to the coastal areas, despite the dramatic decision made in the late 1950s to move the capital (previously Rio de Janeiro) several hundred miles inland to the purpose-built city of Brasília in an attempt to develop the heart of Brazil.

The southern agricultural heartland is about the size of Spain, Portugal, and Italy combined and is much flatter than the rest of the country. It is relatively well watered, but most of it is in the interior of the region and lacks properly developed transport routes.

The same is true of most of Brazil. If you look at many of the Brazilian coastal cities from the sea there is usually a massive cliff rising dramatically out of the water either side of the urban area, or directly behind it. Known as the Grand Escarpment, it dominates much of Brazil's coast; it is the end of the plateau called the Brazilian Shield, of which most of Brazil's interior is comprised.

Because the country lacks a coastal plain, to connect its major coastal cities you need to build routes up and over the escarpment, along to the next urban area and then back down. The lack of decent modern roads is compounded by a similar deficiency of rail track. This is not a recipe for profitable trading or for unifying a large space politically.

It gets worse. Brazil does not have direct access to the rivers of the Rio de la Plata region. The River Plate itself empties out into the Atlantic in Argentina, meaning that for centuries traders have moved their goods down the Plate to Buenos Aires rather than carry them up and down the Grand Escarpment to get to Brazil's under-developed ports. The Texas-based geopolitical intelligence company Stratfor.com estimates that Brazil's seven largest ports combined can handle fewer goods per year than the single American port of New Orleans.

Therefore Brazil lacks the volume of trade it would like and, equally important, most of its goods are moved along its inadequate roads rather than by river, thus increasing costs. On the plus side, Brazil is working on its transport infrastructure, and the newly discovered offshore gas reserves will help pay for this, reduce reliance on Bolivian and Venezuelan energy imports, and cushion the inevitable economic dips all nations suffer. Nevertheless, Brazil will require a Herculean effort for it to overcome its geographical disadvantages.

Around 25 percent of Brazilians are thought to live in the infamous favela slums. When one in four of a state's population is in abject poverty it is difficult for that state to become rich. This does not mean Brazil is not a rising power, just that its rise will be limited.

A shortcut to growth could be soft power, hence Brazil's efforts to gain a permanent seat on the UN Security Council and its habit of building regional economic alliances such as Mercosur, which loosely ties together Brazil, Argentina, Paraguay, Uruguay, and Venezuela.

Every few years, often led by Brazil, the South Americans attempt to launch their version of the EU—the latest incarnation being UNASUR, of which twelve South American nations are members. Its headquarters are in Ecuador but Brazil has the loudest voice. In this it resembles the EU, which has its headquarters in Belgium and a leading power in Germany. And there the comparison stops. UNASUR has an impressive presence on the Internet but it remains more of a website than an economic union. The EU countries have similar political and economic systems and most members share a currency, whereas the Latin Americans differ in their politics, economics, currencies, education levels, and labor laws. They also have to overcome the constraints of distance, as well as the heights of the mountains and the density of the jungles that separate them.

But Brazil will keep working to help create a South American powerhouse by using its diplomatic and increasing economic strength. The country is by nature nonconfrontational, its foreign policy is against intervention in other countries, and war with any of its neighbors seems highly unlikely. It has managed to maintain good relations with all the other eleven South American nations despite having a border with nine of them.

There is a frontier dispute with Uruguay, but it does not look set to become inflamed; and the rivalry between Brazil and Argentina is unlikely to be played out anywhere more politically significant than a soccer field. In recent years Brazil has moved army units away from its border with Argentina and has seen its Spanish-speaking neighbor reciprocate. An Argentinian navy vessel has been welcomed in a Brazilian port whereas a British Royal Navy ship was denied such access a few years ago, thus pleasing the Argentinians in their ongoing diplomatic battle with the UK over the Falkland Islands.

Brazil is included in the BRICS—a group of major countries said to be on the rise both economically and politically, but, while each one may be rising individually, the concept is more fashion than reality. Brazil, Russia, India, China, and South Africa are not a political or geographical grouping in a meaningful way and have very little in common with one another. If the letters had not spelled what sounds like a word, then the BRICS theory would not have caught on. The BRICS hold an annual conference and Brazil does sometimes liaise with India and South Africa on international issues in a sort of vague echo of the Cold War nonaligned movement, but it does not join Russia and China in taking a sometimes hostile stance toward the United States.

The North and South American giants did fall out in 2013 over an issue that still rankles in Brazil. The news that the US National Security Agency had spied on the Brazilian president, Dilma Rousseff, led her to cancel a state visit to Washington. That an apology was not forthcoming from the Obama administration was testament to the fact that the Americans are irritated that China has supplanted them as Brazil's main trading partner. Brazil's subsequent decision to buy Swedish fighter jets for its air force rather than ones from Boeing is thought to have been informed by the disagreement. However, the state-to-state relationship has partially recovered, albeit not at the presidential level. Confrontation is not Brazil's style, unlike Venezuela under the late President Chavez. The Brazilians know the world thinks they are a coming power, but they also know that their power will never match that of the Americans.

Neither will that of Argentina; however, in some ways it is better placed to become a First World country than is Brazil. It lacks the size and population to become *the* primary regional power in Latin

America, which looks to be Brazil's destiny, but it has the quality of land to create a standard of living comparable to that of the European countries. That does not mean it will achieve this potential—simply that if Argentina gets the economics right, its geography will enable it to become the power it has never been.

The foundations for this potential were laid in the nineteenth century with military victories over Brazil and Paraguay that resulted in control of the flat agricultural regions of the Rio de la Plata, the navigable river system, and therefore the commerce that flows down it toward Buenos Aires and its port. This is among the most valuable pieces of real estate on the whole continent. It immediately gave Argentina an economic and strategic advantage over Brazil, Paraguay, and Uruguay—one it holds to this day.

However, Argentina has not always used its advantages to the fullest. A hundred years ago it was among the ten richest countries in the world—ahead of France and Italy. But a failure to diversify, a stratified and unfair society, a poor education system, a succession of coups d'état, and the wildly differing economic policies in the democratic period of the last thirty years has seen a sharp decline in Argentina's status.

The Brazilians have a joke about their snobbish neighbors, as they see them: "Only people this sophisticated could make a mess this big." Argentina needs to get it right, and a dead cow may help it.

The Dead Cow, or Vaca Muerta, is a shale formation that, combined with the country's other shale areas, could provide Argentina's energy needs for the next 150 years with excess to export. It is situated halfway down Argentina, in Patagonia, and abuts the western border with Chile. It is the size of Belgium—which might be relatively small for a country but is large for a shale formation. So far so good, unless you are against shale-produced energy—but there is a catch. To get the gas and oil out of the shale will require massive foreign investment, and Argentina is not considered a foreign-investment-friendly country.

There's more oil and gas farther south—in fact, so far south it's offshore in and around islands that are British and have been since 1833. And therein lies a problem, and a news story that never goes away.

What Britain calls the Falkland Islands are known as Las Malvinas by Argentina, and woe betide any Argentine who uses the F word. It is an offense in Argentina to produce a map that describes the islands as anything other than the "Islas Malvinas," and all primary school children are taught to draw the outlines of the two main islands, west and east. To regain the "Little Sisters" is a national cause for successive generations of Argentines and one that most of their Latin neighbors support.

In April 1982, the British let their guard down and the Argentinian military dictatorship under General Galtieri ordered an invasion of the islands—which was considered a huge success until the British task force arrived eight weeks later and made short work of the Argentinian army and reclaimed the territory. This in turn led to the fall of the dictatorship.

If the Argentine invasion had happened in the present decade, Britain would not have been in a position to retake the islands, as it currently has no functioning aircraft carriers, a situation that will be remedied by 2020, at which time Argentina's window of opportunity closes. However, despite the lure of oil and gas, an Argentinian invasion of the Falklands is unlikely for two reasons.

First, Argentina is now a democracy and knows that the vast majority of Falkland Islanders wish to remain under British control;

second, the British, once bitten, are twice shy. They may temporarily lack an aircraft carrier to sail the eight thousand miles down to the South Atlantic, but they do now have several hundred combat troops on the islands, along with advanced radar systems, ground-to-air missiles, four Eurofighter jets, and probably a nuclear attack submarine lurking nearby most of the time. The British intend to prevent the Argentinians from even thinking they could get onto the beaches, let alone take the islands.

The Argentine air force uses planes that are decades behind the Eurofighter, and British diplomacy has ensured that an attempt by Argentina to buy up-to-date models from Spain was called off. Buying from the United States is a nonstarter due to the Special Relationship between the UK and United States, which is indeed, at times, special; so the chances of Argentina being in a position to mount another attack before 2020 are slim.

However, that will not calm the diplomatic war, and Argentina has sharpened its weapons on that front. Buenos Aires has warned that any oil firm that drills in the Falklands/Malvinas cannot bid for a license to exploit the shale oil and gas in Patagonia's Vaca Muerta field. It has even passed a law threatening fines or imprisonment for individuals who explore the Falklands' continental shelf without its permission. This has put many big oil companies off, but not of course the British. However, whoever probes the potential wealth beneath the South Atlantic waters will be operating in one of the most challenging environments in the business. It gets somewhat cold and windy down there, and the seas are rough.

We have traveled as far south as you can go before you arrive at the frozen wastelands of the Antarctic. While plenty of countries would like to exert control there, a combination of the extremely challenging environment, the Antarctic Treaty, and lack of obtainable and valuable resources together largely prevent overt competition, at least for the present. The same cannot be said of its northern counterpart. Heading straight up from Antarctica to the northernmost part of the globe, you reach a place destined to be a diplomatic battleground in the twenty-first century as countries great and small strive to reach pole position there—the Arctic.

S I A

Sa

Kara
Sea

Novaya
Zemlya

Archangel•

LATVIA

ESTONIA

FINLAND

Murmansk•

Barents
Sea

SWEDEN

Franz Josef
Land

Svalbard

Tromsø•

NORWAY

Gakkel Ridge

Spitsbergen

•Longyearbyen

Norwegian
Sea

osov Ridge

C ∨ North Pole

Greenland
Sea

Nares Strait

Hans
Island

oeth Islands

Ellesmere
Island

G R E E N L A N D
(Denmark)

ICELAND

•Reykjavík

Denmark Strait

N

•Thule

Devon
Island

Baffin Bay

Arctic Circle

A T L A N T I C

D A

Baffin Island

O C E A N

1000 miles   1000 km

10

THE ARCTIC

There are two kinds of Arctic problems, the imaginary and the real.
Of the two, the imaginary are the most real.
—Vilhjalmur Stefansson, *The Arctic in Fact and Fable*

When the icemen come, they will come in force.

Who has the force? The Russians. No one else has such a heavy presence in the region or is as well prepared to tackle the severity of the conditions. All the other nations are lagging behind and, in the case of the United States, do not appear to be even trying to catch up: America is an Arctic nation without an Arctic strategy in a region that is heating up.

The effects of global warming are now showing more than ever in the Arctic: the ice is melting, allowing easier access to the region, coinciding with the discovery of energy deposits and the development of technology to get at them—all of which has focused the Arctic nations' attention on the potential gains and losses to be made in the world's most difficult environment. Many of the countries in the region have competing claims that they haven't bothered to press—until now. But there is a lot to claim, and a lot to argue about.

The word *arctic* comes from the Greek *arktikos*, which means "near the bear," and is a reference to the Ursa Major constellation, whose last two stars point toward the North Star.

The Arctic Ocean is 5.4 million square miles; this might make it the world's smallest ocean but it is still almost as big as Russia, and one and a half times the size of the United States. The continental shelves on its ocean bed occupy more space proportionally than any other ocean, which is one of the reasons it can be hard to agree on areas of sovereignty.

The Arctic region includes land in parts of Canada, Finland, Greenland, Iceland, Norway, Russia, Sweden, and the United States (Alaska). It is a land of extremes: for brief periods in the summer the temperature can reach 26 degrees Celsius in some places, but for long periods in winter it plunges to below minus 45. There are expanses of rock scoured by the freezing winds, spectacular fjords, polar deserts, and even rivers. It is a place of great hostility and of great beauty that has captivated people for millennia.

The first recorded expedition was by a Greek mariner named Pytheas of Massalia in 330 BCE who found a strange land called Thule. Back home in the Mediterranean, few believed his startling tales of pure white landscapes, frozen seas, and strange creatures, including great white bears; but Pytheas was just the first of many people over the centuries to record the wonder of the Arctic and to succumb to the emotions it evokes.

Many also succumbed to its deprivations, especially those voyaging to the edge of the known world in search of what doubters said was the "mythical" Northwest Passage from the Atlantic to the Pacific Ocean. One example is Henry Hudson. He may have the second-largest bay in the world named after him, but back in 1607 he probably would have preferred to have lived into old age rather than being cast adrift and almost certainly sent to his death by a mutinous crew sick of his voyages of discovery.

As for the first person to reach the North Pole, well, that's a tricky one, given that even though there is a fixed point on the globe denoting its position, below it, the ice you are standing on is moving, and without GPS equipment it is hard to tell exactly where you are. Sir William Edward Parry, minus a GPS, tried in 1827, but the ice was moving south faster than he could move north and he ended up going backward; but he did at least survive.

Captain Sir John Franklin had less luck when he attempted to cross the last non-navigated section of the Northwest Passage in 1848. His two ships became stuck in the ice near King William Island in the Canadian archipelago. All 129 members of the expedition perished, some on board the ships, others after they abandoned the vessels and began walking south. Several expeditions were sent to search for survivors, but they found only a handful of skeletons and heard stories from Inuit hunters about dozens of white men who had died walking through the frozen landscape. The ships had vanished completely, but in 2014, technology caught up with geography and a Canadian search team using sonar located one of the vessels, HMS *Erebus*, on the seabed of the Northwest Passage and brought up the ship's bell.

The fate of Franklin's expedition did not deter many more adventurers from trying to find their way through the archipelago, but it wasn't until 1905 that the great Norwegian explorer Roald Amundsen charted his way across in a smaller ship with just five other crew. He passed King William Island, went through the Bering Strait and into the Pacific. He knew he'd made it when he spotted a whaling ship from San Francisco coming from the other direction. In his diary he confessed his emotions got the better of him, an occurrence perhaps almost as rare as his great achievement: "The Northwest Passage was done. My boyhood dream—at that moment it was accomplished. A strange feeling welled up in my throat; I was somewhat overstrained and worn—it was weakness in me—but I felt tears in my eyes."

Twenty years later, he decided he wanted to be the first man to fly over the North Pole, which, although easier than walking across it, is no mean feat. Along with his Italian pilot, Umberto Nobile, and fourteen crew, he flew a semirigid airship over the ice and dropped Norwegian, Italian, and American flags from a height of three hundred feet. A heroic effort this may have been, but in the twenty-first century it was not seen as one giving much legal basis to any claims of ownership of the region by those three countries.

That also applies to the impressive effort of Shinji Kazama of Japan, who in 1987 became the first person to reach the North Pole on a motorcycle. Mr. Kazama was so intrepid as not to have relied on a shrinking polar ice cap, and is the sort of man who would have ridden through a blizzard in order to get into the history books, but there is no doubt that there is now less ice to cross.

That the ice is receding is not in question—satellite imaging over the past decade clearly shows that the ice has shrunk—only the cause is in doubt. Most scientists are convinced that man is responsible, not merely natural climate cycles, and that the coming exploitation of what is unveiled will quicken the pace.

Already villages along the Bering and Chukchi coasts have been relocated, as coastlines are eroded and hunting grounds lost. A biological reshuffle is under way. Polar bears and Arctic foxes are on the move, walruses find themselves competing for space, and fish, unaware of territorial boundaries, are moving northward, depleting stocks for some countries but populating others. Mackerel and Atlantic cod are now being found in Arctic trawler nets.

It is clear from satellite images that the ice in the Arctic is receding, making the sea-lanes through the region more accessible for longer periods of the year.

The effects of the melting ice won't just be felt in the Arctic: countries as far away as the Maldives, Bangladesh, and the Netherlands are at risk of increased flooding as the ice melts and sea levels rise. These ramifications are why the Arctic is a global, not just a regional, issue.

As the ice melts and the tundra is exposed, two things are likely to happen to accelerate the process of the graying of the ice cap. Residue from the industrial work destined to take place will land on the snow and ice, further reducing the amount of heat-reflecting territory. The darker-colored land and open water will then absorb more heat than the ice and snow they replace, thus increasing the size of the darker territory. This is known as the albedo effect, and although there are negative aspects to it there are also positive ones: the warming tundra will allow significantly more natural-plant growth and agricultural crops to flourish, helping local populations as they seek new food sources.

There is, though, no getting away from the prospect that one of the world's last great unspoiled regions is about to change. Some climate-prediction models say the Arctic will be ice-free during the summer by the end of the century; there are a few that predict it could happen much sooner. What is certain is that, however quickly it happens and dramatic the reduction will be, it has begun.

The melting of the ice cap already allows cargo ships to make the journey through the Northwest Passage in the Canadian archipelago for several summer weeks a year, thus cutting at least a week from the transit time from Europe to China. The first cargo ship not to be escorted by an icebreaker went through in 2014. The *Nunavik* carried twenty-three thousand tons of nickel ore from Canada to China. The polar route was 40 percent shorter and used deeper waters than if it had gone through the Panama Canal. This allowed the ship to carry more cargo, save tens of thousands of dollars in fuel costs, and reduced the ship's greenhouse emissions by 1,300 metric tons. By 2040, the route is expected to be open for up to two months each year, transforming trade links across the High North and causing knock-on effects as far away as Egypt and Panama in terms of the revenues they enjoy from the Suez and Panama Canals.

The northeast route, or Northern Sea Route as the Russians call it, which hugs the Siberian coastline, is also now open for several months a year and is becoming an increasingly popular sea highway.

The melting ice reveals other potential riches. It is thought that vast quantities of undiscovered natural gas and oil reserves may lie in the Arctic region in areas that can now be accessed. In 2009, the US Geological Survey estimated that 1,669 trillion cubic feet of natural gas, 44 billion barrels of natural gas liquids, and 90 billion barrels of oil are in the Arctic, with the vast majority of it offshore. As more territory becomes accessible, extra reserves of the gold, zinc, nickel, and iron already found in part of the Arctic may be discovered.

ExxonMobil, Shell, and Rosneft are among the energy giants that are applying for licenses and beginning exploratory drilling. Countries and companies prepared to make the effort to get at the riches will have to brave a climate where for much of the year the days are endless night, where for the majority of the year the sea freezes to a depth of more than six feet, and where, in open water, the waves can reach forty feet high.

It is going to be dirty, hard, and dangerous work, especially for anyone hoping to run a year-round operation. It will also require massive investment. Running gas pipelines will not be possible in many places, and building a complex liquefaction infrastructure at sea, especially in tough conditions, is very expensive. However, the financial and strategic gains to be made mean that the big players will try to stake a claim to the territories and begin drilling, and that the potential environmental consequences are unlikely to stop them.

The claims to sovereignty are not based on the flags of the early explorers but on the United Nations Convention on the Law of the Sea (UNCLOS). This affirms that a signatory to the convention has exclusive economic rights from its shore to a limit of two hundred nautical miles (unless this conflicts with another country's limits), and can declare it an exclusive economic zone (EEZ). The oil and gas in the zone are therefore considered to belong to the state. In certain circumstances, and subject to scientific evidence concerning a country's continental shelf, that country can apply to extend the EEZ to 350 nautical miles from its coast.

The melting of the Arctic ice is bringing with it a hardening of attitude from the eight members of the Arctic Council, the forum where geopolitics becomes geopolarctics.

The "Arctic Five," those states with borders on the Arctic, are Canada, Russia, the United States, Norway, and Denmark (due to its responsibility for Greenland). They are joined by Iceland, Finland, and Sweden, which are also full members. There are twelve other nations with Permanent Observer status, having recognized the "Arctic States' sovereignty, sovereign rights, and jurisdiction" in the region, among other criteria. For example, at the 2013 Arctic Council, Japan and India, which have sponsored Arctic scientific expeditions, and China, which has a science base on a Norwegian island as well as a modern icebreaker, were granted Observer status.

However, there are countries not on the council that say they have legitimate interests in the region, and still more that argue that under the theory of the "common heritage of mankind" the Arctic should be open to everyone.

There are currently at least nine legal disputes and claims over sovereignty in the Arctic Ocean, all legally complicated, and some with the potential to cause serious tensions between the nations. One of the most brazen comes from the Russians: Moscow has already put a marker down—a long way down. In 2007, it sent two manned submersibles 13,980 feet below the waves to the seabed of the North Pole and planted a rust-proof titanium Russian flag as a statement of ambition. As far as is known, it still "flies" down there today. A Russian think tank followed this up by suggesting that the Arctic be renamed. After not much thought, they came up with an alternative: "the Russian Ocean."

Elsewhere, Russia argues that the Lomonosov Ridge off its Siberian coast is an extension of Siberia's continental shelf, and therefore belongs to Russia exclusively. This is problematic for other countries, given that the ridge extends all the way to the North Pole.

Russia and Norway have particular difficulty in the Barents Sea. Norway claims the Gakkel Ridge in the Barents as an extension of its Economic Exclusion Zone (EEZ), but the Russians dispute this, and they have a particular dispute over the Svalbard Islands, the northernmost point on earth with a settled population. Most countries and international organizations recognize the islands as being under (limited) Norwegian sovereignty, but the biggest island, Svalbard, formerly known as Spitsbergen, has a growing population of Russian migrants who have assembled around the coal-mining industry there. The mines are not profitable, but the Russian community serves as a useful tool in furthering Moscow's claims on all of the Svalbard Islands. At a time of Russia's choosing it can raise tensions and justify its actions using geological claims and the "facts on the ground" of the Russian population.

Norway, a NATO state, knows what is coming and has made the High North its foreign policy priority. Its air force regularly intercepts

Russian fighter jets approaching its borders; the heightened tensions have caused it to move its center of military operations from the south of the country to the north, and it is building an Arctic battalion. Canada is reinforcing its cold-weather military capabilities, which includes five new navy warships with moderate ice-breaking capability to be delivered between 2018 and 2022. Announcing the increase in the spring of 2015, Prime Minister Stephen Harper said, "Canada has a choice when it comes to defending our sovereignty over the Arctic. We either use it or lose it." Denmark has also reacted to Moscow's muscle flexing by creating an Arctic Response Force.

Russia meanwhile is building an Arctic army. Six new military bases are being constructed and several mothballed Cold War installations—such as those on the Novosibirsk Islands—are reopening, and airstrips are being renovated. A force of at least six thousand combat soldiers is being readied for the Murmansk region and will include two mechanized infantry brigades equipped with snowmobiles and hovercraft.

It is no coincidence that Murmansk is now called Russia's northern energy gateway and that President Putin has said that, in relation to energy supply, "Offshore fields, especially in the Arctic, are without any exaggeration our strategic reserve for the twenty-first century."

The Murmansk brigades will be Moscow's minimum permanent Arctic force, but Russia demonstrated its full cold-weather fighting ability in 2014 with an exercise that involved 155,000 men and thousands of tanks, jets, and ships. The Russian Defense Ministry said it was bigger than exercises it had carried out during the Cold War.

During the war games, Russian troops were tasked with repelling an invasion by a foreign power named "Missouri," which clearly signified the United States. The scenario was that "Missouri" troops had landed in Chukotka, Kamchatka, the Kurils, and Sakhalin in support of an unnamed Asian power that had already clashed with Russia. The unnamed power was Japan, and the scenario's conflict was provoked by a territorial dispute said by analysts to be over the South Kuril Islands. The military display of intent was then underlined politically when President Putin for the first time added the Arctic region as a sphere of Russian influence in its official foreign policy doctrine.

Despite Russia's shrinking economic power, resulting in budget cuts in many government departments, its defense budget has increased and this is partially to pay for the boost in Arctic military muscle taking place between now and 2020. Moscow has plans for the future, infrastructure from the past, and the advantage of location. As Melissa Bert, a US Coast Guard captain, told the Center for Strategic and International Studies in Washington, DC: "They have cities in the Arctic, we only have villages."

All this is, in many ways, a continuation, or at the least a resurrection, of Russia's Cold War Arctic policies. The Russians know that NATO can bottle up their Baltic Fleet by blockading the Skagerrak Strait. This potential blockade is complicated by the fact that up in the Arctic their Northern Fleet has only 180 miles of open water from the Kola coastline until it hits the Arctic ice pack. From this narrow corridor it must also come down through the Norwegian Sea and then run the potential gauntlet of the GIUK gap to reach the Atlantic Ocean. During the Cold War, the area was known by NATO as the Kill Zone, as this was where NATO's planes, ships, and submarines expected to catch the Soviet fleet.

Fast-forward to the new cold war and the strategies remain the same, even if now the Americans have withdrawn their forces from their NATO ally Iceland. Iceland has no armed forces of its own and the

American withdrawal was described by the Icelandic government as "short-sighted." In a speech to the Swedish Atlantic Council, Iceland's Justice Minister Björn Bjarnason said: "A certain military presence should be maintained in the region, sending a signal about a nation's interests and ambitions in a given area, since a military vacuum could be misinterpreted as a lack of national interest and priority."

However, for at least a decade now, it has been clear that the Arctic is a priority for the Russians in a way it is not for the Americans. This is reflected in the degree of attention given to the region by both countries, or in the case of the United States, its relative inattention since the collapse of the Soviet Union.

It takes up to $1 billion and ten years to build an icebreaker. Russia is clearly the leading Arctic power with the largest fleet of icebreakers in the world, thirty-two in total, according to the US Coast Guard Review of 2013. Six of those are nuclear-powered, the only such versions in the world, and Russia also plans to launch the world's most powerful icebreaker by 2018. It will be able to smash through ice more than ten feet deep and tow oil tankers with a displacement of up to seventy thousand tons through the ice fields.

By contrast, the United States has a fleet of one functioning heavy icebreaker, the USCGC *Polar Star*, down from the eight it possessed in the 1960s, and has no plans to build another. In 2012, it had to rely on a Russian ship to resupply its research base in Antarctica, which was a triumph for great-power cooperation, but simultaneously a demonstration of how far behind the United States has fallen. No other nation presents a challenge, either: Canada has six icebreakers and is building a new one; Finland has eight; Sweden, seven; and Denmark, four. China, Germany, and Norway have one each. In the fall of 2015, President Obama made the first trip by a sitting president to Alaska and did call for more US icebreakers to be built. However, this was almost a passing remark on a trip built around the issue of climate change. The security and energy aspects of the Arctic were barely mentioned. Washington, DC, remains way behind the curve.

The United States has another problem. It has not ratified the UNCLOS treaty, effectively ceding two hundred thousand square miles of undersea territory in the Arctic because it has not staked a claim for an EEZ.

Nevertheless, it is in dispute with Canada over potential offshore oil rights and access to the waters in the Canadian archipelago. Canada says they are an "internal waterway," the United States says they are a strait for international navigation not governed by Canadian law. In 1985, the United States sent an icebreaker through the waters without informing Canada in advance, causing a furious row to break out between the two neighbors whose relationship is simultaneously friendly but prickly.

The United States is also in dispute with Russia over the Bering Sea, Arctic Ocean, and northern Pacific. A 1990 Maritime Boundary Agreement was signed with the then Soviet Union in which Moscow ceded a fishing region. However, following the breakup of the Soviet Union, the Russian parliament refuses to ratify the agreement. The area is treated by both sides as being under US sovereignty, but the Russians reserve the right to return to this issue.

Other disputes include the one between Canada and Denmark over Hans Island, located in the Nares Strait, which separates Greenland from Ellesmere Island. Greenland, with its population of fifty-six thousand people, has self-government but remains under Danish sovereignty. A 1953 agreement between Denmark and Canada left the island still in dispute, and since then both countries have taken the trouble to sail to it and plant their national flags on it.

All the sovereignty issues stem from the same desires and fears— the desire to safeguard routes for military and commercial shipping, the desire to own the natural riches of the region, and the fear that others may gain where you lose. Until recently the riches were theoretical, but the melting ice has made the theoretical probable, and in some cases certain.

The melting of the ice changes the geography and the stakes. The Arctic states and the giant energy firms now have decisions to make about how they deal with these changes and how much attention they pay to the environment and the peoples of the Arctic. The hunger for energy suggests the race is inevitable in what some Arctic specialists have called the New Great Game. There are going to be a lot more ships in the High North, a lot more oil rigs and gas platforms—in fact, a lot more of everything. The Russians not only have their nuclear-powered icebreakers, but are even considering building a floating nuclear power plant capable of withstanding the crushing weight of ten feet of ice.

However, there are differences between this situation and the "scramble for Africa" in the nineteenth century or the machinations of the great powers in the Middle East, India, and Afghanistan in the original Great Game. This race has rules, a formula, and a forum for decision making. The Arctic Council is composed of mature countries, most of them democratic to a greater or lesser degree. The international laws regulating territorial disputes, environmental pollution, laws of the sea, and treatment of minority peoples are in place. Most of the territory in dispute has not been conquered through nineteenth-century imperialism or by nation states at war with one another.

The Arctic states know that theirs is a tough neighborhood, not so much because of warring factions but because of the challenges presented by its geography. There are five and a half million square miles of ocean up in the Arctic; they can be dark, dangerous, and deadly. It is not a good place to be without friends. They know that for anyone to succeed in the region they may need to cooperate, especially on issues such as fishing stocks, smuggling, terrorism, search and rescue, and environmental disasters.

It is plausible that a disagreement over fishing rights could escalate into something more serious, given that the UK and Iceland almost came to blows during the "Cod Wars" of the 1950s and 1970s. Smuggling occurs wherever there are transit routes, and there is no reason to believe the Arctic will be any different; but policing it will be difficult due to the conditions there. And as more commercial vessels and cruise ships head into the area, the search-and-rescue and anti-terrorism capabilities of the Arctic nations will need to grow accordingly, as will their capacity to react to an environmental disaster in increasingly crowded waters. In the 1960s, the icebreaker *Lenin* had an accident in its reactor while at sea. After returning to shore, parts of the reactor were cut out and, along with damaged fuel, placed in a concrete container with a steel liner that was then dumped into the sea. Such incidents are likely to occur more frequently as the Arctic opens up, but they will remain difficult to manage.

Perhaps the Arctic will turn out to be just another battleground for the nation states—after all, wars are started by fear of the other as well as by greed; but the Arctic is different, and so perhaps how it is dealt with will be different. Our history has shown us the rapacious way of the zero-sum game. Arguably, a belief in partial geographic determinism, coupled with human nature, made it difficult for it to have been any other way. However, there are examples of how technology has helped us break out from the prison of geography, that technology was made by us, and, in our newly globalized world, can be used to give us an opportunity in the Arctic. We can overcome the rapacious side of our nature, and get the Great Game right for the benefit of all.

CONCLUSION

We finished at the top of the world and so the only way is up.

The final frontier has always called out to our imagination, but ours is the age in which humanity has lived the dream and pushed out into space, a millimeter into infinity, on our way to the future. Humanity's restless spirit ensures that our boundaries are not confined to what Carl Sagan famously called the "Pale Blue Dot."

But we must come back down to earth, sometimes with a bump, because we have neither conquered our own geography yet nor our propensity to compete for it.

Geography has always been a prison of sorts—one that defines what a nation is or can be, and one from which our world leaders have often struggled to break free.

Russia is probably the clearest example, naturally expanding from the small region of flatland it controlled until its heartland covered a huge space ringed mostly by mountains and the sea—with just one vulnerable point across the North European Plain. If the Russian leaders wanted to create a great nation, which they did, then they had little choice as to what to do about that weak spot. Likewise, in Europe no conscious decision was made to become a huge trading area; the long, level networks of rivers made it possible, and to an extent inevitable, over the course of millennia.

As the twenty-first century progresses, the geographical factors that have helped determine our history will mostly continue to determine our future: a century from now, Russia will still be looking anxiously westward across what will remain flatland. India and China will still be separated by the Himalayas. They may eventually come into conflict with each other, but if that does happen, then geography will determine the nature of the fight: either they will need to develop technology to allow a huge military force to cross over the mountains, or, if that remains impossible and neither side wants to descend into nuclear war, to confront each other at sea. Florida will continue to guard the exit of and entrance to the Gulf of Mexico. It is the Gulf's location that is key, not who controls it. To take an extreme and unlikely scenario: imagine a majority Hispanic Florida has seceded from the United States and allied itself with Cuba and Mexico. This would alter only the dynamics of who controlled the Gulf, not the importance of the location.

Of course, geography does not dictate the course of all events. Great ideas and great leaders are part of the push and pull of history. But they must all operate within the confines of geography. The leaders of Bangladesh might dream of preventing the waters from flooding up the Bay of Bengal, but they know that 80 percent of the country is on a floodplain and cannot be moved. It is a point the Scandinavian and English leader King Canute made to his sycophantic courtiers in the eleventh century, when ordering the waves to retreat: nature, or

God, was greater than any man. In Bangladesh all that can be done is to react to the realities of nature: build more flood defenses and hope that the computer modeling of rising waters due to global warming is overstated.

New geographical realities such as climate change present new opportunities and challenges. Global warming may well result in the mass movement of people. If the Maldives, and many other islands, really are destined to be lost to the waves, the impact will not just be on those leaving before it is too late but also upon the countries to which they flee. If the flooding of Bangladesh becomes worse, the future of the country and its 160 million people is dire; if the water levels rise much higher, this impoverished country may go under. And if the desertification of the lands just below the Sahel continues, then wars such as the one in Darfur, Sudan (partially caused by the desert encroaching on nomads in the north, which in turn pushed them southward toward the Fur people), will intensify and spread.

Water wars are another potential problem. Even if stable democracies were to emerge in the Middle East in the coming decades, if the waters of the Murat River, which rises in Turkey before feeding the Euphrates, were to diminish considerably, then the dams Turkey would have to build to protect its own source of life could quite easily be the cause of war with Syria and Iraq downstream.

Looking further ahead, as we continue to break out of the prison of our geography into the universe, the political struggles will persist in space, at least for the foreseeable future.

A human being first burst through the top layer of the stratosphere in 1961 when twenty-seven-year-old Soviet cosmonaut Yuri Gagarin made it into space aboard Vostok 1. It is a sad reflection on humanity that the name of a fellow Russian named Kalashnikov is far better known.

Gagarin, Buzz Aldrin, and many others are the descendants of Marco Polo and Columbus, pioneers who pushed the boundaries and who changed the world in ways they could not have imagined in their own lifetimes. Whether for better or worse is not the point; they discovered new opportunities and new spaces in which people would compete to make the most of what nature had put there. It will take generations, but in space, too, we will plant our flags, "conquer" territory, claim ground, and overcome the barriers the universe puts in our way.

There are now about 1,100 functioning satellites in space, and at least 2,000 nonfunctioning ones. The Russians and Americans launched approximately 2,400 of the total, Japan has about 100, China a similar number, followed by a host of other countries with far fewer. Below them are the space stations, where for the first time people live and work semipermanently outside the confines of earth's gravity. Farther on, at least five American flags are thought to be still standing on the surface of the moon, and farther still, much farther, our machines have made it out past Mars and Jupiter, some heading way beyond what we can see and are trying to understand.

It is tempting to think of our endeavors in space as linking humanity to a collective and cooperative future. But first there will continue to be competition for supremacy in outer space. The satellites are not just there to beam back our TV pictures, or to predict the weather: they also spy on other countries, to see who is moving where and with what. In addition, America and China are engaged in developing laser technology, which can be used as weapons, and both seek to ensure that they have a missile system that can operate in space and nullify the competition's version. Many of the technologically advanced nations are now making preparations in case they need to fight in space.

When we are reaching for the stars, the challenges ahead are such that we will perhaps have to come together to meet them: to travel the universe not as Russians, Americans, or Chinese but as representatives of humanity. But so far, although we have broken free from the shackles of gravity, we are still imprisoned in our own minds, confined by our suspicion of the "other," and thus our primal competition for resources. There is a long way to go.

ACKNOWLEDGMENTS

Many thanks to all those who freely gave of their time, advice, and encouragement.

I would like to thank my wife, Joanna, for her patience and natural spell-check abilities; Pippa Crane and Jennie Condell at Elliott and Thompson for giving shape and direction to my geographic wanderings; and Ollie Dewis for her encouragement and ideas.

I am grateful to the following for casting their experienced eyes over sections of the book and would like to reiterate that any errors contained therein are my doing and responsibility: James Richards (former official Chinese interpreter to the UK government, chairman of China Association), Professor James D. Boys (Visiting Senior Research Fellow, King's College London), David Slinn (former UK ambassador to North Korea), Joel Richards MA (South American specialist), Kelvin O'Shea (Sky News), Tim Miller (Sky News), Jaksa Scekic (Reuters, Belgrade), and Aleksander Vasca (Reuters, Belgrade).

Thanks to Scribner editor Colin Harrison for guidance and reminding me that the US and UK are two countries separated by a common language, and to Katrina Diaz at Scribner, whose lines of communication bridged the Atlantic Ocean.

Also, thanks to those serving members of governments and the civil service who kindly gave me their expertise, but preferred it to be used without attribution.

BIBLIOGRAPHY

General References

Diamond, Jared. *Guns, Germs, and Steel*. New York: W. W. Norton, 2005.

Dodds, Klaus. *Geopolitics: A Very Short Introduction*. Oxford: Oxford University Press, 2007.

Ikenberry, G. John. "The Illusion of Geopolitics." *Foreign Affairs* 93, no. 3 (May/June 2014), 80–90.

Keegan, John. *Atlas of World War Two*. London: Harper Collins, 2006.

Mackinder, Halford John. "The Geographical Pivot of History." *Geographical Society* 23, no. 4 (April 1904), 421–37. https://en.wikisource.org/wiki/Democratic_Ideals_and_Reality:_A_Study_in_the_Politics_of_Reconstruction.

Mackinder, Halford John. *Democratic Ideals and Reality*. London: Constable and Company Limited, 1919.

Mead, Walter Russell. "The Return of Geopolitics." *Foreign Affairs* 93, no. 3 (May/June 2014), 69–79.

Monmonier, M. *How to Lie with Maps*. Chicago: University of Chicago Press, 1996.

Parry, Chris. *Super Highway: Sea Power in the 21st Century*. London: Elliott & Thompson, 2014.

Pickles, John. *A History of Spaces: Cartographic Reason, Mapping and the Geo-Coded World*. London: Routledge, 2004.

Roberts, S., A. Secor, and M. Sparke. "Neoliberal Geopolitics." *Antipode* 35, no. 5 (November 2003), 886–97.

Times Atlas of World History, The. London: Times Books, 2000.

Times Universal Atlas of the World, The. London: Times Books, 2008.

Weigley, Russell F. *The American Way of War*. Bloomington, IN: Indiana University Press, 1973.

Russia

Eberstadt, Nicholas. "Russia's Peacetime Demographic Crisis: Dimensions, Causes, Implications." National Bureau of Asian Research, 2010.

Kennan, George F. "The Sources of Soviet Conduct." *Foreign Affairs* (July 1947). http://www.academia.edu/6987967/_The _Long_Telegram_and_Sources_of_Soviet_Conduct_George_F. _Kennan_Father_of_the_Cold_War_.

"Russia's Accusations—Setting the Record Straight." NATO Fact Sheet, April 2014.

China

Beardson, Timothy. *Stumbling Giant: The Threats to China's Future*. New Haven, CT: Yale University Press, 2013.

Boehm, Dana Carver. "China's Failed War on Terror: Fanning the Flames of Uighur Separatist Violence." *Berkeley Journal of Middle Eastern and Islamic Law* 2, no. 1:3, 2009.

De Crespigny, Rafe. *China This Century*. Oxford: Oxford University Press, 1992.

Holmes, James. "When China Rules the Sea." *Foreign Policy*, September 2015.

Kaplan, Robert D. *The Revenge of Geography*. London: Random House, 2012.

Lewis, Martin. "East Asia." Stanford University Global Geopolitics Lectures, East Asia, January 15, 2008.

Shaughnessy, Edward L., ed. *China: Empire and Civilization*. London: Duncan Baird Publishers, 2005.

Theroux, Paul. *Riding the Iron Rooster*. London: Hamish Hamilton, 1988.

United States

Commager, S. *Documents of American History Volume 1: to 1898* (10th Edition). New Jersey: Prentice Hall, 1988.

"The Geopolitics of the United States, Part 1: The Inevitable Empire." Stratfor.com, July 4, 2014. https://www.stratfor.com /analysis/geopolitics-united-states-part-1-inevitable-empire.

Kagan, Robert. *Dangerous Nation: America and the World, 1600–1898*. London: Atlantic Books, 2006.

Pei, Minxin. "How America and China See Each Other." *Foreign Affairs* (March/April 2014). https://www.foreignaffairs.com /reviews/review-essay/how-china-and-america-see-each-other.

"Rise to World Power, 1867–1913," A Short History of the Department of State, US Department of State website. history.state.gov /departmenthistory/short-history-worldpower.

Western Europe

Kagan, Robert. *Of Paradise and Power*. New York: Random House, 2003.

Ottens, Nick. "Too Big for Europe: The Recurring German Problem." *Atlantic Sentinel*, April 28, 2014.

Simon, Luis, and James Rogers. "The Return of European Geopolitics? All Roads Run Through London." *RUSI Journal* 155, no. 3 (2010), 57–63.

Speck, Ulrich. "Power and Purpose: German Foreign Policy at a Crossroads." CarnegieEurope.eu, November 3, 2014.

Turchin, Peter. *War and Peace and War*. London: Plume Books, 2007.

Africa

Bloom, David E., and Jeffrey D. Sachs. "Geography, Demography, and Economic Growth in Africa." Harvard Institute for International Development, Harvard University, October 1998.

Chaves, Isaias, Stanley L. Engerman, and James A. Robinson. "Reinventing the Wheel: The Economic Benefits of Wheeled Transportation in Early Colonial British West Africa." February 2012. http://scholar.harvard.edu/jrobinson/publications/reinventing -Wheel-Economic-Benefits-Wheeled-Transportation-Early -Colonial-0.

Kasperson, Roger E., and Julian V. Minghi. *The Structure of Political Geography*. New Brunswick, NJ: Transaction Publishers, 2011.

The Middle East

Fisher, Max. "40 Maps Which Explain the Middle East." Vox.com, May 5, 2014. http://www.vox.com/a/maps-explain-the-middle-east.

Iraq: A Geography. West Point: United States Military Academy, 2004.

India/Pakistan

French, Patrick. *India: A Portrait*. London: Allen Lane, 2011.

"Geography of India." MapsofIndia.com, November 12, 2014. http:// www.mapsofindia.com/geography/.

Kreft, Dr. Heinrich. "The Geopolitical Importance of Pakistan." Institut für Strategie- Politik- Sicherheits- und Wirtschaftsberatung (ISPSW), February 15, 2008. http://www.ispsw.com/en/publications.

Musharraf, Pervez. *In the Line of Fire: A Memoir*. New York: Free Press, 2008.

"Pakistan and Afghanistan." Institute for the Study of War, 2009. http://www.understandingwar.org/pakistan-and-afghan.

Korea/Japan

Chang, Gordon G. *Nuclear Showdown: North Korea Takes on the World*. London: Hutchinson, 2006.

Oberdorfer, Don. *The Two Koreas*. New York: Basic Books, 2001.

Latin America

Keen, Benjamin, and Keith Haynes. A *History of Latin America, Volume 1*. Wadsworth: Cengage Learning, 2012.

Sorrell, Martin. "Latin America's Decade" (lecture, World Economic Forum on Latin America, Rio de Janeiro, April 27–29, 2011. http://www.weforum.org/events/world-economic-forum-latin-america-2011.

Zovatto, Daniel. "Elections in the Southern Cone: Citizens Chose Continuity." Brookings, October 30, 2014. http://www.brookings.edu/research/opinions/2014/10/30-democracy-alternation-latin-america-zovatto.

The Arctic

Bjarnason, Björn. "Climate Change and Iceland's Role in North Atlantic Security," speech. Belfer Center, John F. Kennedy School of Government, Harvard, November 26, 2007.

Conant, Eve. "Breaking the Ice: Russian Nuclear-Powered Ice-Breakers." *Scientific American* blog, September 8, 2012. http://blogs.scientificamerican.com/guest-blog/2012/09/08/breaking-the-ice/.

Grydehøj, Anne, Adam Grydehøj, and Maria Akrén. "The Globalization of the Arctic: Negotiating Sovereignty and Building Communities in Svalbard, Norway." *Island Studies Journal* 7, no. 1 (2012), 99–119.

United Nations Convention of Law of the Sea, Part V: Exclusive Economic Zone, UNCLOS Treaty. http://www.un.org/depts/los/convention_agreements/texts/unclos/part5.htm.

Woods Hole Oceanographic Institution, The Arctic: Exploration Timeline, Polar Discovery, 2009. http://polardiscovery.whoi.edu/arctic/330.html.

INDEX

Note: *Italicized* page numbers indicate maps.

Abbottabad, 198
Abe, Shinzo, 63–64
Abkhazia, *30*, 32, 112
Abraham, 163
Aconcagua Mountain, 232
Adams, Henry, 72
Adams, John Quincy, 73–74
Adriatic Sea, *95*
Aegean Sea, 23, *90–91*, 97–98, 174
Afghanistan, 8–9, 16, 28, 38–39,
    48, 80, 81, 106, *141*, 167, 169,
    180–81, 186, 187, *188*, 191,
    192, 193–96, *194*
  artificial borders in, 193, *194*
  heroin trade, 238–39
  NATO troops in, 4–5, 195–200
  Soviet invasion (1979), 18–19,
    189, 193
  Taliban, 4–5, 193–201, 238–39
  and the United States, 4–5, 88,
    201
Africa, *115*, 116–40. *See also names
    of specific countries*

artificial borders in, 6, *115*,
    121–27, 144
and China, 64, 88, 125, 129, 132,
    133 37
civil wars and ethnic conflicts,
    123–27, 130–33
climate and terrain, 116–20, 121,
    127–29, 136–37, 139
colonial period, 121–27, 130,
    132, 137, 138
and Cuba, 133
energy resources, 64, 128, 129–30,
    132, 133–35, 139
and France, 131–32
Homo sapiens origins, 116, 118, 125
independence movement, 122
Islamists, 123, 128, 130–31, 136
isolation of, 6, 116–17, 121
languages, 119–20, 124, 139
natural resources, 64, 119–20,
    124–25, 133–37, 139
rivers, *115*, 119, 120, 121,
    127–29, 139

Africa (*cont.*)
  and Russia, 36, 132–33
  size, 117–19, 140
  and the United States, 88,
    131–32
aircraft carrier battle groups, 7, 40–41
Aksai Chin, *38–39*, 49
Alaska, 8–9, 16–17, 57, 76, 186,
  254–55, 257, 260
Alawites, 151–53, 169
Albania, 3–4, 14, 21, *90–91*, 95, 102
albedo effect, 261
Aldrin, Buzz, 276
Alexander the Great, 5, 147
Algeria, 144
Ali (son-in-law of Muhammad),
  145, 146, 152–53
Alps, *90–91*, 93, 95
al-Qaeda, 4–5, 53, 154–55, 160, 195,
  196, 198, 201
Amazon Rainforest, 124, *229*, 245
Amazon River, *229*, 232, 245–46
American Revolutionary War (1775-
  83), 70–71
Amman, *141*, *149*, 150, *162*, 166
Amundsen, Roald, 258–59
Anatolian Plain, 171
Andaman Sea, *180–81*
Andes Mountains, *229*, 232–33
Angola, 64, *115*, 118, 122, 124,
  125–26, 132–33, 135, 137–38
Appalachian Mountains, 66–67, 69,
  70–72
Aqaba, *162*
Arabian Desert, 143
Arabian Sea, *141*, *180–81*, 183,
  188, 190, 192, *194*
Arab Spring, 45, 175–77
Arctic/Arctic Circle, 8–9, *254–55*,
  256–71

  climate and terrain, 257
  energy resources, 6–7, 35–36, 76,
    256, 262–63, 265, 268, 269–71
  expeditions, 257–59
  global warming effects, 256,
    259–61, *260*, 269, 275
  icebreakers, 267–68, 270
  New Great Game, 269–71
  and Russia, 6–7, 15, 16, 19, 256,
    257, 263, 264–68
  sovereignty disputes, 264–68
  and the United States, 256, 257,
    263, 267–68
Arctic Council, 263, 269–70
Arctic Ocean, 57, *254–55*, 257, 268
Arctic Sea, 8–9, 15
Argentina, *229*, 231, 234, 235, 243,
  246, 247–48, 249–52
Arizona, 66–67, 75, 236
Armenia, 8–9, 20–21, *30*, 32,
  90–91, *141*, *149*, 167
Armitage, Richard, 195
Arunachal Pradesh, 49, 202
Assad, Bashar al-, 153, 173
Assad, Hafez al-, 153
Assam, *188*, 190, 203
Atacama Desert, *229*
Atatürk, 172, 175
Athenian Empire, 1
Atlantic Ocean, 66–67, 70, *90–91*,
  115, 116–17, 120, *229*, 260
Australia, 5, 80, 83
Austria, 33, *90–91*, 95
Austro-Hungarian Empire, 94
Azerbaijan, 8–9, 18, 20, *30*, *141*,
  149

Babylonian Empire, 1
Baffin Island, *254–55*
Baghdad, 159

Bahamas, 66–67
Bahrain, 7, 82, 87, *141*
Balboa, Vasco Núñez de, 240
Balkan states, 3–4, 101–2
Baltic Sea, 8–9, 12, 16, 23, 29, 33,
    90–91, 96, 100, 112
Baltic States, 8–9, 14, 16, 18, 21,
    27–29, 32–33, *90–91*, 214
Baluchistan, *180–81*, 183, 187, *188*,
    189–90, 200
Bangladesh, *38–39*, 63, *180–81*,
    183–86, *188*, 274–75
Banks Island, *254–55*
Barents Sea, 8–9, *254–55*, 260, 264
Bashir, Omar al-, 135
Basra, *141*, 147
Bay of Bengal, *38–39*, 63, *180–81*,
    183, *188*, 205, 274
Bedouins, 150
Beijing, *38–39*
Belarus, 8–9, 20, 33, *90–91*
Belearic Islands, *90–91*
Belgium, *90–91*, 124, 126
Belize, 235, 237, *240*
Benghazi, 122–23
Bering Sea, 8–9, 11–12, 259, 268
Bering Strait, 8–9, 16–17, 57, 233,
    254–55, 258
Berlin Wall, 14
Bert, Melissa, 266
Bessarabia, 31
Bhutan, *38–39*, *180–81*, 183, *188*,
    202
Bhutto, Benazir, 196
bin Laden, Osama, 198, 201
Bismarck, Otto von, 89, 102
Bjarnason, Björn, 267
Black Sea, 8–9, 15, 16, 21, 23–24,
    27, 31, 33, *90–91*, 94, 95, *141*,
    173–74

Boko Haram/Wilayat al Sudan al
    Gharbi, 130–31
Bolivar, Simón, 234
Bolivia, *229*, 234–35
Borneo, *58*
Bosnia-Herzegovina, 3, *90–91*, 95
Bosporus, 23, 174
Botswana, *115*, 137
Brahmaputra River, 184
Brasília, 246
Brazil, 88, *229*, 231, 232, 233, 234,
    243, 245–49, 250
Brazilian Shield, 246
BRICS (Brazil, Russia, China, and
    South Africa), 249
Brunei, *58*, 61
Buenos Aires, 247, 250, 252
Bulgaria, 14, 21, *30*, 33–34, *90–91*,
    94, 95, 102, *141*
Burma, *38–39*, 44, 48, 63–64, 82,
    180–81, 183, *188*, 202, 204
Burundi, *115*, 125, 126–27, 138–39
Bush, George W., 5, 199
Byrnes, James, 213

Calcutta, 186, 187
California, 66–67, 71, 73, 75–76,
    236
Cambodia, *58*
Cameroon, *115*, 131–32
Canada
    and Arctic/Arctic Circle, *254–55*,
        257, *260*, 263, 265, 268–69
    and the United States, 66–67,
        69, 70
Canadian Shield, 69
Canute, King, 274–75
Cape Horn, *229*, 232
Cape of Good Hope, *115*, 117, 138
Carey, Mariah, 135

Caribbean Sea, 63, 76–77, 88, *229*, 240

Carpathian Mountains, 8–9, 12, 16, *30*, 30–31, *90–91*, *95*, 100, 112

Carter, Ash, 62

Caspian Sea, 8–9, 15, 16, *141*, *149*, 167, 173–74, 189

Catherine the Great, 15–16, 26

Caucasus, 15, 16, *30*, 32

Celebes Sea, *58*

Central African Republic, *115*, 118, 125

Central America, *229*, *240*. *See also* Latin America *and names of specific countries*

Central American Free Trade Agreement, 244

Central Plain/North Central Plan, 41–43

Cerrado, *229*

Chad, *115*, 118, 123, 131–32

Charles XIII, 13

Charlie Hebdo massacre (2015), 111

Cha, Victor, 216

Chechnya, 15, 18, *30*, 196

Chiang Kai-shek, 45

Chile, *229*, *231*, *232*, 234–35, 244–45, 246

China, 8–9, 38–39, *40–65*, 58, *180–81*, *183*, *207*
  and Africa, 64, 88, 125, 129, 132, 133–37
  Air Defense Identification Zone, 59–61, 85, 225
  annexation of Tibet, 7, 43, 45–46, 49–51, 52, 53, 190, 201–2
  and Arctic/Arctic Circle, 263
  as BRICS country, 249

deep-water port investments, 63

energy resources, 52–53, 61–62, 64, 85–87

food production, 55

and India, 2–3, 48–50, 190, 201–5, 274

and Japan, 45, 58–59, 220–22, 224–27

and Korea, 208–10, 212–14, 217–18, 227

land reclamation, 61–62, 85

languages, 42, 52

laser technology, 276–77

and Latin America, 88, 240, 241–43, 244–45, 249

naval capacity, 6, 40–41, 56–63, 61–62, 83, 85, 86, 87, 205

and Pakistan, 48, 52, 53, 61, 63, 189–90, 191

railway to Tibet, 50–51

and Russia, 18, 35–37, 47

size, 41, 42–43, 49, 65

space exploration, 57, 276

and United Kingdom, 45, 46

and the United States, 40–41, 59–65, 82–87

Chou En-lai, 54–55

Christians and Christianity, 75, 95, 147–48, 151, 175, 187, 203

Chukchi Sea, *254–55*, 259

Churchill, Winston, 12

Clinton, Hillary, 83

Cold War, 86, 98, 112, 124–25, 212–14, 219, 235, 249, 265–66

Collective Security Treaty Organization (CSTO), 20–21

Colombia, *229*, *232*, 238, 244–45

Colorado, *66–67*, 75

coltan, 126

Communism, 13–14, 16, 18, 36–37, 45–50, 54–55, 86, 88, 132–33, 176, 209–14, 223

Confucius, 43

Congo, *115*, 118

Congo Rainforest, 124

Congo River, *115*, 119

Congress of Vienna (1815), 103

Conrad, Joseph, 123

Costa Rica, *240*

cotton, 192

Crete, *90–91*

Crimea, 13, *22–27*, *30*, 31, 34, 37, 106–7, 112

Crimean War (1853-56), 13, 31

Croatia, 3, *90–91*, 94, 95, 102

Cuba, 66–67, 85, 88, *240*
    and Africa, 133
    and the United States, 76–77, 85, 88, 209
    culture wars, 109–11
    Cyprus, *90–91*, *141*, *149*, 174
    Cyrenaica, 123
    Czech Republic, 14, 21, 33, 34, *90–91*, 95

DAESH (*Dawlat al-Islamiya f'al-Iraq wa al-Shams*), 155–56

Dagestan, 18

Dalai Lama, 49, 53, 190, 201–2

Damascus, 153, 166, 169

Danube River, 31, *90–91*, 93–94, 95, 119

Dardanelles Strait, 174

Dead Sea, *162*

Declaration of Independence (1776), 71

demilitarized zone (DMZ), in Korea, 214–18

Democratic People's Republic of Korea (DPRK). *See* North Korea

Democratic Republic of the Congo (DRC), *115*, 122, 123–26, 133–35, 137–38

Deng Xiaoping, 46

Denmark, 8–9, *23*, *90–91*, 102, 105, 110, 263, 265, 268–69

Destroyers for Bases Agreement, 79, 82

"developing world," 123–24

Devon Island, *254–55*

Dharamsala, 202

Diamond, Jared, 116, 119

Diaoyu/Senkaku Islands, *38–39*, 59, 225

Diego Garcia, 7

Dnieper River, 14, 27, *30*, *30*

Dniester River, 31

Dokdo/Takeshima Islands, *207*, 220

Dominican Republic, 76

drones, 131, 156–58, 195–96, 199

drugs, 237–39

Durand Line, 194, *194*

Durand, Mortimer, 194

East African Community (EAC), 134, 138

East China Sea, *38–39*, *40–41*, 47–48, 57, 59, 79, 219, 220, 225

East Coast Plain (U.S.), 66–67, 69

East Siberian Sea, *254–55*

East Turkestan, 53–54

economic crisis of 2008, 81, 97, 98–99, 105, 109, 112–13

Economic Exclusion Zone (EEZ), 263, 264, 268

Ecuador, *229*, 232, 235, 243

EEZ (Economic Exclusion Zone), 263, 264, 268
Egypt, *115*, 127–28, *141*, 144, *149*, *162*, 164, 166–67, 169, 173, 174, 177–78
   Grand Ethiopian Renaissance Dam, 129
   Suez Canal, 23, 80, *115*, 117, 127–28
   Suez Crisis (1956), 80
Elbe River, *90–91*, 104
Elburz Mountains, 167
Elizabeth Islands, *254–55*
Ellesmere Island, *254–55*, 268
El Salvador, *240*
energy resources
   in Africa, 64, 128, 129–30, 132, 133–35, 139
   in Arctic/Arctic Circle, 6–7, 35–36, 76, 256, 262–63, 265, 268, 269–71
   and China, 52–53, 61–62, 64, 85–87
   hydroelectricity, 64, 127, 129, 139, 232
   in Japan, 222–23
   in Latin America, 237, 241, 247, 250–51, 252
   liquefied natural gas (LNG), 34, 35
   in the Middle East, 143, 159, 167, 168–69, 170, 174
   nuclear production, 168–69, 170, 267, 269
   in Pakistan, 189, 192
   and Russia, 26, 29, 31–37
   shale gas production, 34, 87, 241, 250–51, 252
   in United States, 34, 86–87, 89
English Channel, 102–3, 107–8
Erdoğan, Recep Tayyip, 173, 175, 183

Eritrea, *115*, 118, 125, 127, *141*
Estonia, 8–9, 14, 16, 18, 21, 27–29, 33, *90–91*, *254–55*
Ethiopia, 64, *115*, 127, 128–29, 136, *141*
ethnic Russians, 24–29, 31
Euphrates River, *141*, 143, 147, 275
Eurasian Economic Union, 20
Europe. *See* Western Europe
European Union (EU), 68–69, 81, 104–13
   Brexit vote (2016), 81, 109
   challenges, 109–12
   formation, 104–5
   members, 97, 99–100, 102, 104–13, 171–72, 175
   and Russia, 21–22, 26
   "Schengen Area," 110
   and the United Kingdom (UK), 81, 104–5, 107–8, 109–10
ExxonMobil, 262

Falkland Islands/Las Malvinas, 248, 251–52
Federally Administered Tribal Areas, 188
Fezzan, 123
Finland, 8–9, 32–33, *90–91*, 102, *254–55*, 257, 260, 263
First World War, 78, 143, 144, 148, 149–51, 161, 172
Florida, *66–67*, 73–74, 76–77, 274
fracking, 87
France, *90–91*, 93, 100–101, 172
   and Africa, 131–32
   climate and terrain, 96, 102–4
   and Germany, 102–4, 111–12
   Louisiana Territory, 72–73, 74
   in the Middle East, 144, 151, 152–53

and Russia, 13, 35–36, 173–74
terrorist attacks, 109–11, 157
Triple Entente (1907), 103–4, 144
and the United Kingdom, 80
Franco, Francisco, 97
Franco-Prussian War, 103
Franklin, John, 258
Franz Josef Land, 8–9
Free Tibet Movement, 49–51, 52
French Guiana (France), 229, 232

Gagarin, Yuri, 275–76
Gambia, 115, 118
Ganges River, 180–81, 184, 186
Gaza Strip, 162, 163, 164–65
geopolitics, nature and importance
    of, 2–7
Georges-Picot, François, 144
Georgia (country), 8–9, 18, 21,
    27–28, 30, 32, 82, 90–91, 112,
    141
Georgia (U.S.), 70
Gere, Richard, 49–50
Germany, 14, 90–91, 95, 98–107,
    113
  Catholicism versus Protestantism,
    95
  and the European Union (EU),
    105–6
  and France, 102–4, 111–12
  and Greece, 95, 98–99, 105–6
  reunification, 111, 218
  and Russia, 13, 26, 33, 100, 106,
    112
  Triple Entente (1907), 103–4,
    144
  and the United States, 79
Gilgit, 194
GIUK (Greenland/Iceland/UK) gap,
    23, 90–91, 108, 266

global warming effects, 256, 259–61,
    260, 269, 275
Gobi Desert, 38–39, 42, 46–47
Golan Heights, 162, 167
gold, 76
Gorbachev, Mikhail, 14
Grand Canal, 38–39, 43
Grand Escarpment, 246, 247
Grand Ethiopian Renaissance Dam,
    129
Great Britain. See United Kingdom
    (UK)
Great Lakes, 66–67, 75
Great Plains (U.S.), 66–67, 69
Great Rift Valley, 125
Great Wall/Long Wall of China,
    43–44
Great Zimbabwe, 120
Greece, 33, 90–91, 97–99, 174
  and the European Union (EU),
    105, 106
  and Germany, 95, 98–99, 105–6
  and Russia, 36, 98
Greek Empire, 123
Greenland, 36, 117, 254–55, 257,
    260, 263, 268
  GIUK (Greenland/Iceland/
    UK) gap, 23, 90–91, 108,
    266
Greenland Sea, 254–55, 260
Gregorian calendar, 172
Guam, 77, 79
Guatemala, 235, 237, 240
Guiana, 235
Gujarat, 185
Gulf of Aden, 141
Gulf of Mexico, 66–67, 69, 72–73,
    77, 237, 240, 274
Gulf of Thailand, 58
Gulf Stream, 92

Guyana, 229
Gwadar, 53, 61, 63, *180–81*, 189, 205

Hainan, *38–39*, 45–46, 58
Hama, 5, 153
Hanbal, Ahmad ibn, 145–46
Han Chinese, 41–46, 49–56
Hannibal, 5
Hans Island, 268–69
Harper, Stephen, 265
Hashemite Kingdom (Jordan), 149–50, 160–61, 163
Hassan (grandson of Muhammad), 145
Hausa, 130–31
Hawaii, 77
Herodotus, 127
heroin, 237–39
Hezbollah, 151–52, 166, 169
Himachal Pradesh, 202
Himalayas, 2–3, *38–39*, 48–50, *180–81*, 183, 184, 192, 201, 204, 274
Hindu Kush, 3, 19, *180–81*, 183
Hindus and Hinduism, 185–86, 187
Hiroshima, *207*, 223
Hispanic ethnic group, 75, 88, 236
Hitchens, Christopher, 208
Hitler, Adolf, 13, 99
HIV, 119
Hokkaido, *38–39*, 58–59, *207*
Holocaust, 162
Holy Roman Empire, 103
Homestead Act (1862), 76
Honduras, *240*
Hong Kong, *38–39*, 46, 58, 60
Honshu, *38–39*, *207*
Hudson, Henry, 257
Hu Jintao, 50

human rights, 49–50, 54–55, 64, 75–76, 82, 109–10, 135, 171–72, 175
Hungary, 3–4, 14, 21, 33, *90–91*, 94, 95
Hussein (grandson of Muhammad), 145, 146
Hussein, Saddam, 147–48, 170
Hutu, 125–27
hydroelectricity, 64, 127, 129, 139, 232

Iberian Peninsula, *90–91*, 93
icebreakers, 267–68, 270
Iceland, 8–9, 80, *90–91*, *254–55*, 257, *260*, 263, 266–67, 270
  GIUK (Greenland/Iceland/UK) gap, 23, *90–91*, 108, 266
immigrant populations, 109–10, 151
India, *38–39*, 83, 117, 178, *180–81*, 182–205, *188*, *194*. *See also* Pakistan
  and Arctic/Arctic Circle, 263
  as BRICS country, 249
  and China, 2–3, 48–50, 190, 201–5, 274
  climate and terrain, 183–84
  colonial period, 184, 185–86, 194
  languages, 184, 185
  naval capacity, 205
  nuclear weapons, 182–83, 184, 190–91
  rivers, *180–81*, 184, 185
  separatist movements, 203
  size, 182, 203
  and the United States, 204–5
Indian Ocean, 19, 56, 61, 63, *115*, 116–17, 119, 120, 183
individual rights, 54–55
Indochina, 44, 47–48, 61, 222–23

Indonesia, 5, 55, *58*, 61, 83, 86
Indus River, *180–81*, 184, 185, 186, 192, *194*
Inner Mongolia, *38–39*, 41, 45–47, 51
Inter-American Democratic Charter, 244
International Criminal Court, 135–36
Internet, 7, 155, 248
Iran, *8–9*, 30, *141*, 144, *149*, 166–71, 178, *180–81*, *194*
nuclear capabilities, 87, 168–70
and Turkey, 173
Iraq, 7, *8–9*, 81, 88, *141*, 143, 144, 146–49, *149*, 152, 156–59, 169, 170, 178
Ireland, *90–91*
ISIS. *See* Islamic State/ISIS
Islam. *See also* Muslims
  Salafi, 145–46, 159–60
  Shia, 145–47, 151–52, 159, 168–69, 170–71, 187
  Sunni, 145–47, 151–54, 156, 158–59, 170–71
Islamabad, 192–93, *194*, 195–96, 198–201
Islamic State/ISIS, 110, 142, 154–61
Islamists, 88
  in Africa, 123, 128, 130–31, 136
  in India/Pakistan, 184, 186–87
  in the Middle East, 142, 154–61, 175, 176, 178
Israel, 128, *141*, 143, 144, *149*, 150, 151, 161–62, *162*, 163–66, 174
  Iranian nuclear capabilities, 87, 168–70
  lack of strategic depth, 166
  and the United States, 87
Istanbul, 171

Italy, 33, 36, 80, *90–91*, 95, 96
Ivan the Great, 15
Ivan the Terrible, 15, 37

Jamaica, *240*
Japan, *8–9*, *38–39*, 40–41, 204, *207*, 220–27
  and Arctic/Arctic Circle, 263
  and Burma, 63–64
  and China, 45, 58–59, 220–22, 224–27
  climate and terrain, 221
  energy resources, 222–23
  and Korea, 208, 212, 213, 218–20, 221–22
  lack of natural resources, 6
  remilitarization, 85, 224–27
  and Russia, 58–59, 213, 222, 226
  space exploration, 276
  and the United States, 78, 79, 82–83, 85, 214, 222–24
Jefferson, Thomas, 72
Jerusalem, *141*, *149*, 161, *162*, 163–64
jihadists, 145–46, 154–61. *See also* Islamic State/ISIS
Jinnah, Muhammad Ali, 182
Jordan, *141*, 143, 144, *149*, 149–50, 160–61, *162*, 163

Kabul, 193, *194*, 198, 200
Kagan, Robert, 112
Kaliningrad, *8–9*, *90–91*, 112
Kamchatka Peninsula, *8–9*, *207*
Kang, David, 216
Kanuris, 130–31
Kaplan, Robert D., 63, 105
Karachi, 192, *194*
Karakoram Range, *38–39*, 48, *180–81*, 183

Kara Sea, 35, *254–55*

Kashmir, *188*, 188–89, 190, 191–92, 200

Kazakhstan, 8–9, 20, *30*, 36, *38–39*, 52, 82

Kazama, Shinji, 259

Kemal, Mustafa, 172

Kenya, 56, 64, *115*, 122, 127, 133–34, 136, 138

Khrushchev, Nikita, 24

Khuzestan, 168

Kiev, 14, 21, 22, 25, 27

Kill Zone, 266

Kim Jong-il, 211

Kim Jong-Un, 211

King William Island, *254–55*, 258

Kissinger, Henry, 101

Klitschko, Vitali, 22

Kohl, Helmut, 113

Korea, 8–9, *38–39*, 83, *207*, 208–20
 artificial borders in, *207*, 212–15, *215*
 and China, 208–10, 212–14, 217–18, 227
 founding story, 211
 and Japan, 208, 212, 213, 218–20, 221–22
 Korean War (1950-53), 80
 North/South division, 6, 208–20
 and the United States, 83–84, 208, 212–14, 227

Korea Strait, 220

Kosovo, 3–4, 106

Kublai Khan, 44

Kunlan Range, 50

Kunlun Shan, *38–39*

Kurds/Kurdistan, *141*, 144, 146–49, 154, 159, 171–72, 175

Kuril Islands, 58–59, *207*, 226, 266

Kuwait, 87, *141*, 143, 148

Kyrgyzstan, 8–9, 20–21, *38–39*, 52

Kyushu, *38–39*, *207*

Lake Baikal, 8–9

Lake Nicaragua, 242

Laos, *38–39*, 48, *58*, *180–81*

Laptev Sea, *254–55*

laser technology, 276–77

Las Malvinas/Falkland Islands, 248, 251–52

Latin alphabet, 172

Latin America, *229*, 230–53. *See also names of specific countries*
 agricultural lands, 246
 artificial borders in, 233–34
 border disputes, 234–35
 and China, 88, 240, 241–43, 244–45, 249
 climate and terrain, 230, 232, 236, 237, 246–47
 colonial development patterns, 230–32, 233–34
 compared with North America and Western Europe, 231–32
 energy resources, 237, 241, 247, 250–51, 252
 exploration period, 240
 independence movements, 234
 internal geography as problem, 6
 languages, 232–33, 236
 regional economic alliances, 244, 247–48
 rivers, *229*, 232, 245–46, 247
 and Russia, 35
 size, 230–31
 and the United States, 87–88, 240–41, 243–44, 245, 249

Latvia, 8–9, 14, 16, 18, 21, 27–29, 33, 90–91, *254–55*

Lebanon, 90–91, 128, *141*, *149*, 150–52, *162*, 166
Leopold, King of Belgium, 124, 125
Lhasa, *38–39*, 50, 51
Liberia, *115*, 133
Libya, 106, *115*, 122–23, 144, 176, 178
Liechtenstein, *90–91*
Limpopo River, 120
liquefied natural gas (LNG), 34, 35
Lithuania, 8–9, 14, 16, 21, 27–29, 33, 34, *90–91*
Little Diomede Island, 17
Louisiana Territory, 72–73, 74
Luzon, *38–39*, 58
L'viv, 22

Macau, 46
Macedonia, *90–91*, 95
Maginot Line, 100–101
malaria, 119, 137
Malawi, *115*, 137
Malaysia, 58, 61, 83, 86
Maldives, 275
Mali, *115*, 122
Mali Empire, 120
Manchuria, 36, *38–39*, 41, 45, 47, 51, 212, 222
Mandela, Nelson, 116
Mao, 45–46
Maoism, 202
Margvelashvili, Giorgi, 32
Marshall Plan (1948-51), 79
Mazar-e-Sharif, 4–5
Mbundu tribe, 132–33, 135
Mecca, *141*, 150, 168
Medina, *141*, 168
Mediterranean Sea, 36, *90–91*, 97, 98, *115*, 117–18, 120, *141*, *149*, *162*, 166, 174

Mekong River, *38–39*, 49
Melville Island, *254–55*
Mercator world map, 117
Mercosur, 247–48
Merkel, Angela, 99
Meseta Central, *90–91*, 95, 96–97
Mesopotamia, 143
Mexican War (1846-48), 75
Mexico, 231, 235–39, *240*, 244–45
    drugs, 237–39
    and the United States, 66–67, 70, 74–75, 235–37
Mexico City, 237, 239
Middle East, *141*, 142–79. *See also names of specific countries*
    African trade, 120
    Arab Spring, 45, 175–77
    artificial borders in, 6, *141*, 142–46, 150, *162*
    climate and terrain, 143, 166–68
    colonial period, 144–45, 149–51, 152–53, 160, 161–62
    energy resources, 143, 159, 167, 168–69, 170, 174
    and France, 144, 151, 152–53
    Gulf War conflicts, 148, 167, 169
    Islamists, 142, 154–61, 175, 176, 178
    Kurds/Kurdistan, *141*, 144, 146–49, 154, 159, 171–72, 175
    languages, 166, 168, 172, 177
    Ottoman Empire, 3, 15, 26, 31, 94, 121, 123, 144, 146–47, 149–50, 161, 173, 186
    Persian Empire, 15, 147, 169–70
    and Russia, 13, 35–36, 173–74
    Shia Islam, 145–47, 151–52, 159, 168–69, 170–71
    size, 143
    Suez Crisis (1956), 80

Middle East (*cont.*)
  Sunni Islam, 145–47, 151–54,
    156, 158–59, 170–71
  United Kingdom in, 144, 149–50,
    160, 161–62
  water supplies, 275
Mischief Islands, 61
Mississippi Basin, 66–67
Mississippi River, 66–67, 68, 72–74,
  75
Mitrovica, 3–4
Moldova, 8–9, 21, 28, 29–32, *30*,
  90–91, *95*
Mongolia, 8–9, 18, 38–39, 42–43,
  52
Mongols, 14–15, 44, 45–46, 167,
  212, 220
Monroe Doctrine (1823), 74–75,
  243–44
Monroe, James, 74–75, 243–44
Montenegro, *90–91*, *95*
Montreux Convention (1936), 23
Morales, Evo, 235
Moscow, 8–9, 12–16, 18, 33
Mouillot, Miranda Richmond, 92
Mozambique, *115*, 119, 137
Mubarak, Gamal, 177–78
Mubarak, Hosni, 177–78
Muhammad, 145, 163
Multan, *194*
Murat River, 275
Murmansk, 8–9, 19, *254–55*, 265
Musharraf, Pervez, 195–96
Muslim Brotherhood, 153, 173,
  177–78
Muslims
  in Africa, 118, 130–31
  in Albania, 3–4
  in European countries, 109–10,
    160

  in India/Pakistan, 184–86, 203
  in the Middle East, 88, 145–47,
    151–54, 156–60, 169–71
  Salafi, 145–46, 159–60
  Shia, 145–47, 151–52, 159,
    168–69, 170–71, 187
  Sunni, 145–47, 151–54, 156,
    158–59, 170–71
  Xinjiang, 44–45, 51–54

Nagaland, 203
Nagasaki, *207*, 223
Namibia, *115*, 118, 126
Napoleon, 13, 73, 96
Native Americans, 71, 73–74,
  75–76
NATO. *See* North Atlantic Treaty
  Organization (NATO)
Nepal, *38–39*, *180–81*, 183, *188*,
  202
Neruda, Pablo, 230
Netherlands, *90–91*
Nevada, 66–67, 75
New Cold War, 30
New Great Game, 269–71
New Mexico, 75, 236
New Orleans, 66–67, 72–73, 74, 75,
  77, 247
"New Russia," 26
New Zealand, 80
Nicaragua, *240*
Nicaragua Grand Canal (develop-
  ment site), 88, *240*, 241–43
Niger, *115*, 118, 134–35
Nigeria, *115*, 120, 122, 129–32
Niger River, *115*, 119, 130
Nile River, 42, *115*, 119, 127–28
Nimr al-Nimr, 170–71
Nixon, Richard, 54–55, 238
Nkurunziza, Pierre, 126–27

Nobile, Umberto, 259
North American Free Trade Association, 244
North Atlantic Treaty Organization (NATO)
  in Afghanistan, 4–5, 195–200
  in Balkan states, 3–4
  formation, 13–14, 79–82, 104
  members, 13–14, 23, 26, 27–29, 32, 36, 79–82, 89, 101, 102, 107, 111, 174, 192, 264–65, 266
  and Russia, 21–32, 36, 100
North China Plain/Central Plain, 41–43
Northern Sea Route, 260, 261–62
North European Plain, 1, 8–9, 12–13, 19, 21–22, 31, 37, 79, 90–91, 94, 96, 100, 102, 103, 112, 273–74
North Korea, 209–14. See also Korea
  isolation of, 210–12
  nuclear weapons, 209, 215–18
North Pole, 258, 259, 264
North Sea, 23, 90–91, 96, 112
North-West Frontier, 183, 186, 188, 193, 195–96, 199, 200
Northwest Passage, 257–59, 260, 261–62
Norway, 8–9, 23, 80, 90–91, 254–55, 257, 260, 263, 264–65
Norwegian Sea, 8–9, 90–91, 254–55
Novaya Zemlya, 8–9
Novorossiysk, 23
Novosibirsk Islands, 8–9, 265
nuclear energy, 168–69, 170, 267, 269
nuclear weapons, 52–53, 84, 112, 201, 223

and India, 182–83, 184, 190–91
and Iran, 87, 168–70
and North Korea, 209, 215–18
and Pakistan, 182–83, 184, 190–91

Obama, Barack, 50, 63–64, 81, 87, 127, 136, 199, 204–5, 249, 267–68
Oberdorfer, Don, 213
Odessa, 30
Ohio, 66–67
Ohio River, 66–67, 71–72
oil. See energy resources
Okinawa, 38–39, 59, 79, 85, 223, 225, 226, 227
Oman, 141, 143
Oregon, 66–67, 73
Organization of American States (OAS), 244
"Orientalism," 177
Ortega, Daniel, 242
Ottoman Empire, 3, 15, 26, 31, 94, 121, 123, 144, 146–47, 149–50, 161, 173, 186
Özal, Turgut, 173

Pacific Ocean, 8–9, 58, 64, 66–67, 69, 71, 73, 77, 207, 229, 240, 254–55, 260
Pakistan, 38–39, 180–81, 182–205, 188, 194. See also India
  artificial borders in, 6, 190–91, 194, 194
  and China, 48, 52, 53, 61, 63, 189–90, 191
  colonial period, 190
  energy resources, 189, 192
  lack of strategic depth, 192
  languages, 187–88

Pakistan (*cont.*)
  nuclear weapons, 182–83, 184, 190–91
  Taliban, 197–201
Palawan, *58*
Palestine, *141*, 144, *149*, 150, 151, 161–62, *162*
Palin, Sarah, 16–17
Panama, *240*, 240–41
Panama Canal, 77, 88, *240*, 240–41, 242–43, 261–62
Pan-American Highway, 238
Papoulias, Karolas, 98–99
Paracel Islands, *58*
Paraguay, *229*, 247–48, 250
Parry, William Edward, 258
Pashtuns, 187, 188, 194–95, 196, 197–99, 200, 201
Pearl Harbor, 223
People's Republic of China (PRC). *See* China
Persian Empire, 15, 147, 169–70
Persian Gulf, *141*, 169
Peru, *229*, 231, 232, 235, 244–45
Peshawar, *194*, 194–95, 200
Peter the Great, 15–16, 19, 37
petroleum. *See* energy resources
Philippines, *38–39*, *58*, 61, 77, 85, 204, 214, 223
Poland, 8–9, 12–13, 14, 21, 22, 28, 31, 33, 34, *90–91*, 95, 100–101, 214
Portugal, *90–91*, 93, 94, 132, 137, 233–34, 246
Powell, Colin, 195
Pratas Reef, *58*
Puerto Rico, 76, 77
Punjab, 184, 185, 187, 188, *188*, 193, 199, 200, 203
Putin, Vladimir, 1, 12, 14, 21–29, 34, 35, 37, 81, 101, 265, 266

Pye, Lucian, 40
Pyongyang, *207*, 211, *215*, 217, 219
Pyrenees, *90–91*, 93, 94, 97
Pytheas of Massalia, 257

Qaradawi, Yusuf al-, 178
Qatar, 87, *141*, 178
Quetta, *194*

railways, 11–12, 18, 50–51, 64, 76, 133–35, 137, 139–40
rainforests, 124, *229*, 245–46
Ramadi, *141*, 156, 157, 159
Red Sea, 118, *141*
Reid, John, 197
Republic of Korea (ROK). *See* South Korea
Rhine River, *90–91*, 104, 119
Rhodesia, 122
Rhône River, *90–91*, 95, 96
rice, 42–43
Rio de Janeiro, *229*, 246
Rio de la Plata region, 247, 250
Rio Grande River, 66–67, 75, 236, *240*
River Ibar, 3–4
Rocky Mountains, 66–67, 69
Roman Empire, 94, 123
Romania, 14, 21, 24, 30, *90–91*, 94, 95, 102, *141*
Roosevelt, Theodore "Teddy," 77–78, 84, 244
Rosneft, 262
Rousseff, Dilma, 249
Rub al Khali, *141*, 143
rubber, 125, 223
Russia, 11–37, *30*, *38–39*, *90–91*, *141*, *207*, 233, *254–55*, 260. *See also* USSR
  and Africa, 36, 132–33

and Arctic/Arctic Circle, 6–7, 15, 16, 19, 256, 257, 263, 264–68
artificial borders in, 8–9
as BRICS country, 249
and China, 18, 35–37, 47
and Crimea, 22–27, 34, 106–7, 112
economic problems of 1990s, 81–82
energy resources, 26, 29, 31–37
ethnic Russians, 24–29, 31
and Georgia, 32
and Germany, 13, 26, 33, 100, 106, 112
and Greece, 36, 98
and Japan, 58–59, 213, 222, 226
lack of warm-water port, 19, 22–27, 34, 81, 106–7, 112, 189
languages, 24–29, 31
and Latin America, 35
and Middle East, 13, 35–36, 173–74
and Moldova, 21, 28, 29–32
and NATO, 21–32, 36, 100
naval capacity, 23–24, 29, 108, 174, 266–67
North European Plain, 1, 8–9, 12–13, 19, 21–22, 31, 37, 100, 273–74
size, 14–18, 36–37
strategic depth, 12–13, 69
and Syria, 23, 36
Triple Entente (1907), 103–4, 144
and Turkey, 34, 85, 173–74
and Ukraine, 1, 8–9, 14–16, 20, 21–22, 24–27, 30, 31, 33–34, 47, 81, 100, 106–7, 112
and the United States, 29, 32, 81–82
and Western Europe, 99–100

Russian Far East, 13, 47
Russian Federation, 18
Russo-Japanese War (1904-5), 213
Rwanda, 115, 125–26, 127, 133–34, 138–39
Ryukyu Islands, 38–39, 59, 207, 223, 225

Saakashvili, Mikheil, 32
Sagan, Carl, 273
Sahara Desert, 115, 116–17, 118, 120, 131
Sahel, 115, 118, 121, 131, 275
Said, Edward, 177
Sakhalin, 8–9, 38–39, 207
Salafi Islam, 145–46, 159–60
salt, 120, 121
San Martín, José de, 234
Santos, José Eduardo dos, 135
São Tomé and Principe, 60, 115
Saudi Arabia, 87, 115, 132, 141, 143, 149, 150, 160, 170–71, 178
Sava River, 90–91, 93–94, 95
Schäuble, Wolfgang, 98–99
Scotland, 108, 109
Sea of Azov, 27
Sea of Galilee, 162, 166
Sea of Japan, 8–9, 19, 47, 58–59, 207, 215, 217–19, 220
Sea of Marmara, 174
Sea of Okhotsk, 8–9, 207, 220
Second World War, 13–14, 16, 45, 78–79, 96–99, 100–101, 104, 106, 113, 126, 162, 222–26
Seine River, 90–91, 95, 96
Senkaku Islands/Diaoyu, 38–39, 59, 225
Seoul, 207, 215, 215–18
September 11, 2001 terrorist attacks, 28, 195, 199, 201

Serbia, 3–4, 33, 90–91, 94, 95, 101
Sevastopol, 22–27, 30
Severnaya Zemlya, 8–9
Seward, William, 76
shale gas production, 34, 87, 241, 250–51, 252
Shanghai, 44, 59
Shatt al-Arab, 167, 168
Shell, 262
Shia Islam, 145–47, 151–52, 159, 168–69, 170–71, 187
Shihezi, 53
Shikoku, 207
Siachen Glacier, 190
Siberia, 8–9, 11–12, 15, 17–18, 254–55
Sierra Madre Occidental, 237, 240
Sierra Nevada Mountains, 66–67, 69
Sikhs, 184, 185–86, 203
Silk Route, 52–53
Sinai Peninsula, 162, 166
Sindh, 187, 188, 188, 200
Singapore, 58, 61, 83, 86
Singh, Amarjit, 183
Skagerrak Strait, 23, 266
slavery
    in Africa, 121
    in China, 43–44
Slovakia, 14, 21, 33, 90–91, 94, 95
Slovenia, 90–91, 95, 102
Somalia, 115, 122, 136, 141
South Africa, 115, 118, 132, 136–39, 249
South African Development Community (SADC), 138
South America, 229. See also Latin America and names of specific countries
South China Sea, 38–39, 43, 47–48, 57–58, 58, 59–63, 85, 204
Southern Cone, 233, 246

South Korea, 83, 209, 212–22. See also Korea
South Ossetia, 32, 112
Soviet Union, former. See USSR
soybeans, 42–43, 246
space exploration, 57, 275–76
Spain, 90–91, 93, 94, 96–97, 172
    in Latin America, 233
    and the United States, 71, 73–77
Spratly Islands, 58, 61, 62, 85
Sri Lanka, 63, 180–81, 188
Stalin, Joseph, 20, 31, 37
Stefansson, Vilhjalmur, 256
St. Petersburg, 8–9, 17
Strait of Dover, 108
Strait of Gibraltar, 23
Strait of Hormuz, 108, 141, 167, 169
Strait of Malacca, 58, 61, 63, 86, 108, 189, 205
Straits of Florida, 77
Sudan, 115, 121, 122, 127, 128, 129, 133–34, 135, 141, 275
Suez Canal, 23, 80, 115, 117, 127–28
Sulu Sea, 58
Sumatra, 58
Sunni Islam, 145–47, 151–54, 156, 158–59, 170–71
Sunni Triangle, 159
Sun Tzu, 5
Surinam, 229
Svalbard Islands (Norway), 8–9, 264
Sweden, 8–9, 13, 90–91, 102, 110, 254–55, 257, 260, 263
Switzerland, 90–91, 95
Sykes, Mark, 144
Syria, 7, 8–9, 82, 90–91, 141, 143, 144–45, 149, 149–54, 156, 157, 162, 166, 173–74, 178. See also Islamic State/ISIS

civil war, 5
and Russia, 23, 36

Taiwan/Republic of China (ROC),
    38–39, 40–41, 45–46, 57–58,
    58, 59–61, 61, 86, 222, 243
Tajikistan, 4–5, 8–9, 20–21, 38–39,
    48, 52, 53
Takeshima/Dokdo Islands, 207, 220
Taliban, 4–5, 193–201, 238–39
Tamil Nadu, 184
Tanzania, 115, 118, 120, 125, 126,
    127, 134, 137, 138
Tehran, 87, 141, 167–68, 171, 176
Tel Aviv, 162, 165
terrorism, 28, 109–11, 130–31, 157,
    195, 199, 201, 270
Texas, 66–67, 71, 74–75, 236
Thailand, 38–39, 55, 58, 83,
    180–81, 204
Thar Desert, 180–81, 192
Theroux, Paul, 50
Thule, 254–55, 257
Tiananmen Square massacre (1989), 46
Tibet, 7, 38–39, 43, 45–46, 49–51,
    52, 53, 190, 192, 201–2
Tibetan Plateau, 38–39, 42, 49
Tierra del Fuego, 229, 232
Tigris River, 141, 143, 147
Tikrit, 141, 147, 156, 159
Transjordan, 150
Transnistria, 30, 31, 112
Transylvanian Alps, 30–31
Treaty of Paris (1856), 31
Treaty of Tordesillas (1494), 233–34
Triple Entente (1907), 103–4, 144
Tripolitania, 122–23
Truman, Harry, 213
Turkey, 8–9, 30, 33, 90–91, 97, 141,
    149, 154, 167, 169, 171–75

control of Bosporus, 23, 174–75
and Iran, 173
and Russia, 34, 85, 173–74
water supplies, 275
Turkmenistan, 8–9, 20, 141, 167
Tutsi, 125–27
Twain, Mark, 68

Uganda, 115, 118, 125, 127, 133–34,
    138–39
Uighur people, 51–54
Ukraine, 1, 6, 8–9, 14–16, 20,
    21–22, 24–27, 30, 30, 31,
    33–34, 47, 81, 90–91, 95, 100,
    106–7, 112
Umayyid Caliphate, 147, 185
UNASUR, 248
United Arab Emirates (UAE), 87,
    141, 156
United Kingdom (UK), 90–91,
    100–101, 107–9
in Afghanistan, 196–97
Brexit vote in EU (2016), 81, 109
and China, 45, 46
colonial period, 46, 70–71
energy dependency, 33
and the European Union (EU),
    81, 104–5, 107–8, 109–10
Falkland Islands/Las Malvinas,
    248, 251–52
and France, 80
GIUK (Greenland/Iceland/UK)
    gap, 23, 90–91, 108, 266
and Iceland, 270
immigrants, 109–10
in India/Pakistan, 184, 185–86,
    190, 194
in the Middle East, 144, 149–50,
    160, 161–62
naval capacity, 79, 82, 108–9

United Kingdom (UK) (*cont.*)
  Triple Entente (1907), 103–4, 144
  and the United States, 70–71, 79, 82, 252
United Nations (UN)
  Convention on the Law of the Sea (UNCLOS), 263, 268
  Human Development Index, 125
  and Korea, 214
  peacekeeping missions, 126
  Security Council, 27, 135, 138, 247
  Taiwan and, 243
United States, 66–67, 68–89. *See also names of specific states*
  and Afghanistan, 4–5, 88, 201
  and Africa, 88, 131–32
  and Arctic/Arctic Circle, 256, 257, 263, 267–68
  and Canada, 66–67, 69, 70
  and China, 40–41, 59–65, 82–87
  Cold War, 86, 98, 112, 124–25, 212–14, 219, 249, 265–66
  colonial period, 70–71
  and Cuba, 76–77, 85, 88, 209
  drones, 131, 156–58, 195–96, 199
  and drugs, 237–39
  energy resources, 34, 86–87, 89
  geography in dictating foreign policy, 7
  and Germany, 79
  Hispanic population, 75, 88, 236
  and India, 204–5
  and Iran, 87
  and Iraq, 88
  and Israel, 87
  and Japan, 78, 79, 83, 85, 214, 222–24
  and Korea, 84, 208, 212–14, 227
  languages, 75, 87, 93, 236
  laser technology, 276–77
  and Latin America, 88, 240–41, 242–43, 243–44, 245, 249
  and Mexico, 66–67, 70, 74–75, 235–37
  Native American nations, 71, 73–74, 75–76
  naval capacity, 40–41, 56–57, 76–78, 79, 82, 83, 87–88, 169, 227, 237
  prospects for, 68, 89
  and Russia, 29, 32, 81–82
  September 11, 2001 terrorist attacks, 28, 195, 199, 201
  size, 42–43, 72–73
  space exploration, 276
  and Spain, 71, 73–77
  strategic depth, 6, 66–67, 68–77
  and United Kingdom, 70–71, 79, 252
U.S. Geological Survey, 262
Ural Mountains, 8–9, 11–13, 15–17, 29, 96
Uruguay, 229, 244–45, 246, 247–48, 250
Ürümqi, 38–39, 53, 60
USSR, 13–14, 16. *See also* Russia
  Afghanistan invasion (1979), 18–19, 189, 193
  Cold War, 86, 98, 112, 124–25, 212–14, 219, 249, 265–66
  collapse of, 17, 19–21, 29, 31, 36, 52, 99, 267
  Cuban Missile Crisis (1962), 76–77, 85
  space exploration, 275–76

Utah, 66–67, 75
Uzbekistan, 8–9, 20, *141*

Vaca Muerta shale formation,
    250–51, 252
Venezuela, 35, *229*, 232, 234, 235,
    241, 243, 244–45, 247–48, 249
Victoria Island, *254–55*
Vietnam, *38–39*, 48, *58*, 61, 80, 83,
    85, 204
Vladivostok, 8–9, 19, *38–39*, 47, 208
Voltaire, 110–11

Wang Jing, 241–42
War of the Pacific (1879), 234
Warsaw Pact, 13–14, 21, 101
Washington, George, 78
water supplies, 49, 92, 127–29, 139,
    192, 221, 232, 246, 247, 275
West Bank, 150, *162*, 163–65
Western Europe, *90–91*, 92–113. *See
    also* European Union (EU) *and
    names of specific countries*
  climate and terrain, 6, 92–96,
    102–4
  industrialization and trade,
    93–94, 96–97, 104–5, 107–8
  Latin America compared with,
    231–32
  north-south divide, 92–106

West Siberian Plain, 8–9, 18
Wilayat al Sudan al Gharbi/Boko
    Haram, 130–31
wine, 31–32
World Bank, 35

Xhosas, 122
Xi Jinping, 57
Xinjiang, *38–39*, 44–45, 51–54

Yalu River, *207*, 209, 212, 214,
    217
Yangtze River, *38–39*, 41, 43, 49
Yanukovych, Viktor, 21–22, 106–7
yellow fever, 119
Yellow River, *38–39*, 41–42, 43, 49
Yellow Sea, 8–9, *38–39*, 47–48,
    58–59, *207*
Yeltsin, Boris, 101
Yemen, *115*, *141*, 143, 178
Yugoslavia, 3–4, 101

Zagros Mountains, *141*, 167, 168
Zaire, *115*, 124–25
Zambezi River, *115*, 119, 120
Zambia, *115*, 125, 133, 134, 137
Zheng He, 56
Zhrinovsky, Vladimir, 19
Zimbabwe, *115*, 122, 126, 137
Zulus, 122

Turn the page for a sample chapter from Tim Marshall's new book,

A Flag Worth Dying For:
The Power and Politics of National Symbols

Coming from Scribner in hardcover and ebook in summer 2017

INTRODUCTION

I am no more than what you believe me to be,
and I am all that you believe I can be.
—The American flag in a conversation as imagined by Franklin K. Lane,
United States secretary of the interior, Flag Day, 1914

On the day of 9/11, after the flames had died down and the dust had mostly settled, three FDNY firefighters clambered onto the still-smoking wreckage of the World Trade Center in New York City and raised the Stars and Stripes.

The event was not planned; there were no official photographers. The three men just felt that amid such death and destruction they should do "something good." A local newspaper photographer called Thomas Franklin captured the moment. Later he commented that his picture "said something to me about the strength of the American people."

How could a piece of colored cloth say something so profound that the photo was reproduced not only across the United States, but in newspapers around the world? The flag's meaning comes from the emotion it inspires. Old Glory, as the Americans know it, speaks to them in ways that a non-American simply cannot share; but we can understand this because many of us will have similar feelings about our own symbols of nationhood and belonging. You may have overtly positive, or indeed negative, opinions as to what you think your flag stands for, but the fact remains: that simple piece of cloth is the embodiment of the nation. A country's history, geography, people, and values—all are symbolized in the cloth, its shape, and the colors in which it is printed. It is invested with meaning, even if the meaning is different for different people.

Each of the world's flags is simultaneously unique and similar. They all say something—sometimes perhaps too much.

That was the case in October 2014 when the Serbian national football team hosted Albania at the Partizan Stadium in Belgrade. It was Albania's first visit to the Serbian capital since 1967. The intervening years had witnessed the Yugoslav civil war, including the conflict with the ethnic Albanians in Kosovo. That ended in 1999 with the de facto partition of Serbia, following a three-month NATO bombing of Serb forces, towns, and cities. Then, in 2008, Kosovo unilaterally declared itself an independent state. The move was supported by Albania and recognized by many countries—but, notably, Spain was one that did not. It understood that the sight of the Kosovar flag flying above the capital of an independent Kosovo might galvanize the Catalonian independence movement.

Fast-forward six years and tensions between Serbia and Kosovo, and by extension Albania, were still high. In the certain knowledge that they would be attacked, away fans had not been allowed to attend.

It was a slow-paced game, albeit with a highly charged atmosphere, punctuated by loud chants of "Kill the Albanians" ringing out from the stands. Shortly before halftime, fans and then some players began to notice that a remote-controlled drone was approaching slowly out of the night sky toward the halfway line on the field. It was later discovered to have been piloted by a thirty-three-year-old Albanian nationalist named Ismail Morinaj, who was hiding in a tower of the nearby Church of the Holy Archangel Gabriel, from where he could see the field.

As the drone came lower, a stunned silence began to descend around the stadium and then, as it hovered near to the center circle, there was a sudden explosion of outrage. It was carrying an Albanian flag.

This wasn't merely the flag of the country, which alone would likely have caused problems. This flag bore the double-headed Albanian black eagle, the faces of two Albanian independence heroes from the early twentieth century and a map of Greater Albania, incorporating parts of Serbia, Macedonia, Greece, and Montenegro. It was emblazoned with the word *autochthonous*, a reference to indigenous populations. The message was that the Albanians, who consider themselves to be of ancient Illyrian origin from the fourth century BCE, were the real people of the region—and the Slavs, who only arrived in the sixth century CE, were not.

A Serbian defender, Stefan Mitrović, reached up and grabbed the flag. He later said he began folding it up "as calmly as possible in order to give it to the fourth official" so that the game could continue. Two Albanian players snatched it from him, and that was that. Several players began fighting with one another, then a Serbian fan emerged from the stands and hit the Albanian captain over the head with a plastic chair. As more Serbs poured onto the field, the Serb team came to their senses and tried to protect the Albanian players as they ran for the tunnel, the match abandoned. Missiles rained down on them as the riot police fought fans in the stands.

The political fallout was dramatic. The Serbian police searched the Albanian team's dressing room and then accused the brother-in-law of the Albanian prime minister of operating the drone from the stands. The media in both countries went into nationalistic overdrive; Serbia's foreign minister, Ivica Dačić, said his country had been "provoked" and that "if someone from Serbia had unveiled a flag of Greater Serbia in Tirana or Pristina, it would already be on the agenda of the UN Security Council." A few days later the planned visit of the Albanian prime minister to Serbia, the first in almost seventy years, was canceled.

George Orwell's aphorism that football is "war minus the shooting" was proved right and, given the volatility in the Balkans, the mix of football, politics, and a flag could even have led to a real conflict.

Planting the United States flag at the site of the twin towers did presage a war. Thomas Franklin said that when he took his shot he had been aware of the similarities between it and another famous image from a previous conflict—the Second World War, when United States Marines planted the American flag atop Iwo Jima. Many Americans will have recognized the symmetry immediately and appreciated that both moments captured a stirring mix of powerful emotions: sadness, courage, heroism, defiance, collective perseverance, and endeavor.

Both images, but perhaps more so the 9/11 photograph, also evoke the opening stanza of the American national anthem, "The Star-Spangled Banner," particularly its final lines:

> *O say does that star-spangled banner yet wave*
> *O'er the land of the free and the home of the brave?*

At a moment of profound shock for the American people, the sight of their flag yet waving was, for many, reassuring. That the stars of the fifty states were held aloft by men in uniform may have spoken to the streak of militarism that tinges American culture, but to see the red, white, and blue amid the awful gray devastation of Ground Zero will also have helped many ordinary citizens to cope with the other deeply disturbing images emerging from New York City that autumn day.

———

Where did these national symbols, to which we are so attached, come from? Flags are a relatively recent phenomenon in mankind's history. Standards and symbols painted on cloth predate flags and were used by the ancient Egyptians, the Assyrians, and the Romans, but it was the invention of silk by the Chinese that allowed flags as we know them today to flourish and spread. Traditional cloth was too heavy to be held aloft, unfurled and fluttering in the wind, especially if painted; silk was much lighter and meant that banners could, for example, accompany armies onto battlefields.

The new fabric and custom spread along the Silk Route. The Arabs were the first to adopt it and the Europeans followed suit, having come into contact with them during the Crusades. It was likely these military campaigns, and the large Western armies involved, that confirmed the use of symbols of heraldry and armorial markings to help identify the participants. These heraldic bearings came to be linked with rank and lineage, particularly for royal dynasties, and this is one of the reasons why European flags evolved from being associated with battlefield standards and maritime signals to becoming symbols of the nation state.

Every nation is now represented by a flag, testament to Europe's influence on the modern world as its empires expanded and ideas spread around the globe. As Johann Wolfgang von Goethe told Francisco de Miranda, the designer of the Venezuelan flag: "A country starts out from a name and a flag, and it then becomes them, just as a man fulfills his destiny."

What does it mean to try to encapsulate a nation in a flag? It means trying to unite a population behind a homogeneous set of ideals, aims, history, and beliefs—an almost impossible task. But when passions are aroused, when the banner of an enemy is flying high, that's when people flock to their own symbol. Flags have much to do with our traditional tribal tendencies and notions of identity—the idea of "us versus them." Much of the symbolism in flag design is based on that concept of conflict and opposition—as seen in the common theme of red for the blood of the people, for example. But in a modern world striving to reduce conflict and promote a greater sense of unity, peace, and equality, where population movements have blurred those lines between "us and them," what role do flags now play?

What is clear is that these symbols can still wield a great deal of power, communicating ideas quickly and drawing strongly on emotions. There are now more nation states than ever before, but non-state actors also use flags as a kind of visual sound bite to convey concepts ranging from the banality of cheap commercial goods to the depravity of religious and racial violence. This is something we've continually witnessed in recent history, from Hitler and the Nazi swastika—an image that even today evokes a powerful reaction—to the emergence of the Islamic State (IS) and its emphasis on religious or prophetic symbols that can grab attention and, sometimes, garner support.

This book could have told hundreds more stories, for example that of each of the 193 nation states, but that would have turned it into a reference work, and a very, very thick one at that. Instead, the stories recounted are those of some of the major national flags, some of the more obscure ones, and some that simply have the most interesting histories. In most cases the original meanings of the patterns, colors, and symbols are important, but sometimes, for some people, those meanings have morphed into something else, and that is what they believe the flag stands for now. The meaning is in the eye of the beholder.

We open with what is probably the most recognizable flag in the world: the Stars and Stripes, a visual representation that captures the American dream. Deeply revered by the vast majority of the population, it is the strongest example of how a symbol can come to define and unite a country. From the world's current empire we move to one of the past: the influence of the Union Jack extended to the farthest reaches of the globe, the flag representing the united front of a vast empire, but beneath the surface strong national identities persisted within the British Isles, and they haven't gone away.

The flag of the European Union also struggles to unify; in a continent with deeply rooted identities many Europeans are more attached to their national flags than ever. While some of these flags are based on Christian imagery, over the years the religious associations have mostly faded. Not so in the Arab nations to the south: their flags often feature powerful Islamic symbols and ideas that speak to the population. The symbolism is strong, but the nation states are weaker. The future may yet bring further change to the forms of these nations and their flags. A possible catalyst for this is the various terror cells operating in the region;

the actions and influence of these organizations, ever present on our screens, are important to understand. Groups such as IS also use religious symbolism to great effect, instilling fear and creating global recognition.

Moving eastward across Asia, we find an array of flags that reflect the sweeping movements of ideas, peoples, and religions, in the twentieth century and well before. Many of these modern nation states have reached back to the roots of their ancient civilizations for their flags, often in response to a turning point in their history, in a fusion of old and new. In Africa, by contrast, we see the colors of a very modern conception of the continent, one that has thrown off the shackles of colonialism and faces the twenty-first century with increasing self-awareness.

Latin America's revolutionaries kept closer cultural ties to the colonizers who shaped our world, and many of the continent's flags reflect the ideals of the nineteenth-century nation builders.

Flags are powerful symbols, and there are plenty of other organizations that have used them to great effect—they may embody messages of fear, peace, or solidarity, for example, becoming internationally recognizable in the shifting landscapes of identity and meaning.

We wave flags; we burn them; they fly outside parliaments and palaces, homes, and showrooms. They represent the politics of high power and the power of the mob. Many have hidden histories that inform the present.

We appear to be in the midst of a resurgence of identity politics at the local, regional, national, ethnic, and religious levels. Power shifts, old certainties fall away, and at such times people reach for familiar symbols as ideological anchors in a turbulent, changing world. The reality of a nation does not necessarily live up to the ideals embodied in its flag; nevertheless the flag can be, as Secretary of the Interior Franklin K. Lane "quoted" the Stars and Stripes as saying, "all that you believe I can be."

This is the emotion-charged emblem that is a flag. It has the power to evoke and embody sentiments so strong that sometimes people will even follow their colored cloth into gunfire and die for what it symbolizes.